Prisons and the Voluntary Sector

A BRIDGE INTO THE COMMUNITY

Shane Bryans works in the Criminal Policy Group of the Home Office. His previous post was as Governor of HM Young Offender Institution Aylesbury. He joined the Prison Service in 1986, having gained a law degree and a masters degree in Criminology from the University of Cambridge. Whilst working in the Prison Service he gained a Master of Business Administration degree from the Open University and a Master of Education degree from the University of Sheffield. In 1998 he was seconded to Cambridge University for a Cropwood Fellowship and in 1999 was elected a Fellow of the Royal Society of Arts. Shane Bryans has published numerous articles on prisons and a book *The Prison Governor: Theory and Practice* (with David Wilson) (1998), now in its second edition. He also edited *Prisons and the Prisoner: An Introduction to the Work of Her Majesty's Prison* Service (with Rachel Jones) (2001). He has led human rights delegations to Mongolia and Romania to inspect prison conditions.

Clive Martin is Director of CLINKS (Prisons Community Links), the national body that supports the work of the voluntary and community-based sector in prisons. He conducted the pilot study *Community-based Organizations and Four Prisons in England* published by CLINKS in 1999. He is also the author of *The Good Practice Guide: Prisons and the Voluntary and Community-based Sector* published jointly by CLINKS and HM Prison Service (2001). He taught in prisons for ten years and has developed European Union prison and community projects to bring about multi-agency approaches to constructive prison regimes and effective resettlement. His education includes teacher training in South Africa and he is also a graduate of London University.

Roma Walker was formerly Deputy Director of the Inside Out Trust (IOT) and has been involved with this penal voluntary sector organization from 1995, shortly after it was established. Having gained a masters degree in Criminal Justice Studies from the University of Leicester, she is now undertaking research for a PhD on the role and influence of penal reform organizations. She is on the management committee of CLINKS, an umbrella organization working to strengthen the role of the voluntary sector in prisons. She has contributed to various journals, and is a trustee of a grant-making trust. She has been a justice of the peace since 1995.

Prisons and the Voluntary Sector
A Bridge into the Community

Edited by Shane Bryans, Clive Martin and Roma Walker

Published 2002 by
WATERSIDE PRESS
Domum Road
Winchester S023 9NN
Telephone or Fax: 01962 855567
E-mail: watersidepress@ cs.com
Web-site: watersidepress.co.uk

Copyright © Shane Bryans, Clive Martin and Roma Walker. Contributions to the work are the copyright of the individual contributor concerned as noted in individual chapters. All rights reserved. No part of this book may be reproduced, stored in any retrieval system or transmitted in any form or by any means, including via the Internet, without prior permission. The right of the copyright holders to be identified as the author of the work in question has been asserted by them in accordance with the Copyright, Designs and Patents Act 1988.

ISBN Paperback 1 872 870 95 3

Cataloguing-in-publication data A catalogue record for this book can be obtained from the British Library

Printing and binding Antony Rowe Ltd, Chippenham

Cover design Waterside Press in association with John Good Holbrook Ltd, Coventry

Prisons and the Voluntary Sector

A BRIDGE INTO THE COMMUNITY

Edited by

Shane Bryans, Clive Martin and Roma Walker

With a Foreword by Terry Waite CBE

WATERSIDE PRESS

Acknowledgements

This book would not have been possible without the hard work of many people. The editors are particularly grateful to the authors of the various chapters for contributing to the book and for their patience and enthusiasm in responding to our many queries.

We should also like to put on record our thanks to the other people who have contributed to the book in various ways: in particular friends and colleagues; Margaret Carey and Marion Janner, both of whom have inspired us with their energy, innovation and humour and Una Padel whose consistent vision has guided this field of work over many years.

Our gratitude also goes to Catherine Fell and Rebecca Mann of the Prison Service library, for tracking down many references, to Jenny Gordon for typing some of the text and to Jo Maguire for compiling the list of voluntary sector organizations.

Finally, we would like to acknowledge the dedication of the many hundreds of individuals working in the penal voluntary sector, either as staff or volunteers, whose efforts this book highlights.

Shane Bryans, Clive Martin and **Roma Walker**

February 2002

Dedication

This book is dedicated to

Elizabeth, Jamie, Hannah and Jemma Bryans

and

Rex, Andrew and Tom Walker

and

Anne, Amy and Robin

Glossary and Abbreviations

Accreditation The process through which offending behaviour courses have to go in order to become 'accredited' programmes. The courses are considered by a panel of experts who look at the methodology, content and impact of the courses. Only those courses which are cost effective and have a positive impact are accredited.

Adjudication An internal prison disciplinary hearing, before the governor, at which prisoners are charged with breaking prison rules. The member of staff making the charge and the prisoner give evidence and question witnesses. The governor decides on the prisoner's guilt or innocence and gives an appropriate punishment.

ACF Association of Charitable Foundations

ACU Active Community Unit, a Home Office unit responsible for promoting active citizenship

BPSG Black Prisoners' Support Groups

BoV Board of Visitors—A board of lay people attached to each prison which independently monitors the prison premises, its administration and treatment of prisoners.

CARAT Drug rehabilitation service (Counselling, Assessment, Referral, Advice and Throughcare)

CCJS Centre for Crime and Justice Studies

CLINKS An umbrella organization established in 1998 specifically to support the role of the voluntary and community sector working in prisons and with ex-offenders

Compact 'Compact on Relations between Government and the Voluntary and Community Sector in England' (Home Office, 1998)

FPFSG Federation of Prisoners' Families Support Groups

KPI Key Performance Indicator, uses to assess the performance of a prison

NLCB The National Lottery Charities Board, now restyled 'The Community Fund', but more widely referred to as 'The National Lottery'.

NADPAS National Association of Discharged Prisoners' Aid Societies

NCVO National Council for Voluntary Organizations

NCWMP National Council for the Welfare of Muslim Prisoners

PGA Prison Governors Association

POA Prison Officers Association

PSI Prison Service Instruction

PSO Prison Service Order

RAPt Rehabilitation for Addicted Prisoners Trust

RRLO Race Relations Liaison Officer

RRMT Race Relations Management Team

SOVA Society of Voluntary Associates

SMT Senior Management Team (or Group) of a penal establishment

YJB Youth Justice Board for England and Wales which monitors the provision of youth justice services and the youth justice system

Contributors

Editors A note appears on page i

Other contributors

Yousif Al-Khoei is a founding member of the National Council for the Welfare of Muslim Prisoners and a member of the Religious Affairs Advisory Group on Detention Centres. He is a director of the Al-Khoei foundation which was established by the Shi'a Muslim spiritual leader, Imam Abualqasim al-Khoei, in 1989. Al-Khoei Foundation runs a number of educational, social and religious programmes and is in General Consultative Status with the Economic and Social Council of the United Nations. It is also involved in regular consultations with the Council of Europe and various government departments in the UK and Europe on issues affecting Muslims. Mr Al-Khoei is a Commissioner for The Runnymede Trust and the Uniting Britain Trust's Commission on British Muslims and Islamophobia, a Trustee of the Forum against Islamophobia and Racism (FAIR) and a founding member of the Association of Muslim Social Scientists (AMSS). Mr Al-Khoei is a co-founder of the English monthly, *Dialogue*. He is also a member of the Royal Institute of International Affairs and the Religious Education Council.

Margaret Carey is Founder Director of the Inside Out Trust. She believes that people in prison, whose lives have usually been unrewarding, need opportunities to link positively to the community. She previously worked in overseas development, travelling extensively in Africa and Asia. Matching the needs of prisoners for skills and self-esteem with the needs of disadvantaged people all over the world is the rationale supporting the Inside Out Trust. Margaret won the *Guardian* Jerwood Award for charities in 1996 which included funding for study visits to prisons throughout Europe. She has also visited prisons in the USA, Ghana, Uganda and Australia. She is vice-chair of the Restorative Justice Consortium, and member of the IPPR's Criminal Justice Forum 2000, the Penal Affairs Consortium, the Alliance for Reducing Offending, and is working with the International Centre for Prison Studies on the Restorative Prison Project. She is a magistrate in Mid-Sussex, and is married with two children and seven grandchildren. She was awarded the MBE in July 2001.

Richie Dell joined the Prison Service in 1988 and was posted to Ashford Remand Centre to work with male adult remand prisoners until its closure in 1990. He transferred to Portland Young Offender Institution, spending the first five years working with young offenders on pre-release and offending behaviour programmes. He was the Race Relations Liaison Officer and Race Relations trainer for that establishment. In 1995, he moved on to work with juvenile offenders, again doing offending behaviour courses and became the Equal Opportunities Officer and trainer. Seconded to NACRO for three years in 1999 as a Project Development Officer on the 'On-Side' project, he facilitated intense and targeted through-care and resettlement for a number of juvenile offenders in custody at Portland Young Offender Institution. In December 2000 he took over the role of Prisons Development Manager within NACRO, with overall responsibility for race issues. He has been responsible for assisting a number of prison establishments improve their links with Black and Minority Ethnic communities as well as continuing to train both NACRO and Prison Service staff in race and diversity issues.

Stuart Etherington was appointed Chief Executive of the National Council for Voluntary Organizations (NCVO) in 1994. NCVO is a membership organization which represents the interests of charities and voluntary bodies. Previously he was Chief Executive of the Royal National Institute for Deaf People, a major UK charity. He has four degrees: BA in Politics, MA in Social Planning, MBA from the London Business School and an MA in International Relations and Diplomacy. He has also been awarded an honorary doctorate from Brunel University. Throughout his career he has been involved in the leadership of voluntary organizations and policies surrounding them and as such become a leading commentator, both through his writing and his media profile. He is Chairman of Heritage Care, a Housing Association providing care and support for vulnerable people. He is a trustee of the Charities Aid Foundation, Business in the Community and English Churches Housing Group. His government appointments include the Economic and Social Research Council and the Welfare to Work Advisory Group.

Jo Gordon took up her post as HM Prison Service Voluntary Sector Co-ordinator in January 2001. Jo has worked in and with the voluntary sector at both a national and local level. Immediately before joining the Prison Service she was the Director of Social Investment Foundation for Metropolitan Housing Trust, a charitable trust supporting projects working with socially excluded groups. Her career has included both policy and practical work. She was an advisor to the Active Community Unit of the Home Office for three and a half years, a role that combined policy development and monitoring of grants. She established and ran Waste Watch, the national agency for waste reduction and recycling and set up Groundwork Hackney—the first Groundwork Trust in Inner London. Jo worked for a number of years for NACRO, initially with young offenders and then helped to set up the Women Prisoners Resource Centre which offered resettlement and other support to women leaving prison.

Robert Green was born in Walsall and raised there in the 1960s. After completing a degree in Law and English he became a retail manager working along the south coast, and in London's West End. Disillusioned with the pursuit of profit over social responsibility he left and took up a post as a Development Officer for an African-Caribbean community centre in Bolton. After 18 successful months developing a raft of community-based initiatives he left to take up the Project Co-ordinators's role in what was then a newly formed Leicester-based Black Prisoners Support Project. With the help of committed staff and volunteers the project grew into one of the leading organizations looking at the treatment of Black prisoners. He became a member of the Prison Service's Race Advisory Group and led the first ever Black voluntary sector/Prison Service audit team looking at the services and provision for Black prisoners in Glen Parva Young Offender Institution. He has given lectures and training on many aspects on race and criminal justice. In 2000 he left the Black Prisoners Support Project to join Crime Concern as a consultant. Based in Nottingham he specialises in many aspects of community safety including racially-motivated crimes.

Roma Hooper became involved with the voluntary sector in 1979 when she joined Contact a Family as fundraiser and assistant director. In 1987, with a colleague, she established Hooper McMillan, a charity consultancy working with small grassroots organizations. Whilst bringing up a family between 1992 and 2001 she obtained her degree in English and Sociology and has now completed her MSc in Criminal Justice Policy at the London School of Economics. During this time she became involved with Feltham Young Offenders Institution as a volunteer and has become the voluntary sector co-ordinator there. She is secretary of Friends of Feltham, and helped to establish the UK's first prison radio station there; a trustee of the Foundation Training Company; Chairman of the trustees for Trailblazers, the UK's only prison mentoring scheme, and a trustee of the Griffins Society, working on behalf of female offenders. She also established Investors in Children, with Linda McDonald, which intends to create a new grant-making trust to support young people.

Rachel Jones works as a Grade 7 in the Accountancy and Finance Unit of the Home Office. She joined the Prison Service on the Accelerated Promotion Scheme in 1996 and has worked at a variety of establishments including Wormwood Scrubs, Coldingley and HMYOI Aylesbury, where she was Head of Security, Operations and Estates. She spent a year on secondment to the International Centre for Prison Studies, King's College, London, where she completed a variety of projects including work on TB in prisons in the former Soviet Union and international comparisons of life sentence prisoners. She has also been involved in a prison reform project in Mongolia. Prior to moving to the Home Office, her last Prison Service post was as Staff Officer to an Assistant Director. She co-edited *Prisons and the Prisoner: An introduction to the Work of HM Prison Service* (with Shane Bryans) (2001).

Peter Kilgarriff has worked for charitable grant-making trusts for more than 17 years and has been the Director of the Lankelly Foundation since 1989. The decade prior to that was shared evenly between Capital Radio (1979-84) and Community Service Volunteers (1964-1979). Prior to that he worked as a priest in Staffordshire and Oxfordshire. Peter Kilgarriff has been involved with serving and former prisoners on both a personal and professional basis for many years. Between 1980-1990 he was Chair of Norman House, a prototype resettlement project founded by Mervyn Turner 25 years earlier which become a model for many others. He currently chairs the Prison Service Voluntary Sector Strategy Group and is a Trustee of the Swan Mountain Trust and on the Management Committee of CLINKS.

The Venerable William Noblett was appointed Chaplain General and Archdeacon to HM Prisons in July 2001. He served as a chaplain for 14 years in Wakefield, Norwich and Full Sutton prisons. At Wakefield prison he was instrumental in creating an ecumenical team, and at Full Sutton he started an inclusive, multi-faith approach to chaplaincy working that forms the basis of his vision for the future of chaplaincy. He is the author of *Prayers for People in Prison,* published by Oxford University Press, and a number of articles. He is a graduate of Southampton and Oxford Universities, and a Canon and Prebend of York Minster. He is married to Margaret and they have one son.

Kate Nutley has worked as a probation officer and as a manager of a Community Safety Programme in the London Borough of Merton, working with statutory agencies, the voluntary sector and resident's organizations. She joined the Prison Service in 1998 as a Governor Grade, initially working at HMP Coldingley. She became Head of Throughcare at HMP Wandsworth in March 2000 and her responsibilities include co-ordination of the community sector organizations working in the prison.

Una Padel is Director of the Centre for Crime and Justice Studies (formerly ISTD) at King's College London. She started her career as a probation officer and subsequently worked for the Prison Reform Trust in 1985 and the Standing

Conference on Drug Abuse where she managed an HIV Education Project in Prisons. In 1993, she became co-ordinator of London Prisons Community Links, a small organization with the aim of improving visiting conditions at the London Prisons. She played a major role in establishing Prison Visitor Centres. She briefly became Director of CLINKS (Prisons Community Links), a national organization she had helped to establish in order to develop the role of the voluntary sector in prisons, before moving to the Centre for Crime and Justice Studies. She was a member of the Laming Committee.

Andrew Passey is Head of Research at NCVO, where his role is to design, develop and seek funding for research projects to progress the objectives of NCVO in promoting the effectiveness and efficiency of the voluntary sector in the UK. He leads NCVO's Third Sector Foresight research programme, which is now an associate member of the Office for Science and Technology's Foresight programme. Current research priorities are: issues of public trust and confidence in voluntary organizations; a programme of strategic planning research in the voluntary sector; voluntary organizations and knowledge management; and, measuring the economic and social impacts of the sector. He has produced a number of NCVO publications and academic papers, including *Trust and Civil Society* (2000) (Macmillan: co-editied with F. Tonkiss), 'Trust Confidence and Voluntary Organizations: Between Values and Institutions', *Sociology* (May 1999: with F. Tonkiss) and *The UK Voluntary Sector Almanac 2000* (NCVO, 2000).

Stephen Rimmer has been a bureaucrat for most of his career, serving since 1984 in various posts in the Home Office, Prison Service HQ, Cabinet Office and Northern Ireland Office. Following the first market test of HMP Manchester—on which he was a member of the bid team—he worked there as Governor 3/Deputy Governor from 1993 to 1995. He spent three years working on the Government's drug strategy before returning to the 'real world' at HMYOI Glen Parva in 1998, becoming Governor of HMP Gartree later that year. He became Governor of HMP Wandsworth in January 2000 and is now Director of policing in the Home Office.

Adam Sampson has been Chief Executive of RAPt, one of the country's major providers of drugs services in the criminal justice system, for the past three-and-a-half years. Starting out as an academic at Oxford University, he worked in the Probation Service before spending five years as Deputy Director of the Prison Reform Trust and three as Assistant Prisons Ombudsman. He remains involved in the issue of prisoners' rights as Treasurer of the Prisoners' Advice Service. Over the past ten years, he has researched, written and broadcast extensively on the penal system. Consequently, by his own admission, his views are tired, out-of-date and probably worth ignoring.

Nick Sanderson is a deputy director in the Prison Service and responsible for a range of policy matters which concern the rights and responsibilities of prisoners. He has worked in the Prison Service since 1999. Before that he worked on Balkan and Northern Ireland matters in the Cabinet Office. He has held posts in the Home Office dealing with asylum, policing policy and broadcasting amongst others. He has also worked in the Northern Ireland Office.

Foreword

Recently I went to visit a prison hidden away in what might be called 'commuter country'. At one time it had been a Country House and I drove along a tree-lined road before I saw any indication that I was approaching a secure establishment. 'You know' said the Governor as we chatted over tea, 'many of the local people hardly know there is a prison here'. Well, I suppose that might be regarded as a positive sign. Clearly the prison was causing no trouble to local residents, the vast majority of whom were happy not to have to think about the prisoners and what went on in that establishment.

There is, however, another point of view which sees prisons as being very much a communal responsibility and rejects the attitude, sometimes crudely put as 'lock 'em up and throw the key away'. At the time of writing this foreword I am engaged in conducting a series of open days in prisons throughout England. Local people, the majority of whom have never been inside a prison before, are invited to spend several hours in the establishment meeting staff, prisoners and voluntary workers and learning something of what goes on behind the prison wall. One of the main aims of such days is to emphasise that prisons are very much a community responsibility.

As this book shows the work of the Voluntary Sector in Prisons is extensive and as prisons develop it is likely to become even more important in the future. This book is timely and will prove to be a valuable resource for people who seek to play a constructive role in the development of a just and humane penal system.

I warmly commend it.

Terry Waite CBE

CONTENTS

Acknowledgements iv
Dedication v
Glossary and Abbreviations vi
Contributors vii
Foreword xi
Introduction Shane Bryans and Roma Walker 13

Part I: The Operating Context
1. **The UK Voluntary Sector** Stuart Etherington and Andrew Passey 17
2. **Understanding the Prison Service** Rachel Jones 27

Part II: Historical Development
3. **The Penal Voluntary Sector** Margaret Carey and Roma Walker 50
4. **Recent Progress in Community-based Voluntary Sector Work with the Prison Service** Clive Martin 63

Part III: Current Policy and Practice
5. **Prison Service Policy on Voluntary and Community Sector Partnerships** Nick Sanderson and Jo Gordon 74
6. **Voluntary Sector Provision in the Penal System** Una Padel 82
7. **The Contribution of Volunteers in the Penal System** Roma Hooper 92
8. **The Faith-based and Minority Ethnic Voluntary Sector** Yousif Al-Khoei, Richie Dell, Robert Green and The Venerable William Noblett 106
9. **A Governor's Perspective** Katie Nutley and Stephen Rimmer 121
10. **Principles and Pragmatism: Surviving Working with the Prison Service** Adam Sampson 130
11. **Funding the Penal Voluntary Sector** Peter Kilgarriff 138

Part IV: Working Partnerships: Looking to the Future
12 **Practical Steps for a Successful Partnership** Shane Bryans 149
13 **The Road Ahead: Issues and Strategies for Future Joint Working** Shane Bryans, Clive Martin and Roma Walker 162

Appendices
1. Voluntary Sector Organizations Working with the Prison Service 174
2. Charitable Trusts Working in the Penal Affairs Field 184
3. The Laming Report 185
4. Chronological Development of the Penal Voluntary Sector 188
5. Further Reading 190

References 191
Index 196

Introduction

Shane Bryans and Roma Walker

Despite their longstanding presence, and the crucial role that they play in the lives of prisoners and their families, voluntary sector agencies delivering services in prisons have been hitherto largely invisible to and overlooked by Prison Service headquarters and individual establishments. However, for a number of social, political, ideological and pragmatic reasons (not least those of financial expediency), which are explored in greater detail in this book, the role of the penal voluntary sector has recently assumed a much greater prominence and significance. A former prisons minister, Paul Boateng, claimed that the voluntary sector had 'responded to the challenge' and that 'signs of change are emerging ... the voluntary sector ... has the potential to make a real impact upon the way prisons are perceived' (Boateng, 2000, pp. 16-17).

The critical role played by the voluntary sector has also been emphasised by former chief inspector of prisons, Sir David Ramsbotham:

> I have said it before, and will no doubt say it again, but I do not believe that the public at large realises just how much it owes to the voluntary sector, for what it does in prison, both in terms of what the public purse would otherwise have to provide, or in terms of what would be removed from the treatment and condition of prisoners.
>
> (HM Inspectorate of Prisons, 1999, p.39)

The growth of the voluntary sector has not been confined to the penal environment. Indeed, rather than voluntary services being seen as redundant in an age of increased statutory involvement, government enthusiasm has led to a resurgence of interest in the voluntary sector (Gill and Mawby, 1990, p.7). The government's support for voluntary involvement is critical as government policy has a significant influence, either directly through funding or indirectly by creating a more conducive environment within which voluntary organizations operate (Billis and Harris, 1996, p.46).

The active promotion of the penal voluntary sector continues to be a ministerial priority. It is within the context of the growth of that sector and its raised profile that this book was conceived. The editors share a passion for, and commitment to, the work of the voluntary sector in prisons. Whilst coming from very different traditions (one is a prison governor, the others senior managers in penal voluntary sector organizations) they have seen the positive impact that the voluntary sector can have on prisons, as well as some of the difficulties which it can face working in the penal environment.

The aim of this book is to explain both the theoretical framework which underpins the work of the penal voluntary sector and, at the same time, to give practical advice on how to improve joint working. For these reasons contributors were sought from very different backgrounds and perspectives. They have all been involved with either the voluntary sector or the Prison Service, and have practical experience of the issues surrounding joint working. The result, we hope, is a book that is 'grounded in reality' rather than one which gives some idealised and fictional view of the Prison Service partnership with the voluntary sector. However, it is not our aim to be definitive and the book is by no means the last word. Nor can we claim to cover every issue. Instead our intention is to stimulate debate and discussion, and to provide some much needed literature upon the subject. Hopefully this book will contribute towards the process of enhancing constructive working practices between the two sectors.

Whilst encompassing all voluntary organizations involved in penal affairs, the emphasis of the book is primarily upon those voluntary organizations whose main function is to provide some sort of direct *service* to prisoners or their families. The focus is less upon pressure groups which *campaign*, on behalf of prisoners, for a more just and humane penal system. Obviously there is a considerable overlap between the two groups, with the service providers supporting the campaigning activities and pressure groups involved in some limited service provision. Voluntary sector activity is a continuum; Pahl (1979) distinguishes the two extremes by referring to the 'social movement' goals of pressure groups and the 'social provision' goals of service providers. However, the various penal pressure groups may choose to be either 'thorns in the flesh' or 'critical friends' of the Prison Service in pursuit of their aims. This can obviously have an impact upon the attitude of the Prison Service to the wider penal voluntary sector and upon the relationship between the two sectors.

Scheme of the book

The book consists of four parts. *Part I* deals with the **operating context** in which the voluntary sector and Prison Service function. *Chapter 1* gives an overview of the voluntary sector, including: an exploration of definitions; the role of government in setting voluntary sector policy; the voluntary sector and partnerships; national agreement, codes and compacts; and a vision for the future of the voluntary sector. *Chapter 2* provides an introduction to the other half of the partnership, the Prison Service. It begins with a short history of imprisonment and goes on to describe the relationships between the Prison Service and the Home Office. The structure and organization of the Prison Service at national and local level is then discussed. The chapter concludes with an exploration of Prison Service establishments including an outline of: management structures, governors, prison officers and prisoners.

Part II considers the **historical development** of the penal voluntary sector. *Chapter 3* traces the historical development of that sector from its early roots in pioneering penal reform, to the work of charities, aid societies, discharged prisoners societies and police court missionaries. It concludes with a discussion of the work of the modern penal voluntary sector. *Chapter 4* brings matters up-to-date by tracing more recent developments and the growth of the sector. The chapter considers the influence of government policy, the growth of research on the penal voluntary sector and the seminal work undertaken by CLINKS in 1999 in identifying the nature of the problems encountered in the relationship between the voluntary and statutory sectors.

The **current policy and practice** of joint working by the Prison Service and voluntary sector is described in *Part III*. *Chapter 5* provides a definitive statement of Prison Service policy towards the voluntary and community sector and is written by the policy holder at Prison Service headquarters and the Prison Service Voluntary Sector co-ordinator. The chapter traces the development of the underpinning strategy of joint working and sets the scene for coming years. *Chapter 6* describes the types of current provision by the voluntary sector. It gives details of the characteristics and organization of the penal voluntary sector and identifies the range of projects in place today. It also points to two important recent changes, the accreditation of voluntary sector services and the implementation of the Laming Committee recommendations on the role of the penal voluntary sector. *Chapter 7* outlines the role of volunteers in prisons and debunks the myth of the 'do-gooder' by emphasising the major contribution to the work of prisons which such volunteers make. In particular, the chapter looks at the work of the Boards of Visitors, Prison Visitors, Samaritans and the growth of volunteer mentoring schemes. *Chapter 8* considers how the Prison Service and voluntary sector are attempting, with varying degrees of success and commitment, to meet the challenge of the differing cultural and spiritual needs of prisoners and their families. The contributors present four different perspectives that reflect racial, cultural and spiritual diversity.

Chapter 9 is written by a prison governor and a senior manager in a prison and reflects upon working with the voluntary sector from a prison perspective. Whilst pointing out the benefits of joint working it also highlights some of the potential pitfalls facing both prisons and the voluntary sector. Security and safety issues are considered along with how best to manage the contribution of the voluntary sector. *Chapter 10* provides a voluntary sector perspective of working with the Prison Service. Its author, who has considerable experience of working with the Prison Service, discusses the need to balance principles and pragmatism. The chapter highlights the managerialisation of the voluntary sector, provides advice on 'navigating the choppy waters of Prison Service politics' and comments on the regulation of voluntary sector staff working in prisons.

Chapter 11 covers the key area of the funding of voluntary sector work in prisons. Independent funding (and funding bodies), Prison Service funding policy and funding by other statutory bodies are explored as means of funding prison-related work. The chapter also considers ethical issues surrounding funding and how best to create joined-up provision.

Finally, *Part IV* looks to **future partnership working** and provides practical help to ensure that joint working proves successful for both sectors. *Chapter 12*, written by a prison governor, describes practical steps for a successful partnership and seeks 'to turn rhetoric into reality'. After discussing some of the background issues to do with partnership working, the chapter goes on to provide a 'how to' guide to positive joint working. It identifies areas for joint working; provides criteria for identifying the right partner organization; describes the contractual process and explains how to reach an agreement; and discusses monitoring and evaluation issues. The last chapter seeks to pull together some of the key themes identified elsewhere in the book and to identify the main advantages to both the Prison Service and voluntary sector of working together effectively. It also sets out the potential problems which will need to be addressed if the aim of effective joint working is to be achieved. The chapter concludes by providing 'a map for the road ahead', if the relationship between the Prison Service and voluntary sector is to move from being one of *co-operation* to a more truly *partnership*-based approach.

At the end of the book there are a number of appendices: lists of voluntary sector organizations and charitable trusts working in prisons; the recommendations of the Laming Report on the role of the community in prisons; further reading; a chronology of the key milestones in the development of the penal voluntary sector; and a list of references.

CHAPTER 1

The United Kingdom Voluntary Sector

Stuart Etherington and Andrew Passey

The briefest of historical analyses illustrates that voluntary action has a long history in the UK—for example 500 voluntary hospitals were created in England during the twelfth and thirteenth centuries. The notion of charitable trust emerged in Tudor England, though the nineteenth century saw a major expansion of voluntary association across the UK. This took a range of forms: philanthropic associations developed to help the poorest and most vulnerable members of society; self-help and mutual-aid insured against sickness and raised funds for burial; and campaigning groups acted across a number of causes including prison reform, sanitary improvements, and repeal of the Corn Laws. The first half of the twentieth century was characterised by partnership with government, while post-war the professionalisation of public and social services, and the 'privatisation' of services, have been felt across all kinds of voluntary organization (cf. Davis Smith, 1995; Deakin, 1995).

Partnership features large in the Labour government's political lexicon, and in terms of public policy it represents an obvious continuity between it and its Conservative predecessor. However, for Labour partnership means more, and has been applied by it to a gamut of government-voluntary sector relations, from output-driven contracts for the delivery of public services, through inter-agency regeneration partnerships, to strategic agreements or 'compacts' between government and the voluntary and community sector.

The discussion in this chapter sets the context for the debate in the rest of this book by looking briefly at different definitions and measures of the UK voluntary sector, drawing on a range of quantitative research. It goes on to discuss the role of the voluntary sector in government policy, especially the development of partnership arrangements between government, business, and voluntary organizations. The chapter ends by unpicking where the voluntary sector sits in current policy debates and developments, and in so doing considers its future development.

DEFINING AND MEASURING THE UNITED KINGDOM VOLUNTARY SECTOR

Defining the limits of the voluntary sector often involves bracketing it off from state and market, which tends to underplay the positive features of the voluntary sector itself. Recent analysis has aimed to move beyond such definition by emphasising distinct formal and functional characteristics of voluntary organizations. The focus has shifted from social good to the economic inputs, throughputs and outputs of voluntary organizations (Kendall and Almond, 1999; Hems and Passey, 1998; Passey et al, 2000).

While sharing an emphasis on the economic characteristics of voluntary organizations, such approaches tend to produce rather partial summaries of what 'counts' as the voluntary sector, which can differ markedly between studies (Passey and Tonkiss, 2000). Different numbers can also translate into different messages for policy-makers, which can make problematic consistent lobbying across the voluntary sector.

Hems and Passey (1998) adopted the relatively narrow definition of *general charities* used by the government's Office for National Statistics (ONS), which is explicitly geared to measuring the contribution made by charities to the UK economy. A general charity must be independent (i.e. constitutionally and institutionally separate from government and business); non-profit distributing; and must serve a public benefit (beyond its own membership). Estimates for 1999 reveal an operating income of £14.2 billion, current expenditure of £13.4 billion, and total assets (buildings, land, investments) of £65.1 billion. General charities employ 485,000 paid workers and benefit from the action of over three million unpaid workers (Passey et al, 2000). Significantly, general charities contribute around £5 billion each year to the national wealth, the equivalent of 0.7 per cent of the UK's Gross Domestic Product (GDP). This figure, however, does not account for the significant impact of volunteer effort, which when factored in takes the contribution closer to 1.9 per cent of GDP (*ibid*).

This definition includes 'household-name' national bodies as well as local charities, and by using government definitions it provides a sound basis for policy development. However, it excludes educational establishments, trade unions, professional bodies, arts organizations, campaigning movements, social clubs, self-help and mutual societies that are part of a wider conception of civil society. This partly stems from the criterion of *public benefit* that goes beyond the interests of general charities' own members, which excludes self-help bodies, co-operatives and mutual organizations.

However, the legal basis of whether or not a particular organization is 'charitable' is itself the subject of intense debate. Essentially, the thrust of the argument is that in future a smaller proportion of voluntary organizations may be charitable because of a growth in:

- non-primary purpose trading activity (and therefore perhaps in the establishment of trading subsidiaries which may be engaged in a range of activities including contracting with the state for the provision of services);
- single issue campaigning groups (organizations campaigning for a change in the law or public policy as a primary purpose are ineligible for charitable status);
- funding for partnership-based programmes which require voluntary, public and private sector organizations to work together on service delivery; and
- interest in social enterprise and/or the mutual or self help model (organizations promoting mutual interest rather than operating for the wider public benefit are also ineligible).

Given these environmental changes, one conclusion could be that the category 'charity' appears increasingly irrelevant. However, the concept of a charity (i.e. an institution) continues to have resonance with the public. The status charity in law provides both institutional and individual donors with reassurance that money will be spent for public benefit purposes. It therefore positively promotes giving (NCVO, 1998).

Rather than following the current fashion for trying to squeeze all not-for-profit activity into charity status, a report from an NCVO (National Council for Voluntary Organizations) advisory group published in February 2001 recommends that government should look to give more encouragement to the mutual sector by providing it with an appropriate but separate legal form and tax benefits conducive to its development. A further issue is the need to look at how the different sorts of voluntary organizations that make up the sector can work more creatively and productively together, for example by looking at how charitable funds might be used to promote the development of credit unions.

It is argued above that there are environmental trends that suggest that a smaller proportion of voluntary sector organizations will in the future be charitable. There are, however, some developments which point the other way. The Charity Commission is, for example, undertaking a review to see whether some purposes previously deemed ineligible for charitable status might, given social and economic developments, now be included. They have examined the charitable status of organizations seeking to tackle unemployment, rural and urban regeneration and community development and issued draft guidance for consultation on the circumstances in which these objects could now be charitable. It will also be interesting to see how many of the new partnerships being established to deliver government programmes will be deemed charitable, and the extent to which they will start to compete with established charities for a variety of service contracts. This may have particular relevance in the communities served by existing penal voluntary agencies, and to the grant-making trusts that fund them.

Analysis of the voluntary sector based upon a definition of charity is thus addressing one component of a larger sector of activity. Work elsewhere has sought to focus on other specific sub-components, or to take a broader sweep of voluntary sector activity. However, as with the charitable core of the voluntary sector, there has only been limited research into the size, scope and nature of a *mutual sector*, partly due to problems over definition.

Recent British research suggests 'grass roots' mutualism is alive and well, despite the conversion of many large mutual institutions into public limited companies. Employing a wide definition of mutualism that includes organizations that exhibit a more general 'mutual ethos' as well as those owned and governed by members, Leadbetter and Christie (1999) conclude that the mutual sector has a membership of more than 30 million people, it turns over £25 billion annually, and employs more than 250,000 people. They argue that mutuals can be seen to operate in the 'old' economies (e.g. farming) and the 'new' (e.g. e-commerce).

A more extended definition of the *UK voluntary sector*, based on 'structural-operational' factors (Kendall and Knapp 1996; see also Salamon and Anheier, 1992) was adopted by Kendall and Almond (1999). It is based on five criteria, that organizations should be:

- formally organized;
- institutionally separate from the state;
- non-profit distributing;
- self-governing; and
- based on voluntary membership and contributions.

It extends the official definition adopted by Hems and Passey to include educational establishments, professional bodies, arts organizations, and museums. The estimates it produces of the size and scope of the UK sector are thus much larger—in 1995 operating income was estimated at US$77.3 billion (around £50 billion), paid employment totalled 1.4 million people (6.2 per cent of the total workforce) rising to 2.5 million when volunteers were included (Kendall and Almond, 1999).

These accounts of the voluntary sector fit with growing governmental interest in the sector's role as a 'partner' in economic and social policy. Here, both the role of voluntary organizations in providing services (from pensions to healthcare) *and* in promoting social cohesion in some general sense is foregrounded.

GOVERNMENT AND THE VOLUNTARY SECTOR

Labour's interest in the voluntary sector is representative of a growing government focus on this arena through the 1990s. There were three major reviews of government/third sector relations carried out between 1990 and 1996, each of which conceptualised the voluntary sector in different ways (Lewis, 1999). The 1990 Home Office 'Efficiency Scrutiny' focused on the relationship from the perspective of those government departments funding voluntary organizations, essentially assessing the justification for such resourcing. The Centris Report, published in 1993, distinguished between a 'third force' of voluntary organizations funded by the state, and a 'first force', which it saw as independent of government, and constituting the 'energy that the human being uses in pursuit of the social contract' (Knight, 1993, p.xvii).

The 1996 Deakin Commission reconstituted the first and third forces within a voluntary sector, placing voluntary organizations in a public space between a triangular 'force field' of the market, the state, and the informal sector. Deakin was independent of government, a factor that distinguished it from both the earlier reviews discussed above, and it concluded by making more than 60 recommendations for a range of stakeholders from both within and outside the voluntary sector (Commission on the Future of the Voluntary Sector, 1996). These included changes to charity law (see above), calls for voluntary organizations to develop quality measures and improve standards, and that there should be the development of a 'concordat' between government and the voluntary sector 'laying down basic principles for future relations' (*ibid* p. 4). Two years, and a change of government later, the English *Compact* was published (Home Office, 1998), which Kendall (2000) argues is symptomatic of a 'mainstreaming' of the voluntary sector into public policy. Whether or not this is the case, it certainly illustrates a conception in government of the voluntary sector as a valid arena for government intervention.

THE UK VOLUNTARY SECTOR IN PARTNERSHIP

In a broad range of policy areas co-operation between the statutory and voluntary sectors (and in specific programmes with business too) is seen as the key to achieving real progress in tackling complex social problems. A plethora of partnership programmes now exist, some are based on specific geographical areas, others on population cohorts.

Programmes include the Single Regeneration Budget, the New Deal for Communities, Health Action Zones and Education Action Zones (area-based) plus the New Deal and Sure Start (cohort-based).

Partnerships are perceived to have a number of advantages over traditional methods of delivering public policy programmes, such as: achieving economies of scale; facilitating innovation; preventing duplication; addressing complex needs; promoting sustainable benefits to the local community; delivering local responses to local problems and promoting social cohesion. Again, the relevance to the penal voluntary sector should be noted. However, a recent evaluation of the implications for voluntary organizations of the current expansion in local cross-sectoral partnerships raised a number of concerns, at the centre of which was the need for government to loosen up top-down prescriptions of the ways in which partners should work together and how performance of partnerships should be measured (NCVO, 2000a).

One of the key determinants of partnership effectiveness is the leadership role of highly skilled individuals, who are good at bringing people together and at achieving results. However, these skills are limited, in both government and in voluntary organizations. So, in practice, we see that partnership leaders are often the representatives of the biggest public sector organization involved. Some commentators have called for practical responses to this problem, such as Local Learning Units (LLUs) to share information to promote skills development and innovation (6, P, 1997).

Partnerships need freedom to develop their own structures and ways of working. Controlling activity from the centre may achieve the desired results in the short-term but tends to strangle partnership creativity, making success hard to sustain. In many instances the structures put in place to operate and evaluate partnerships fail to provide the necessary conditions to foster innovation. Central government and partner agencies need to learn to delegate control of *risk-taking*, accept uncertainty and share knowledge and information. Clearly there are implications here in relation to the developing partnership between the Prison Service and the penal voluntary sector.

One key element of this is the need to enable all potential partners to develop their capacity to work together. Resources for capacity building need to be available *before* the introduction of a programme, such as happened in the New Deal for Communities (Carley *et al.*, 2000). NCVO's own review concluded that a proportion of the total annual regeneration budget should be set aside specifically to develop local capacity.

Finally, local partnership programmes need to sit within coherent local development plans, which themselves need to contribute to regional development strategies (Carley *et al*, 2000). This though involves learning from the experience of others to effectively diffuse policy development across partnership programmes and different locations. Government's emphasis on 'evidence-based policy' hints at an understanding of this issue, however an evaluation of policy transfer between local partnership programmes concluded that, to be more effective, there was a 'need for targeting bodies with limited financial and personnel resources' (Wolman and Page, 2000, p.1). Many such bodies will reside in the voluntary sector.

THE COMPACT(S): NATIONAL AGREEMENTS AND CODES

The Compact on Relations between Government and the Voluntary and Community Sector in England was agreed in November 1998, and in the words of one commentator it represents a 'step change' in government-sector relations (Kendall, 2000, p.22). It was negotiated for the voluntary and community sector by the Working Group on Government Relations, whose mandate stemmed from the biggest ever consultation in the sector. The Compact takes a wide definition of voluntary action, not simply focussing on those parts of the sector most closely associated with government (such as social welfare and health). It aims to provide a framework for a new approach to partnership and covers a shared vision and principles, undertakings by government and by the voluntary and community sector (on independence, funding, accountability, policy development and consultation, and good practice), issues relating to community and black and minority ethnic groups, and resolution of disagreements. The Compact also includes a commitment to develop codes of practice and encourage the adoption of Compact principles and undertakings at a local level, where most voluntary and community sector activity takes place.

The Compact recognises the social and economic contributions that voluntary and community groups make and acknowledges their independence. It also sets out what each side will do. For example, government undertakes to give three months' notice of funding decisions and to allow 12 weeks for consultation. Voluntary sector undertakings include accountability, promoting best practice and equality and informing and involving users and volunteers (Home Office, 1998).

While the Compact is not legally binding, it puts forward various ways to deal with difficulties, such as complaints procedures, mutual resolution, mediation and the Parliamentary Ombudsman. An annual survey of the voluntary and community sector and other information supplied to the Working Group on Government Relations during the year feeds into the annual meeting with ministers to review the operation of the Compact. This meeting makes a report to Parliament so that politicians hear the sector's views.

Since being agreed in 1998, work on the Compact has had two main prongs: the development of codes of good practice (funding and consultation have been agreed and published); and the development of local compacts. Codes on funding and consultation were published in May 2000 (Home Office, 2000a and 2000b), while others on volunteering, black and minority organizations, and community groups were published by in early 2001. They aim to make a positive impact on the way in which the government consults and appraises its polices in respect of the voluntary and community sector, and on the funding relationship between government and the voluntary and community sector. Both outline principles and processes, and each set out ten key principles. Those for the funding code include: 'improved sustainability and longer-term planning through, for example, multi-year roll-forward funding', 'recognition of core costs and the different ways these can be met' and 'fair access to strategic, project and contract funding'. In general they should 'make a positive difference to the funding relationship between government and the voluntary and community sector' (Home Office, 2000a). A *Good Practice Guide* for prisons and the voluntary and community-based sector was produced collaboratively in 2000 by CLINKS and the Prison Service (see *Chapter 4* for a more detailed discussion of the guide). It was informed by the Compact. Furthermore, alterations and clarifications around funding arrangements between the Prison Service and the voluntary sector have been instigated as a consequence of the Compact. The Prison Service's relationship with the voluntary sector has now been strengthened by the recently approved HM Prison Service policy document 'Working with the Voluntary and Community Sector'.

Local compacts
The national Compact recognises that most government/third sector relations take place at the local level. The evolving funding relations between local authorities and third sector organizations have already been reviewed above. Local Compact Guidelines, jointly developed with the Local Government Association, were launched in July 2000 (NCVO, 2000b).

At the local level, compacts run alongside an agenda to 'modernise government'. This involves a range of new responsibilities for local government, including community leadership, engagement and planning processes; local democratic renewal; and the scrutiny of service quality and decisions (Best Value), and the new power of local authorities to promote the social, environmental and economic well-being of their areas. These point to the need for a more robust and balanced partnership with the voluntary and community sector.

THE FUTURE OF THE VOLUNTARY SECTOR

Any review of a range of organizations and activities as broad as the UK voluntary sector will be necessarily selective. However, what this brief overview of the development and current state of the UK voluntary sector illustrates is how it now sits within a number of public policy debates and agendas. In the context of the penal voluntary sector, the issues outlined below are particularly pertinent.

The first reflects an instrumental view in government of the voluntary sector. Voluntary organizations are key delivery agents for a range of government-funded services, and while the so-called 'contract-culture' has been viewed by many in the sector as a negative force for organizational development, the new funding codes between government and the sector include provisions to provide overhead and core funding. This represents a major *philosophical* step in government—that voluntary organizations can provide benefits like building trust and social cohesion, which go over and above their operational abilities to deliver and administer services. The new partnership arrangements that seek to tackle social exclusion include examples where government seems more willing to slacken-off central control, to allow the knowledge and experience of voluntary and community organizations to come to bear on tackling deprivation and the long-term decline of particular communities and places. Elsewhere however, central control remains tighter, and so the potential for current partnership arrangements to generate social inclusion and other long-term outcomes remains in question.

There is also a re-emerging civil society agenda, which in general underpins the significance of voluntary association, of networks and norms of behaviour, and of tolerance of difference. Here, it is possible to distil two streams. First, government has sought to stimulate civil society through financial measures aimed at increasing public donations to charities. The 2000 Budget markedly widened the means through which the Treasury will supplement an individual's charitable donation. This, along with the new funding code in the Compact, suggests that government is committed to supporting the *organizational architecture* of civil society. Indeed, in purely practical terms, it is relatively straightforward for government to act upon, and work with, organizations, but changing public attitudes and behaviour is more problematic.

This brings us to the second strand of the civil society agenda, in which 'community' has supplanted society, and where government has adopted a value-laden discourse that privileges supposed attributes of voluntary organizations. The voluntary sector needs to continue challenging these simplistic and normative assumptions about what it is, and what it does. What is more, this debate also sharpens the focus on the legitimacy of voluntary organizations—how do they speak for particular communities? Do they give voice to marginalised people? The events in Seattle in November 1999[1] point to public cynicism towards a range of institutions, feelings to which voluntary organizations are not immune. Public willingness to by-pass institutions and campaign directly is not new, but if it continues to increase in scale then it might further challenge the accountability and legitimacy of the voluntary sector.

In general, however, the sector's future appears relatively buoyant, although at the heart of these public policy initiatives there remains a paradox that will increasingly influence its development. This revolves around how voluntary organizations can successfully negotiate, with different stakeholders, the potential tensions 'between the aim of "doing good" in relation to social issues and causes, and the pressures of "doing well" as organizations in an increasingly professional and competitive environment' (Tonkiss and Passey, 1999, p.261). The potential tensions between 'doing well' and 'doing good' are already manifesting themselves in the relationships between the Prison Service and the penal voluntary sector. These issues are explored more fully in later chapters.

---

[1] During the 1999 World Trade Organization meeting in Seattle, anti-globalisation protesters and police fought running battles in the streets of the city. Protesters formed into a loose coalition for the WTO summit, and in this way at least they differ from more established campaigning groups. This is suggestive of new forms of voluntary action that by-pass more traditional organizations in favour of coalitions developed for a particular event, in a particular place at a particular time.

CHAPTER 2

Understanding the Prison Service

Rachel Jones

> Her Majesty's Prison Service serves the public by keeping in custody those committed by the courts. Our duty is to look after them with humanity and help them lead law abiding and useful lives in custody and after release.
>
> HM Prison Service Statement of Purpose

The Prison Service of England and Wales (referred to throughout this chapter as the Prison Service) remains an object of fascination for the general public, the subject of documentary, comment and drama, of varying accuracy and indeed insight. Behind the popular media conception of Ronnie Barker doing his 'porridge' however, lies a large and complex organization with a diverse history. Understanding the operating context and constraints on the Prison Service is vital to anyone intending to work with that service. This chapter offers a broad overview of the Prison Service, its history, organization and structure, and provides some introduction concerning its purpose within the wider criminal justice system. It also considers developments in the management and measurement of key tasks and standards.[1]

IMPRISONMENT AND THE PRISON SERVICE: A BRIEF HISTORY

There has been much debate over the use of prisons within society. In 1969, *The Times* argued that 'there should be no conflict in an ideal prison system between security and rehabilitation' (Thomas, 1977, p.23). But there is conflict, both in the eyes of the public and the eyes of staff between the so-called primary goal of secure custody and the manifest secondary goals of rehabilitation, reform, and deterrence. The wider community often perceives prisons as coercive institutions, or conversely as 'holiday camps', and measures their effectiveness by escape rate not

---

[1] A more detailed account of the work of the Prison Service can be found in the seminal work *Prisons and the Prisoner: An Introduction to the Work of HM Prison Service* (Bryans and Jones, 2001).

the rate of reoffending after discharge. There are many influences on the way prisons are viewed, and the prison system itself is not a passive player in shaping these views. The statement of purpose set out above is an attempt by the Prison Service to balance these views, and to undertake to deliver the balance.

The origins of imprisonment in England and Wales date back as far as the eleventh century, when William I constructed the Tower of London. Henry II was the first monarch to establish a 'strong public law and administration' (Morris and Rothman, 1995, p.37). The idea of the prison as a place of punishment or reform is relatively recent however. Prior to the eighteenth century, punishment consisted of torture, mutilation and execution. In the early prisons, prisoners were kept in barbaric conditions, with no segregation of the sexes or of children. The majority of prisoners were debtors, who often had to pay for their own food, clothing and even release. With the advent of transportation, between 1715 and 1775 over 50,000 criminals were shipped to the New World.

In 1777, John Howard published *The State of the Prisons in England and Wales*, realising for the first time the potential of a reformed prison system, and marginalising other forms of punishment.

It was not until 1877 however that the foundations of the modern Prison Service were laid with the introduction of the Prisons Act, and the passing of control of the prisons to the home secretary. This most Victorian of Acts emphasised the importance of deterrence and punishment over rehabilitation, and sought to bring order to the society of prisons. The first chairman of the new Prison Commission was Sir Edmund Du Cane, who placed great emphasis on the need for centralised standards and total compliance from prisoners, who were to have no recognition of their individuality. This stance lead to much criticism, particularly given the high reoffending rate of those who passed through the hands of the prison system which mixed long-term criminals with new offenders and young criminals with the most experienced.

As a result of public anxiety about the punishment of offenders, Parliament set up a committee to examine the state of the prison system, chaired by Herbert Gladstone. The report of the committee in 1895 marked a move away from the oppressive regimes of Du Cane, towards deterrence and reform, just as the period itself marked a move towards increased liberalism. Unproductive labour, such as the treadmill, originally introduced by Cubbitt in 1818 was halted and better conditions for prisoners were introduced, with less emphasis on solitary confinement. Following the report, Du Cane resigned and was replaced by Sir Evelyn Ruggles-Brise who remained head of the Prison Commission until 1921, and who defined the purpose of imprisonment as 'the humanisation of the individual' (Bryans and Wilson, 2000, p.2).

Following this period, many of the recommendations of the Gladstone committee were introduced including borstals (separate training institutions for young prisoners) and open prisons. Borstals were initially thought successful, but rising crime rates resulted in a reaction against their paternalistic approach. Open prisons continue in use today, although their numbers are being reduced following the introduction of early release schemes such as home detention curfew.

Between the wars the use of imprisonment saw a decline, prompted by scepticism as to what prisons could actually achieve. Post-war legislation such as the Criminal Justice Act 1948 took a hard line on crime however, and the use of imprisonment began to rise.

In 1963 the Prison Commission was replaced by the Prison Department of the Home Office. Shortly after this a series of high profile escapes from prisons caused renewed anxiety about security across the prison estate. These included those of the so-called Great Train Robbers Ronald Biggs and Charles Wilson, and the spy George Blake. This led to the appointment of a commission to enquire into security, led by Lord Mountbatten. The Mountbatten Report of 1966 considered that 'the modern policy of humane liberal treatment aimed at rehabilitating prisoners rather than merely exacting punishment, is right' (Mountbatten, 1966, p.4).

The report introduced a new rank, that of senior officer, established dog sections, close circuit television and physical security measures, and introduced a system of categorisation for prisoners to ensure they would be held in appropriate conditions. It led to a large increase in the staffing numbers in prisons (Bryans and Wilson, 2000, p.5). It recommended that all Category A prisoners (the highest security category) should be held together in one prison, to be based on the Isle of Wight. Instead the government opted for a dispersal system, recommended by a committee of experts led by the leading Cambridge academic Sir Leon Radzinowicz, whereby prisoners deemed to require maximum security were 'dispersed' around the country and held in a number of key high security prisons. A similar strategy remains in place today, with Category A prisoners held in five dispersal prisons.

The 1970s marked a period of turbulence for the Prison Service, with disruptions across the dispersal estate and the development of a more militant Prison Service staff lead by the Prison Officers Association (POA). This lead to increasing disputes and arguments about overtime, payment for which made up a high percentage of the salaries of officers and senior officers. In 1978 the May committee was set up to enquire into the state of the service. May proposed that a new regime of positive custody should replace the 1970s philosophy of treatment and training, considering that the service had lost its way over the purpose of imprisonment. It introduced a single staff attendance system, and recommended a reformed prison inspectorate.

1987 saw the introduction of the Fresh Start initiative, which rationalised the grade structure of the service, abolished overtime, and divided the work of the prison into key blocks such as activities, residence and security. For a large number of staff the reform that had the most impact was the abolition of the rank of chief officer, responsible for the discipline of the prison staff and seen by many as the ultimate career goal. Visitors to prisons even today should not be surprised to hear the cry 'Bring back the chief' uttered in response to a surprisingly wide range of problems from litter to prison discipline. In reality the move opened a wider career path for staff to be promoted to most senior ranks of the service. It can also be argued that it reduced the power of the POA.

In 1990 a serious riot at HMP Manchester (Strangeways) which lasted for 25 days, and subsequent disturbances at 25 other prisons including Bristol, Cardiff and Dartmoor, lead to a major enquiry into the work of the Prison Service lead by Lord Justice Woolf. This addressed the fundamental problems of the service at the time; overcrowding, slopping out and the feeling of prisoners that the system was not just. Thereafter, the Woolf report was the most significant report published for over a decade and provided the blueprint for a liberal and just prison system (Woolf and Tumim, 1991). In response to the report and its recommendations, the government published a white paper *Custody, Care and Justice,* which outlined plans to implement the majority of Woolf's recommendations within 25 years.

The Criminal Justice Act 1991 introduced a new sentencing framework for all offenders, setting up in relation to prisoners the system of remission and parole. It also introduced the involvement of the private sector in the building and running of new prisons. This followed consultation reports which stated that private sector involvement would be practical and economic and that 'adequate safeguards could be set up to cover the legitimate public concerns that have been raised' (Deloitte, Haskins and Sells, 1989, p.2).

The debate about private prisons continues today. The argument that the delivery of effective services is the duty of the Prison Service (whether publicly or privately run) is contrasted with that which claims that it is wrong for the state to hand the administration of a key part of its structure to a profit-making organization. Although when in opposition the Labour party had indicated that private prisons would not continue. There are currently nine privately managed prisons now operating, with two more planned. However, Buckley Hall, a privately run prison, was returned to management by the public sector after a public sector in-house bid to run it was successful.[2]

---

[2] Extensive information about all prison establishments, including those which are privately managed, can be found in *The Prisons Handbook 2002* (Waterside Press, 2002).

Following the escapes of Category A prisoners from HMP Whitemoor and HMP Parkhurst in 1994 and 1995, two reports by Sir John Woodcock (Woodcock, 1994) and General Sir John Learmont (Learmont, 1995), caused the Prison Service to reiterate the importance of security issues over rehabilitative elements of imprisonment. The Learmont report particularly ranged far and wide over issues facing the service, and was as symptomatic of its time (the era of Michael Howard, home secretary's, famous assertion that 'prison works') as the 1877 Act before it, emphasising the need for austerity over the approach advocated by Woolf.

The Prison Service conducts its work in the spotlight of criminal justice and government's need to show it is working hard on the question of crime; in consequence the public and media exert considerable influence on policy. Policy has moved from Michael Howard's 'prison works' to Jack Straw's 'prison can be made to work' (Straw, 1998). The importance of the impact this can have on new initiatives should not be underestimated.

Two other recent reports have influenced the development of the service: firstly, the 1997 *Prison Service Review* which looked at the strategic management of the service, and the way forward through business and strategic planning (Prison Service, 1997); secondly, the more recent report of the Targeted Performance Initiative Working Group, chaired by Lord Laming, which examined the management issues facing the service in its attempts to define a failing, or successful prison (Laming, 2000).

The conflict concerning the purpose of imprisonment also continues unabated. The classical interpretation suggests four main purposes to imprisonment: punishment, deterrence, reform and public protection (Walker, 1965). It is perhaps unsurprising that this debate continues, as it has been running for over 100 years. It serves to illustrate the issues surrounding the very public nature of the Prison Service and its work.

MINISTERS AND THE HOME OFFICE

The Prison Service is one of the key components of the Home Office, under the authority of the secretary of state (home secretary). The main function of the Home Office is the development and administration of criminal and other policy through departments such as the Prison Service, National Probation Service, the Police Service and the Immigration and Nationality Department. *Figure 2.1* illustrates the place of the Prison Service within the management structure of the Home Office.

Part I: The Operating Context

Figure 2.1: Management Structure of the Home Office

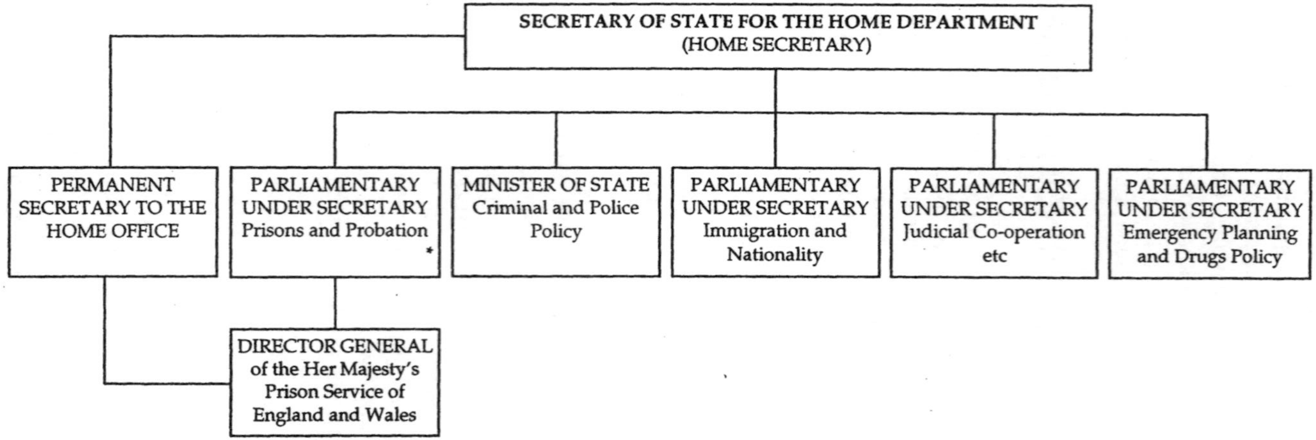

```
                    SECRETARY OF STATE FOR THE HOME DEPARTMENT
                                  (HOME SECRETARY)
                                         |
   ┌─────────────────┬──────────────┬────┴──────────┬──────────────┬──────────────┐
PERMANENT        PARLIAMENTARY   MINISTER OF    PARLIAMENTARY  PARLIAMENTARY  PARLIAMENTARY
SECRETARY TO     UNDER SECRETARY    STATE       UNDER SECRETARY UNDER SECRETARY UNDER SECRETARY
THE HOME OFFICE  Prisons and     Criminal and   Immigration and Judicial       Emergency Planning
                 Probation *     Police Policy  Nationality     Co-operation   and Drugs Policy
                      |                                         etc
              DIRECTOR GENERAL
              of the Her Majesty's
              Prison Service of
              England and Wales
```

* Since renamed Parliamentary Under Secretary Custodial and Community Provision

The Home Office has set two broad aims for the criminal justice system as a whole:

- to reduce crime and the fear of crime and their social and economic costs;
- to dispense justice fairly and efficiently, and promote confidence in the rule of law

Home Office, 2000c, p.4

The Home Office itself has seven aims with the Prison Service being key to the achievement of the fourth: 'effective execution of the sentences of the courts so as to reduce reoffending and protect the public' (Home Office, 2000c). In order to achieve this the Prison Service is expected to work closely with other agencies including the National Probation Service, Youth Justice Board, youth offending teams (YOTs) and secure hospitals.

The Prison Service remains the largest of the Home Office's executive agencies, having been given agency status in 1993 by the then Conservative home secretary Kenneth Clarke. Agency status has meant a greater degree of devolution of management and financial authority than found in most mainstream government departments.

Notably, there is no separate government department within the Home Office dealing with prison policy—as policy and operations are inextricably linked, the Prison Service has responsibility for both (Prison Service, 1997, p.31). The early 1990s saw some conflict in the balance of policy and operational roles, and the division of ministerial and departmental accountability, culminating in the dismissal of the first Director General of the new agency, Derek Lewis, by Michael Howard in 1995, following the escapes from Whitemoor and Parkhurst already mentioned.

A quinquennial review of agency status in 1999 concluded that it had offered

- delegated freedom to the Director General;
- greater focus on outputs and targets; and
- cohesive organization and a visible Director General.

Prison Service, 1999a, p.5

and, in consequence, agency status was retained. A new framework document was issued (Prison Service, 1999b), reflecting the Government's commitment to ensuring proper ministerial accountability for the service, integrating its aims and principles with those of the wider criminal justice system and bringing greater clarity to managerial roles at senior level.

The home secretary is responsible for the Prison Service, and as such is accountable to Parliament. He or she sets the strategic direction of the service, defines its outputs and allocates its resources. The designated minister for the Prison Service is also responsible for the National Probation Service, and acts as the chair of the Strategy Board for Correctional Services (Prison Service, 2000a, p.13).

EXTERNAL ACCOUNTABILITY: INSPECTORATE, OMBUDSMAN AND BOARD OF VISITORS

The home secretary has a number of people monitoring conditions in prisons who are independent of the Prison Service.[3]

HM Chief Inspector of Prisons

The role of the Chief Inspector of Prisons is set out in section 5A Prison Act 1952:

> ... it shall be the duty of the Chief Inspector to inspect or arrange for the inspection of prisons in England and Wales and report to the secretary of state. The Chief Inspector shall in particular report to the secretary of state on the treatment of prisoners and conditions in prisons.

The Inspectorate carries out its work by way of announced and unannounced inspections. Reports of the inspections are published and include lists of good practice, as well as criticisms. A development has been the publication of thematic reviews into areas such as suicides in prisons and young offenders.

Prisons Ombudsman

The first Prisons Ombudsman was appointed in October 1994 and has a Statement of Purpose which reads:

> To provide prisoners with an independent and effective avenue of complaint which is fair and even-handed, has the confidence of prisoners and the Prison Service, and contributes towards a just prison system.

The Ombudsman investigates complaints which are submitted by individual prisoners who have failed to obtain satisfaction from the Prison Service system of requests and complaints. He or she considers the merits of matters complained of as well as the procedures involved and decides whether or not to uphold the complaint. If the complaint is

---

[3] A detailed explanation of the roles of these statutory external monitors can be found in Nicola Padfield's chapter in *Prisons and the Prisoner* (Bryans and Jones 2001, *Chapter 25*).

upheld the Ombudsman can make recommendations either to the Director general of the Prison Service or to the home secretary as appropriate. However, the recommendations do not have to be accepted.

Boards of Visitors

Each prison has an independent Board of Visitors (BoV) whose duties are set out in the Prison Rules 1999. In short, members of BoVs monitor the prison premises, its administration and treatment of prisoners. They have a right to enter an establishment at any time and have free access to every part of it and to see every prisoner.

PRISON SERVICE HEADQUARTERS

The home secretary, with the approval of the prisons and probation minister appoints the director general of the Prison Service. The director general (DG) has designated authority for the day-to-day management of the service and its performance against plans and targets as agreed with ministers. The DG acts as the home secretary's principle advisor on matters relating to Prison Service activities, and has delegated authority on matters of personnel and finance with a budget of £2.465bn (2002-3) which accounts for roughly 16 per cent of the total spending on the criminal justice system. The home secretary also draws on advice from the permanent secretary and other advisors, and from HM Chief Inspector of Prisons, who (as described above) inspects prisons and reports on the treatment of prisoners.

The deputy director general (DDG) has direct managerial responsibility for all Area Managers and two directors—the director of security and the director of high security prisons. The DDG role concentrates on operational and performance management.

In addition to the DG and the DDG, the Prison Services has a number of other directors, each responsible for different areas of service policy. The structure of these directorates changes in response to policy initiatives, for example the Prison Service created the post of director of regimes in response to recommendations made in the *Prison Service Review* (Prison Service, 1997, p.68). *Figure 2.2* illustrates the structure of the service in more detail.

Directorates have also changed as the result of work with outside agencies. For example closer working with the National Health Service has caused the former Directorate of Healthcare to be restructured into two distinct parts. These are the Health Policy Unit, which deals with day-to-day issues, and the Prison Healthcare Task Force, which seeks to provide strategic direction and liaison between prisons and Local Health Authorities (Prison Service, 2000b, p.13).

Part I: The Operating Context

Figure 2.2: Prison Service Organizational Structure (Prison Service, 2000b, p.12)

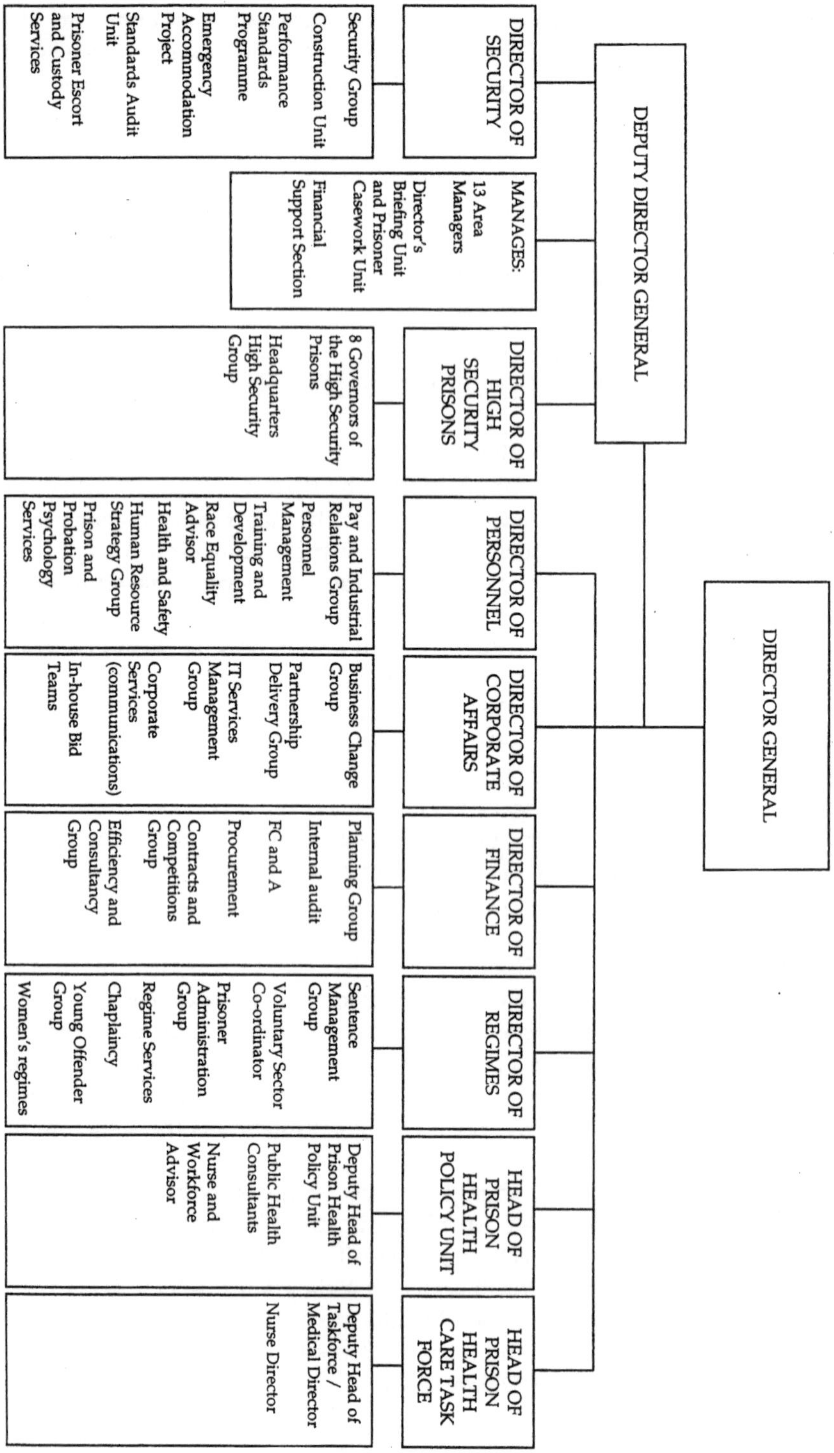

The structure of the senior management of the Prison Service was changed in 1999 with the introduction of two management boards, the Prison Service Management Board and the Prison Service Strategy Board.

Management board
The management board is intended to assist the DG in the day-to-day running of the service, reflecting the 'marked operational focus of the Prison Service' (Prison Service, 2000b, p14). Its day-to-day business includes:

- monitoring performance
- deciding on immediate priorities and expenditure
- authorising projects and initiatives
- approving important internal communications.

The board comprises all executive directors, *ex officio* members appointed by the DG (e.g. the legal advisor and race relations officer), and non-executive directors whose job it is to provide independent advice and oversight.

Strategy board
The Prison Service Strategy Board discusses long-term strategy and high level performance monitoring. Its main purpose is to focus on the contribution of the service to the Home Office policy on crime and criminal justice.

The strategy board was replaced by the Strategy Board for Correctional Services, which advises the home secretary on the strategic direction for the Prison Service and the National Probation Service (Prison Service, 2000a, p14). Chaired by the prisons and probation minister, this board represents a further step towards the integration of policy arrangements for the two services, and perhaps to a Canadian model of a fully integrated Correctional Service. The move has clear implications for the voluntary sector as it will require an understanding of the probation service, and of the challenge that greater integration will bring for outside agencies in terms of consistent delivery and overlap.

PLANNING AND PERFORMANCE MANAGEMENT

Each year the Prison Service, in consultation with the home secretary produces a business plan, setting out the aims and targets for the coming year, based around the high level aims developed in its three year strategic plan. Following the production of this plan, each group in HQ and establishments produces its own business plan, based around the concept of matching objectives to allocated resources.

Funding is allocated centrally from the Treasury. The service can also apply and receive money from the government's spending review (formerly the comprehensive spending review) which determines priorities across government over three years, and which has previously offered considerable sums of money for offending behaviour programmes and work on drugs (Prison Service, 2000a, p.10).

The service is set a number of targets to achieve, against which it will be measured and compared to other government agencies and departments. These measures are known as Key Performance Indicators and for 2000-2001 there were 15 of them as summarised in *Figure 2.3*. They will be judged in the analysis as either being met or not met and the results laid before Parliament.

Figure 2.3 **Key Performance Indicators 2000-2001**[4]

KPI	TARGET
1	Category A escapes
2	Number of escapes from prisons and escorts undertaken by Prison Service staff
3	Number of escapes from contracted out escorts
4	Number of positive adjudications of assault on staff, prisoners and others
5	Number of prisoners held two to a cell designed for one
6	Rate of positive drug tests from the random drug testing policy
7	Number of voluntary drug testing compacts
8	Completions of offending behaviour and sex offender treatment programmes
9	Basic literacy and numeracy targets
10	Purposeful activity hours
11	Cost per uncrowded prisoner place
12	Cost per prisoner
13	Number of staff sickness days
14	Reply deadline for correspondence
15	Response time for call to HQ switchboard and abandoned call numbers

The service has also introduced a number of new performance measures, designed to measure establishments and groups against each other, and to offer an objective view of performance through application of the principles of balanced scorecard analysis (see Kaplan and Norton, 1996). There are 47 of these key performance targets, which include

---

[4] Source: Prison Service, 2000a, p.21.

compliance with internal audits, mother and baby units, programme delivery and with national race relations policy on recruitment.

To encourage a consistent level of performance across the service, a range of performance standards has been introduced. Performance against standards is measured by a Prison Service audit team that visits each establishment every two years. Each prison also has its own internal auditors. There are more than 60 standards covering all aspects of the work of the service from security intelligence to disabled prisoners, and they set out, clearly and concisely, required actions in every area.

AREA STRUCTURE

There are over 130 prisons in England and Wales (Prison Service, 2000b, p.46), of which the management of nine has been contracted out to the private sector. Prisons are divided into 13 geographical areas each with its own manager.[5] The structure of these areas was changed in 2000 to ally the service more closely with other criminal justice agencies, and to ensure co-terminosity with the police and English government regions. The exceptions to this are the high security estate, which contains eight prisons, the female estate and the juvenile estate which are each managed functionally. During 2000, area managers moved out of Prison Service HQ in London to new offices based in their areas.

Area Managers report directly to the DDG and line manage governors. They are responsible for policy implementation, performance management, audit and monitoring and offering support advice and guidance to governors on a myriad of subjects.

The report of the Laming Committee on prison performance places great emphasis on the role of the area manager, and it is likely that the role and its influence over the running of establishments will continue to grow. Laming identified the role of the area manager as key to maintaining a successful prison, and argued that such managers should be fully accountable, when a prison is found to be failing (Laming, 2000, p.3).

PRISON ESTABLISHMENTS

The number and types of prisons in England and Wales is illustrated in *Figure 2.4*.

---

[5] All the prisons in Wales are managed by one area manager.

40 Part I: The Operating Context

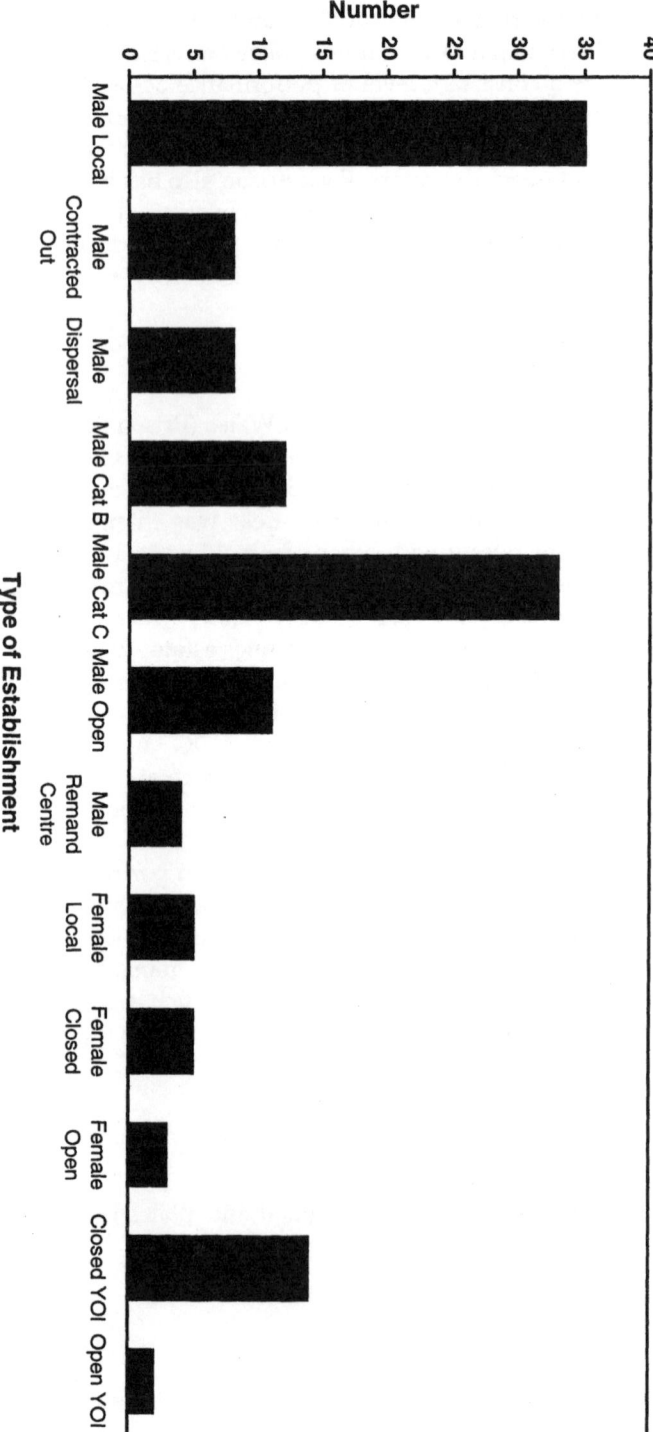

Figure 2.4: Prison Service Establishments (Prison Service, 2000b, p.75)

Security categories and establishments

There are four security categories for adult male prisoners: A, B, C and D, with A being the highest. Unconvicted adult males can be designated as Category A, but if not, they are considered uncategorsied and held in Category B establishments. These categories were introduced after the Mountbatten Report in 1966, and are still in use today. They are defined as follows:

- *Category A:* prisoners whose escape would be highly dangerous to the public, or the police, or the security of the state, no matter how unlikely that escape might be, and for whom the aim must be to make escape impossible (subdivided into standard, high and exceptional risk).
- *Category B:* prisoners for whom the highest conditions of security are not necessary but for whom escape must be made very difficult.
- *Category C:* prisoners who cannot be trusted in open conditions, but who do not have the resources and the will to make a determined escape attempt.
- *Category D:* prisoners who can be reasonably trusted in open conditions.

Prison Service d, 1999, 9.5

Women prisoners can be placed in Category A conditions if necessary, otherwise they are categorised as suitable for closed or open conditions, although they are always held separately from men. Similarly, young prisoners (aged 18-21) can be made 'restricted status' (the equivalent of adult male Category A) but are otherwise placed in open or closed young offender establishments.

Prison establishments reflect these security classifications, with most places being for Category C offenders, but vary considerably in size, shape and design. The oldest prisons still in use today were built in the nineteenth century (Brodie, Croom and Davies, 1999, p.6) to a variety of designs. Some newer prisons are so called 'quick build' or 'ready to use' units which are imported in kit form. HMP The Weare in Dorset has the distinction of being on board a ship; a floating accommodation unit purchased from the USA in 1997, and the first floating prison to be in use since the days of prison hulks. Prisons hold from 150 to around 1,000 prisoners, either in a multifunctional role including those waiting for trial, and those that have been sentenced, or in a single role holding prisoners post conviction and sentence.

The rules governing adult prisons date from the Prison Act 1952 (as amended). Those for young offenders currently date from the Young Offender Institution Rules 1988. The Crime and Disorder Act 1998 set up the Youth Justice Board for England and Wales (YJB), the purpose being to monitor the provision of youth services and the youth justice system. In April 2000, a new sentence, the detention and training order was introduced for 12-17 year olds, and this population was separated out from those under 21. The YJB has responsibility for commissioning and purchasing all juvenile secure accommodation.

Older prisons represent a challenge for the service, both to adapt them to suit modern living conditions (an extensive refurbishment programme ended the practice of 'slopping out' in 1997) but also to keep them in good order. A more recent Prison Service report identified a £30 million maintenance backlog across the prison estate (Prison Service, 2000b, p.10).

Management structure within individual prisons

All prisons have a governor, whose pay scale depends on the size and complexity of the prison. The governor directly manages a number of functional heads and working to each of them are a number of heads of department. This group is often known as the senior management team or group (SMT or SMG). All senior managers in the prison are graded as a Prison Service manager 1, 2 or 3. This term replaced 'governor grades' and administrative/specialist grades in July 2000 as part of a pay and grading initiative. Former governor 5 and higher executive officers (HEO) level staff and above are now referred to by their job (head of regimes, residential etc). A sample establishment structure is shown in *Figure 2. 5.*

Not all establishments are structured in this way, but most will fill key functional roles depending on the wishes of the governor, and indeed the size of the prison. Functional heads also have responsibility for different areas of policy according to their roles, for example the head of activities may have responsibility for the prison's drug strategy.

Governors

It is generally recognised that there is a direct link between what governors believe and value, and how their prisons are run. The job of governor is complex and demanding, needing a wide range of skills and abilities. They make the key difference between the failure or success of a new initiative, and are tasked with maintaining the often difficult balance between operational and policy issues. To understand a prison one could do worse than study its governor.[6] It is also worth noting that governors now have devolved responsibility for managing the budget of the prison. This gives them the flexibility to fund local initiatives, including working with the voluntary sector, provided that they comply with the limitations set out in Prison Service Finance Order.

---

[6] For the work of Governors and how they influence the operation of the prison see *The Prison Governor: Theory and Practice* (Bryans and Wilson, 2000). An explanation of how Governors try to change the culture of their prisons and manage the interface between staff and prisoners is explored in *Chapter 13* of *Prisons and the Prisoner* (Bryans and Jones, 2001).

Understanding the Prison Service **43**

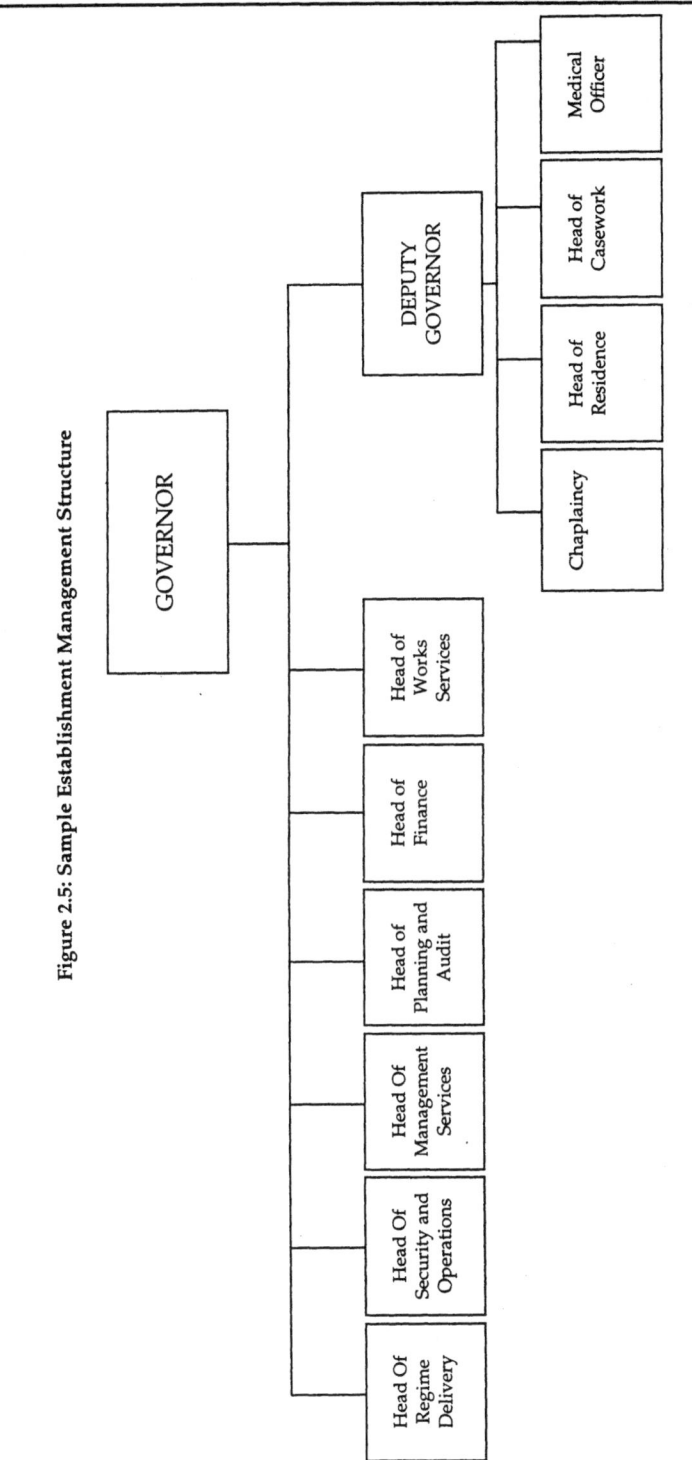

Figure 2.5: Sample Establishment Management Structure

Other Prison Service staff

All the services available in a large community, and indeed more specialist tasks, are delivered in most prisons, from dentistry to hairdressing, from education to religious services, from work and offending behaviour courses to drug counselling. The Prison Service has over 43,000 staff including uniformed staff, administrative staff and specialists such as doctors, chaplains, instructors and psychologists, all employed under civil service conditions. The role of both the medical officer and the chaplain in prisons are enshrined in statute.

Contracted staff provide both education and probation services in all prisons. Education services are bought direct from suppliers, and not from local education authorities. Probation staff are responsible for assisting in the preparation of offenders for release into the community, and their supervision whilst on licence, but their role is very varied, and they will often be involved in prison in the delivery of offending behaviour and other courses. It has already been noted that there are increasingly close links between the National Probation Service and the Prison Service, through the introduction of the Correctional Policy Framework for example (Home Office, 2000c). *Figure 2.6* shows the average number of directly employed full-time staff in the service over the period 1998-2000.

Of these groups it is the uniformed staff (operational support grades, prison officers, senior officers and principal officers) whose culture dominates in a prison. This cultural dominance is reinforced by the power of their union, the POA. In many respects their attitude to new initiatives or progress can heavily influence change.

As the role of prison staff has moved away from that of the mere turnkey, that role has become more complex. As Kauffman observed: 'Prison officials are expected to punish, deter, isolate and rehabilitate offenders, while at the same time maintaining order and inmate productivity' (Kauffman, 1988, p.45). The attempt to strike this balance has lead to different interpretations of how staff carry out their role. Lombardo argues that the work of the prison officer has a number of key themes including human services, order maintenance, security, supervision and rules enforcement (Lombardo, 1989, pp.66-68). The majority of studies on the work of prison staff have been conducted in the USA however, and the prisons of England and Wales are immersed in a very different sort of culture, based closely on tradition and patterns of recruitment that reflected a military bent until the 1980s.

Prison officers, whilst carrying out routine custodial duties, are also involved in the range of activities that prisons offer. In addition to staff who have chosen to specialise in healthcare, dog handling or physical education, officers are also closely involved in sentence management (the process of planning a prisoner's sentence), offending behaviour work, counselling and prisoners' often complex personal problems.

Figure 2.6: Staffing levels: Grade split by gender

	GRADE	FEMALE	MALE	TOTAL	%FEMALE
Unified	Grade 1, B and A	4	16	20	20.0%
	Grade 1, B and B	6	38	44	13.6%
	Grade 1, B and C	13	49	62	21.0%
	Grade 1, B and D	11	45	56	19.6%
	Grade 2, B and A	13	76	89	14.6%
	Grade 2, B and B	39	238	277	14.1%
	Grade 2, B and C	25	184	209	12.0%
	Grade 3, B and A	5	23	28	17.9%
	Grade 3, B and B	41	251	292	14.0%
	Grade 3, B and C	3	8	11	27.3%
	Remaining Governors	5	20	25	20.0%
	Principal Officer	92	1,152	1,244	7.4%
	Principal Officer (APS)	5	6	11	45.5%
	Senior Officer	348	3,444	3,792	9.2%
	Prison Officer	3,313	15,777	19,090	17.4%
	Prison Officer (APS)	5	5	10	50.0%
Unified Total		**3,928**	**21,332**	**25,260**	15.6%
OSG (Operational Support Grade)	Night Patrol	13	76	89	14.6%
	OSG	1,477	4,102	5,579	26.5%
	Prison Auxiliary	75	187	262	28.6%
OSG Total		**1,565**	**4,365**	**5,930**	26.4%
Admin	Senior Civil Servant	9	35	44	20.5%
	Other Admin staff	4,378	1,358	5,736	76.3%
Admin Total		**4,387**	**1,393**	**5,780**	75.9%
Healthcare	Nursing Grades	791	228	1,019	77.6%
	Principal Medical Officer	0	1	1	0.0%
	Senior Medical Officer	4	39	43	9.3%
	Medical Officer	15	106	121	12.4%
	Other Healthcare Staff	74	22	96	77.1%
Healthcare Total		**884**	**396**	**1,280**	69.1%
Chaplaincy	Chaplain	56	215	271	20.7%
	Assistant Chaplain	10	15	25	40.0%
Chaplaincy Total		**66**	**230**	**296**	22.3%

Psychology	Senior Psychology Grades	147	42	189	77.8%
	Psychologist	117	26	143	81.8%
	Psychological Assistant	166	26	192	86.5%
Psychology Total		430	94	524	82.1%
Other Staff		829	4,032	4,861	17.1%
GRAND TOTAL		12,089	31,842	43,931	27.5%

Ethnic origin of staff in post as at 31 October 2000

ETHNICITY	Total	% of staff in post
Asian	492	1.1
Black	845	2.0
Other	184	0.4
White	40,237	91.6
No Data	2,173	4.9
Grand Total	43,931	100

Disabled status of staff in post as at 31 October 2000

DISABLED STATUS	Male	Female	Total
Able Bodied	31,725	12,043	43,768
Status Unknown	2	0	2
Total Disabled	115	46	161

Source: Personnel Corporate Database

They also provide the frontline work in keeping the prison safe and secure, through their vigilance as to physical security issues (checking of cell fabric for example) to their interactions with prisoners which gather vital intelligence to prevent escapes, intercept drugs or detect bullying.[7]

Prison staff are recruited and promoted through a competence-based assessment, with the use of job simulation assessment centres playing an increasing role. These place candidates in situations designed to replicate those faced by staff at all levels, from dealing with a stressed employee to an angry prisoner, although these tests vary with the rank being assessed. Prison officers are recruited on a local basis. In its recruitment policies, the Prison Service plays close attention to equal opportunities. It should be noted that all establishments have a mix of both male and female staff. However, currently women account for only 26 per cent of all staff employed, and 12 per cent of uniform staff. Ethnic minority staff account for only three per cent of all Prison Service staff (Prison Service, 2000c).

Routes for people seeking management roles

Prison Service management grades have a number of routes into the service; either promotion through the ranks or recruitment onto a specialist scheme. These include a scheme for graduate recruitment (Accelerated Promotion Scheme—also open to exceptional existing staff), another for the entry of experienced managers from outside the service (Direct Entry) and lastly one for existing civil servants (Cross Hierarchical Move Scheme). These schemes are designed to quickly move staff into the more senior grades based on competence assessments and the accreditation of key skills and knowledge.

PRISONERS

There were over 68,000 prisoners in England and Wales in 2002.[8] The average population in custody in 2000[9] was 64,600, of whom 11,270 were remand prisoners (Home Office, 2001c, p.1). However, it should be remembered that over 129,700 prisoners were received into custody in 2000. The current Certified Normal Accommodation (uncrowded capacity) is 64,000 and the maximum operational capacity is 72,000 places. The growth of the prison population since 1992 has been particularly rapid, and has been influenced by a number of factors including the Criminal Justice Acts of 1991, 1993, 1994 and 1996, the

---

[7] For a detailed treatment see *The Prison Officer* (Liebling and Price, 2001)
[8] Prisoner categories are described earlier in the chapter in relation to the security categories of prison establishments.
[9] The last complete statistical year on which analysis can be based.

general election, and the murder of Jamie Bulger in 1992 (Home Office, 2000b, p6). The breakdown of the prison population for 2000 is shown in *Figure 2.7*.

Figure 2.7 Main Components of the Prison Population (Averages during 2000)[10]

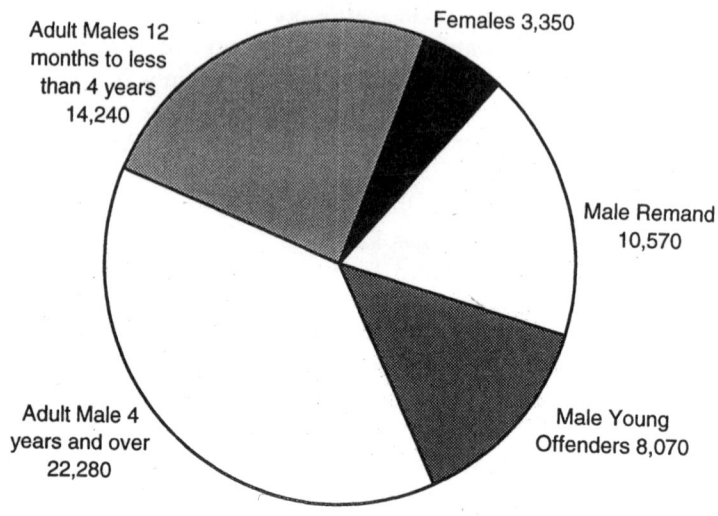

The main offence groups for adult males in 2000 were violence (22 per cent), drug offences (15 per cent), burglary (18 per cent) and robbery (12 per cent) (Home Office, 2001c). For adult women the main sentences were overwhelmingly imposed for drugs (36 per cent) followed by theft and fraud (25 per cent) then violence and sexual crimes (17 per cent) (Home Office, 2001c). Female prisoners make up just 5.2 per cent of the

---

[10] Source: Home Office, 2001c.

overall prison population, while young offenders account for 17 per cent of the male population. Reconviction rates within two years of release are 76 per cent for young offenders, 54 per cent for adult males and 51 per cent for female prisoners (Home Office, 2001c, p.152).

In 2000, prisoners from ethnic groups made up 19 per cent of the male and 25 per cent of the female prison population; nine per cent of the total prison population were foreign nationals. Amongst women serving sentences for drugs, the proportion of foreign nationals is more than 79 per cent (Home Office, 2001, p.107). Of those male prisoners with British nationality, 94 per cent were white, 3 per cent were black, 2 per cent were South Asian and 1 per cent from Chinese and other ethnic groups.

That people from ethnic minorities are over represented in prisons can be illustrated by examining the rate of incarceration per 100,000 of the population. While the proportion for whites is 188 per 100,000, the rate for black people is 1,615 per 100,000, and 199 for members of South Asian groups (Home Office, 2001, p.114).

Prisoners can be segregated from others for a variety of reasons, whether they are under pressure due to the nature of their offence, or are a danger to others through violence or disorder. The basis of this segregation is the prison rule on Good Order and Discipline. Prisoners can also be given a period of cellular confinement following a finding of guilt at an adjudication.

The diversity of the prisoner population means that prisoners have many needs which require attention, from different visits entitlements, to work for convicted prisoners. Thus each prison must carefully tailor its regime to suit its population, catering for prisoners who can happily live amongst others, whilst holding those that for various reasons cannot. Young offenders require particular conditions, as their behaviour is far removed from that of the rest of the population. Prisons are therefore set up to deal with prisoners according to offence, category, sex, age, stage of court appearance or conviction, offending behaviour, release and resettlement needs. The combination of an expanding population that is growing at a greater rate than trends predicted and this diversity makes accommodating prisoners a most challenging task.

A KEY ROLE

The Prison Service has a key part to play in protecting the public and by reducing re-offending. The challenge facing that service is to meet the needs of the prison population, balance the demands of Parliament and the public, achieve targets, implement new policies and effect culture change, amongst others. It is a remarkably complex task carried out against a background of often conflicting stakeholders, and working in the prison system remains one of the most demanding roles in public service.

CHAPTER 3

The Penal Voluntary Sector

Margaret Carey and Roma Walker

This chapter gives a brief outline of the historical development of charitable and voluntary sector activity within the penal system over the last 300 years. A list of the legislative milestones and the development of penal voluntary sector organizations can be found in *Appendix 4*.

It will be apparent to people familiar with current penal sector activity that there are remarkable and striking parallels (and only occasional sharp contrasts) with the present day. There are many areas where little has changed, not least the extent, diversity and innovative nature of activity. The same issues that concerned our predecessors remain today: prisoner numbers, prison conditions and appropriate methods for dealing with young offenders and children within the penal system.

The focus of earlier charitable service provision was similar to what is provided today; for example, support to families, diversion schemes, mentoring and post-release employment. Substance abuse and its consequences generated much energy in the Victorian era, although it was directed towards alcohol rather than drugs. Research, campaigning and the holding of conferences was also prevalent, as was seeking to bring about reform through legislation by the lobbying and support of sympathetic Parliamentarians, and the presentation of evidence to Parliamentary committees. Finally, many of the problems that beset current organizations would have been familiar to earlier ones, including difficulties over access, uneasy relations with prison authorities, funding problems and a sometimes less than well co-ordinated approach between the charities themselves. An interesting feature of the Victorian era was the involvement of prison governors on the committees of the various aid societies.

The development of charitable relief throughout the eighteenth and nineteenth centuries, and in particular during the Victorian era, has to be viewed in the context of the spirit of the age. There was a burgeoning growth of the social conscience and a developing socialist movement. This, when combined with a religious zeal that placed great emphasis upon rescue, moral rehabilitation and reform, led to an approach towards the social problems of the day that was 'unapologetically evangelical' (Newburn, 1995, p.82). Philanthropy was paternalistic in style, with the upper and middle classes in particular, expressing their piety through charity. There was the notion that wealth and status carried a moral responsibility for others. However, there was also a very deep rooted concept of the 'deserving' and 'undeserving' poor, and this underpinned charitable activity. The overarching philosophy was that relief should

> . . . never be given indiscriminately, because such charity 'debauched' or 'pauperised' the recipient, discouraging self-reliance and would encourage fecklessness, laziness and vice. Charity must be only given after careful investigation of each case and a precise assessment of need and moral desert.
>
> Forsythe, 1991, p.219

People in receipt of charitable relief were therefore obliged to prove their worthiness for any munificence. However, some of the aid charities working with prisoners and ex-prisoners applied these principles harshly and judgementally, and their attention and approaches were not always welcomed by the prisoners (Forsythe, 1991, p.227).

PIONEERING PENAL REFORMERS AND SERVICE PROVIDERS

There were a number of individuals in the vanguard of penal reform and philanthropic activity. By exposing conditions, campaigning and providing direct services they brought to public and political attention issues around prisons and prisoners. The most famous, though by no means the only ones, were John Howard and Elizabeth Fry.

John Howard
John Howard was appointed High Sheriff of Bedfordshire in 1773 and as such had responsibility for the local prison. The corruption, squalor and maladministration that he encountered there shocked him. Howard subsequently visited prisons throughout Britain and the continent, travelling a total of over 42,000 miles. His extensive travels, inspections of prisons, and philosophy are well-documented (Freeman, 1978; Ignatieff, 1978; Bryans and Jones, 2001), and his seminal work in 1777 *The State of the Prisons* proved influential. Alongside his meticulous cataloguing of prison conditions, he made proposals for improvements in relation to location, design, hygiene, religious teaching, the separation of offenders (by sex, age and offence) and regulations for the conduct of gaolers. His ideas were innovative, and his recommendations covered all aspects of prison life, including the appointment of inspectors. Whilst liberal and visionary in many areas, he was nonetheless, in accordance with the conventions of the age, a disciplinarian. He advocated that

gentle discipline would be more effective than severe, but for those who did not respond to such leniency he recommended that they should be punished by solitary confinement on bread and water. Howard developed a credo on governing:

> The notion that convicts are ungovernable is certainly erroneous. There is a mode of managing some of the most desperate, with ease to yourself, and advantage to them. Many of them are shrewd and sensible: manage them with calmness, yet with steadiness: show them that you have humanity, and that you aim to make them useful members of society: let them see and hear the rules and orders of the prison, and be convinced that they are not defrauded in the provisions or clothes by contractors or gaolers. When they are sick, let them be treated with tenderness . . . Endeavours should be used to persuade the offender that he is corrected only for his own good.
>
> Howard, 1929, p.40

Howard's efforts resulted in three reformative Acts: the Discharged Prisoners Act 1774, the Health of Prisoners Act 1774, and the Penitentiary Act 1779 (Bryans and Jones, 2001, p.18).

Elizabeth Fry
Elizabeth Fry, a strict Quaker, and following the Quaker tradition of social responsibility, first started visiting women prisoners in 1813. In 1817, with a number of other women Quakers she founded The Ladies' Association for the Improvement of the Female Prisoners in Newgate. She established a school and a chapel within the prison, and supplied food and clothing to the women, and practical assistance upon release. She also developed rules governing behaviour, hygiene and sobriety. This was followed later by the founding of the British Ladies' Society for the Reformation of Female Prisoners. These were the first of many ladies' visiting committees all over the country and were to be a forerunner of the Prison Visitors Association still in existence today. Like John Howard's work before her, Fry's came to the attention of Parliament. She was invited to give evidence to a House of Commons Committee on London Prisons, at which she criticised the practice of mixing the old with the young, and hardened and persistent offenders with those who had committed minor offences or their first crime. At that time, Fry's work was considered inappropriate for a woman to be undertaking and was met with suspicion and opposition (Morris, 1976; Young and Ashton, 1956).

Sarah Martin
Less well known than John Howard and Elizabeth Fry was Sarah Martin, who was born in 1791, in Caister near Yarmouth. Whilst not from a wealthy background, she saved to pay for parties and treats for the

children in the local workhouse. Hearing of the conditions in Yarmouth Jail, she eventually obtained permission to visit. She then raised money to spend on sewing materials to enable prisoners, both men and women, to have some occupation. She visited regularly as she believed that regularity was the main quality of a prison visitor. She moved home to be nearer the prison and extended her work to raising funds to provide food, clothing and employment upon release. Her work presaged that of many current agencies.

CHARITIES AND AID SOCIETIES

As early as 1702 charities were directly involving themselves in penal affairs. In that year Newgate and Marshalsea prisons were inspected by The Society for the Promotion of Christian Knowledge which advocated keeping prisoners in separate cells (Bryans and Jones, 2001, p.17). Charities and aid societies started to proliferate at the end of the eighteenth century, many with pious and worthy titles such as the New Asylum for the Prevention of Vice and Misery amongst the Poor, and the Jewish Ladies' Society for Preventative and Rescue Work, which focused on prostitution. The Philanthropic Society was formed in 1790 to 'educate and reform destitute and depraved children' who were expected to respond to 'a strong religious influence and the irresistible law of kindness' (Young and Ashton, 1956, p.164). Missionary zeal was commonplace from church-based organizations such as the Salvation Army and the Church Army. The focus of their work centred upon the promotion of temperance and the negative impact of alcohol, which was a significant feature of Victorian life. Indeed, between 1860 and 1876, the numbers imprisoned for drunkenness and disorderly behaviour rose from just under 4,000 to almost 24,000 (Newburn, 1995, p.82). In response to this, the Church of England Total Abstinence Society attached missionaries to courts with a view to rescuing and rehabilitating those before the courts (Young and Ashton, 1956, p.174). These missionaries, first established in 1876, would make requests to the magistrates that they bind defendants over into their care and that the missionaries would then undertake to secure their 'restoration and reclamation' (Newburn, 1995, p.82). Such was the extent of the problems of alcohol that by 1900 there were 100 such missionaries, though by then the society had dropped the word 'total' from its title to widen its own support base (*ibid*, p.174). It became the Church of England Temperance Society, and by the 1890s it had a supporters membership of nearly one million (Newburn, 1995, p.82).

The pursuit of such zealous rehabilitation and rescue was not just the aim of the church and the charitable organizations during the Victorian era, but was equally embraced by the prison authorities, which sought 'to improve prisoners morally, spiritually and educationally' (Forsythe, 1991, p.116). The focus of this zeal within prisons was channelled through the chaplaincy. Chaplains had been a presence in prison since Parliament gave authority for their appointment to the old county jails in 1773 (Bryans and Jones, 2001, p.159). Their role was to hold the compulsory Sunday and daily services, supervise the work of visiting educators, and co-ordinate the efforts of the various charities. Additionally they would give lectures to prisoners, typically on subjects such as 'temperance, virtue and the evils of gambling, industry and sexual morality' (Forsythe, 1991, p.120).

By the 1830s 'the chaplain ranked second only to the governor in status and salary if not authority' (Blom-Cooper, 1974, p.9). At Millbank in 1837, the chaplain, the Reverend Daniel Nihil, combined the offices of both chaplain and governor. However, 'his attempt to imbue the prison with high moral fervour was not a success and his rigorous preference for solitary confinement allegedly led to an embarrassing rise in the suicide rate' (Blom-Cooper, 1974, p.9)

Chaplains, along with the prison governors, were very often on the committees of the various charities and Discharged Prisoners' Aid Societies, and were therefore closely involved in their policies and practices. Such close involvement meant that they were in a position to grant or deny access as they so wished, and which sometimes brought them into conflict with the prison authorities.

Innovation and service provision
The range and quality of the service provision of the various charities and aid societies was diverse and often innovative. For example the Church of England Temperance Society provided shelters, missions, homes, colonies and 'labour yards' which generated employment (Forsythe, 1991, p.229). Others provided practical support with clothes, food, the means to return home upon release and tools to assist in a trade. Schools were established for those children considered at risk and early forms of diversion schemes, were developed, such as in Birmingham. There, in 1841, a register of volunteers was instituted to supervise young offenders who would have otherwise been given custodial sentences (Young and Ashton, 1956, p.173). The young offenders were mentored by volunteers who were 'firm but sympathetic morally upright social superiors' who would 'assure the prisoner that he or she was not alone in the world, but that each was cared for by a benevolent paternal society' (Forsythe, 1991, p.218)

The charities and societies often pushed at the boundaries of the conventions of the day, sometimes without official sanction. For example, 'lady visitors' were technically only allowed to visit women prisoners, but if the governor and chaplain approved, the lady visitors also saw young male prisoners. Such activity was described by the Prison Commission as 'a bold experiment' (Lochead, 1993, p.14).

Throughout their history the charities and aid societies have instigated pioneering practices. The following are just a few examples of some of the innovative projects:

- in 1919, the Central Discharged Prisoners' Aid Society pressured the Home Office to extend the regulations to allow them to extend their remit to give assistance to wives and families of prisoners either alone or in co-operation with other charitable organizations. (Hobhouse and Brockway, 1922, pp.468-9)
- in 1922 a full time visitor appointed to the Boys Prison at Wormwood Scrubs instigated a system whereby individual needs were assessed 'beyond the routine medical inspection and admissions questionnaire' (Lochead, 1993, p.15)
- in 1929, with the support of the Howard League for Penal Reform, a pilot scheme was established allowing for a small wage to be paid to working prisoners at Wakefield
- in the 1930s, the Christian Scientist Arnold Hall, consulting closely with the Howard League for Penal Reform, opened a restaurant in London staffed by ex-prisoners. Perhaps somewhat predictably the Home Office was not keen, having 'little faith' in Christian Scientists 'and none at all in those who dabble in penology' (Forsythe, 1991, p.227).
- in 1947 The Women's Voluntary Service provided a 'First Aid' scheme for meeting the immediate domestic problems of women on reception at Holloway (Fox, 1952, p.225).

However, these projects and services not only often met with official opposition, but also faced funding problems that threatened their continuance. Hobhouse and Brockway in their seminal work *English Prisons Today* (1922) note that: 'We know of one of the largest aid societies that has recently been forced owing to financial difficulties, to suspend almost entirely the practice of helping prisoners' families during their sentence' (Hobhouse and Brockway, 1922, p.469)

Research and campaigning
Not all societies and charities were focused exclusively upon service provision or the reclamation of souls. As in the present day, research and campaigning was very much in evidence. Research was undertaken by voluntary organizations on the effects of prison conditions, and they attempted to influence legislation (Hyland, 1993, p.2). For example, in 1808, the Society for the Improvement of Prison Discipline was formed. It carried out prison inspections and published reports of its findings

and pamphlets. As many of its members were MPs it was not without influence and was able to press its case for reform in Parliament, with some tangible successes (Morris, 1976, p.46). Indeed, a campaign for reform by the Prison Discipline Society led to the Gaols Act 1823, and 'although the legislation had little effect on either the nature of regimes or on general conditions, by requiring magistrates to submit annual reports on their prisons to the home secretary it set in motion the process that led to centralised control of the prison system' (Newburn, 1995, p.5).

Penal reformers also enlisted the support of sympathetic MPs whom they lobbied. For example, in 1818, Thomas Foxwell Buxton, Elizabeth Fry's brother-in-law and MP for Weymouth, promoted her work in the House of Commons and spoke of the 107,000 people in British prison, 'a greater number than all the other Kingdoms of Europe put together'.

Other organizations such as the New Asylum for the Prevention of Vice and Misery among the Poor and the Society for Investigating the Causes of the Alarming Increase in Juvenile Delinquency in the Metropolis, formed in 1815, were the forerunners of criminal justice academic research bodies. The latter's prime aim was to research and promote a more 'humane treatment of child offenders than capital punishment and transportation' (Hyland, 1993, p.1). The problems of dealing with child offenders were a real issue, as in 1856 there were 1,990 children aged under 12 in prison (Young and Ashton, 1956, p.164).

Particularly energetic in this field was a pioneering social reformer, Mary Carpenter, who was to have influence on both public opinion and in shaping legislation. Her innovative methods were based on comparative studies of some enlightened methods developing in the USA, Switzerland, Belgium, France and Germany (Young and Ashton, 1956). In 1851 she published *Reformatory Schools for the Children of the Perishing and Dangerous Classes and for Juvenile Offenders*. Such was the response and interest following the publication of her book, that she organized a conference in Birmingham to debate the issues around the institutional care of young offenders. She generated considerable support for her views and methods and consequently was able to open a reformatory school in Bristol that provided accommodation for over 100 children.

LEGISLATION

Legislation affecting the treatment of offenders and prison conditions was influenced by the lobbying activities of the various voluntary organizations. Legislation also paved the way for an extension of service provision from the charities and aid societies. For example, in 1854, the Youthful Offenders Act had provision for reformatory schools to be run by voluntary societies (Hyland, 1993, p.5). These were specifically for the reception and education of young offenders and a school at Feltham was opened that year 'exclusively for convicted cases' (Young and Ashton, 1956, p.165). These reformatories were schools started by voluntary effort, and governed by a board of managers, as an alternative to prison. The Youthful Offenders Act was followed three years later in 1857 by the Certified Industrial Schools Act. This allowed voluntary organizations to run industrial schools, giving trade and vocational training to children at potential risk of delinquency, or whilst still only minor offenders, and so to divert them from prison.

In 1862, Parliament recognised the existence of penal charities with the passing of the Discharged Prisoners' Aid Act (Young and Ashton, 1956, p.158), which enabled charities to be attached to individual prisons. This Act brought more order to the hitherto chaotic system of grant aid to discharged prisoners. Justices now had the power to certify the aid societies connected to each prison and to pay to those societies a sum of £2 per prisoner to help with resettlement. The following year the first of a series of conferences was called by the Reformatory and Refuge Union to discuss the new status of the aid societies as a result of the new act, and to co-ordinate and develop future activity (Young and Ashton, 1956, p.160). By 1895 the Gladstone Committee reported that each prison had two or three such aid societies attached to it.

The Prison Act 1877 transferred the responsibility for prison away from the local justices to a newly created Prison Commission. The Act also made provision for the appointment of Unpaid Visiting Committees to each prison. These were made up of volunteers who had free access to every prisoner and every part of the prison and were later to become the Board of Visitors.

DISCHARGED PRISONERS' AID SOCIETIES

Whilst there were many charitable and philanthropic organizations often providing locally-based services, the most visible concentration of voluntary effort in penal affairs was the Discharged Prisoners' Aid Societies, sanctioned by the 1862 Act. By 1897, there were 56 such societies which employed 'agents' to advise ex-prisoners, and to make recommendations to the committees about an applicant's claim for aid. Where there was no agent, volunteers were used, or local clergy, policemen or police court missionaries were employed for the role on a case-by-case basis. The committees of these societies were made up of local justices and almost always the governor and chaplain were *ex-officio* members (Forsythe, 1991, p.218).

The Discharged Aid Societies worked in addition to, and often in direct and sometimes unhelpful competition with, the other philanthropic organizations. This was not the only problem. Some of the

Discharged Prisoners' Aid Societies had a reputation for being hectoring, moralising, judgmental and often harsh in their approach, which was informed and dominated by the concept of the deserving and undeserving poor. Prisoners did not always welcome their attentions. The Prison Commission similarly was also not impressed by their methods and saw them in need of 'radical reform' (Forsythe, 1991, p.125). Such was the disquiet over some of their practices that they were investigated as part of the Gladstone Committeee Report published in 1895.

Whilst the Gladstone Report emphasised 'the urgent need for aid and aftercare to be available to prisoners on release and for voluntary bodies concerned to have opportunities to establish contact with prisoners before their discharge', it was critical of the local discharged aid societies' methods (Forsythe, 1991, p.219). A subsequent commission ordered pursuant to the Gladstone Report found that they were 'badly organized, underfunded and depending mainly on magistrates' donations. Too many societies gave indiscriminate aid and state monitoring of them was ineffective' (*Report to Her Majesty's Commissioners of Prisons on the Operations of the Discharged Prisoners' Aid Societies*, quoted in Forsythe, 1991, p.219). This report made a number of recommendations for the reform of discharged prisoners' aid. The report concluded that discharged aid societies were in need of reconstruction, but the imposition of such standards was neither welcomed nor instigated by the societies.

A 40 year battle over the issue of reform of the provision of voluntary aid followed (Forsythe, 1991, p.220). Any attempts by the Prison Commission and its inspectors to reform the discharged prisoners' aid societies, by creating central control or increasing efficiency, were resisted by the influential local magistrates who, along with prison governors and chaplains, sat on the aid societies' committees and who all 'tended to eulogise their success and efficiency' (Forsythe, 1991, p.221). The aid societies in turn considered that they were 'the victims of prejudice and hostility and that many of their problems were a direct result of Prison Commission policy' (Forsythe, 1991, p.224)

Ruggles-Brise, the Prison Commissioner from 1895 to 1921, in particular sought to reform the discharged prisoners' aid societies. Ruggles-Brise was an enlightened and reforming commissioner who brought about many positive changes (Bryans and Wilson, 2000, p.2). But he was to have little success in relation to the societies, and throughout his long term in office there was a running battle of bitter schisms, public and private rows, intrigue and high politics in this matter.

This unsatisfactory situation continued well into the 1930s, and in 1935 a further report was commissioned in an attempt to reform the societies (Forsythe, 1991, p.224). Eventually 'the outcome was a compromise between the status quo and central control' (Forsythe, 1991, p.225), and the National Association of Discharged Prisoners' Aid Societies (NADPAS) was set up in 1935 in an attempt to co-ordinate local groups and act as a link between societies and the Prison Commission (Forsythe, 1991, p.225). NADPAS would advise on the allocation of state grants and act as an aftercare agency for those released from prison. In 1963, a report on 'The Organization of Aftercare by the Advisory Council on the Treatment of Offenders', recommended that the work carried out by NADPAS in prison welfare and after-care should be handed over to the Probation Service. However, the report recognised that the voluntary sector still had a role to play in service provision and, in 1966, NADPAS changed its name to NACRO, the National Association for the Care and Resettlement of Offenders (Light, 1984, p.7).

The difficult relations and tensions between the Prison Commission and the Discharged Aid Societies meant that in some cases aid societies were excluded from a number of prisons, in which case they would set up missions opposite offering breakfasts to newly released prisoners in an attempt to attract them (Forsythe, 1991, p.218). It was not just the discharged prisoners' aid societies that encountered access problems. Distrust extended to the other charities and philanthropic organizations. For example Ruggles-Brise, the Prison Commissioner, was unwilling to grant access permits to outside educational groups. He eventually 'only reluctantly admitted the Liverpool School of Cookery after the home secretary insisted' (Forsythe, 1991, p.127). Similarly there was an 'angry dispute between Ruggles-Brise and the Home Office when encouragement was given by the latter to the London School Board's request to give evening lectures on 'commercial, scientific or other subjects' (*ibid*). Ruggles-Brise was also suspicious that suffragette groups may gain access by posing as women's education groups. His reasons for denying access was that there were insufficient prison staff to supervise the growing number of voluntary groups (Forsythe, 1991, p.127).

Relationships were not always good between the discharged aid societies and the other charities either. The established societies often resented newer organizations and felt, for example, as at Wandsworth, 'that these creamed off the most hopeful prisoners and acted without reference to the older aid societies' (Forsythe, 1991, p.125). However, after the creation of NADPAS in 1938 many of the smaller aid societies amalgamated; for example, individual societies in Pentonville, Brixton, Wandsworth and Wormwood Scrubs joined up to form an expanded Royal Society for London's Prisons (Forsythe, 1991, p.225), and the agencies worked together in a more co-operative and co-ordinated fashion than before.

POLICE COURT MISSIONARIES

Apart from the discharged prisoners' aid societies, the other significant bodies involved with offenders were the 'police court missionaries'. The Probation of First Offenders Act 1887 was the first time probation made its appearance in English law, and though the law did not expressly provide for supervision, magistrates could refer the offender to a supervisor, usually a police court missionary attached to a charitable agency. By far the largest of these agencies was the Church of England Temperance Society (Ashton and Young, 1956, p.175) which had appointed its first police court missionary in 1876 (May, 1991). There were other societies too. In Liverpool, for example, in addition to the Church of England Temperance Society, the Wesleyan Mission, the Catholic Aid Society and the Liverpool Ladies Temperance Association all supplied missionaries to cope with the demand that drunken and disorderly behaviour placed on the criminal justice system.

Initially, the police court missionaries' role was the be on hand in court 'to promote temperance, and to try "by personal influence, with material help if necessary, to persuade those who had found their way onto the dock to lead a sober and steady life in the future"' (Young and Ashton, 1956, p.177). However the work eventually extended beyond promoting temperance and magistrates referred an ever-widening caseload to the police court missionaries.

By 1907, there were 146 such missionaries in the courts. Probation was therefore dependent on the voluntary provision of officers by charitable agencies. With the Probation of Offenders Act 1907, the courts were empowered to appoint their own probation officers (Morris, 1976, p.74). Many of the existing police court missionaries were subsequently made probation officers after the 1907 Act, which formed the transition from voluntary to statutory provision.

THE TWENTIETH CENTURY

During the first half of the twentieth century much voluntary sector activity was focused upon post-release supervision. The borstal system, providing reformatory training for young offenders up to the age of twenty-one, was started in 1901. It was based upon a policy and practice of firm discipline and physical exercise, but within a more relaxed and caring regime, and within a structure similar to the English public school (Bryans and Jones, 2001, p.20). Most significantly, the system incorporated supervision upon release. This post-release supervision was provided by the Borstal Association, a largely voluntary organization specifically founded for that purpose and which became an intregal part of borstal training, until the eventual demise of that system.

The provision of education for offenders by voluntary organizations, which had developed during the nineteenth century through the pioneering work of Mary Carpenter and was then legitimised by the passing of the Youthful Offenders Act 1854 and Industrial Schools Act 1857, continued well into the twentieth century. In fact the majority of approved schools before and after World War II were owned and run by voluntary organizations such as National Children's Homes, Barnardos or the Salvation Army. Indeed, by 1967, 93 approved schools were managed by independent or voluntary bodies as opposed to 30 by local authorities (Hyland, 1993, pp.22-23).

Despite the significance of the role played by the voluntary sector within the penal system, with the post-Second World War development of the welfare state, in many fields 'the role of the voluntary sector subsided, to a point where some questioned whether it would survive' (Gill and Mawby, 1990, p.5). However, survive it did, and indeed 'the 1970s were a major period of growth, both of older traditional type voluntary agencies and new forms focusing more on self-help, pressure group activities, community rights' (Gill and Mawby, 1990, p.7). This was particularly true of the penal voluntary sector. Provision proliferated. There was a move away from the evangelical and paternalistic approach to the development of secular and professionally run organizations, many established by individuals who had personal experience of the penal or criminal justice system, either as ex-prisoners, families or those who had suffered as victims. The traditional church-based organizations continued, but they did so alongside those that developed to serve the needs of other faiths and cultures.

Organizations also developed in response to a changing social environment, for example in relation to drug abuse, cultural diversity, recognition of gay rights and the growth of HIV and Aids. The present situation is that the core functions of security, control and discipline are probably now the only aspects of prison life in which the voluntary sector has no input. In all other areas there is some involvement; for example in education, training, throughcare, family ties, spirituality, substance abuse, health, counselling, the arts and issues surrounding race and nationality (Bryans and Walker, 2001, pp.426-427). *The Prisons Handbook* (Leech and Cheney, annually) gives an indication of the range and extent of current service provision available. In 1978 The Wolfendon Committee reported on the voluntary sector and acknowledged that it had a significant role to play in the provision of services that 'complemented, supported, extended and influenced the statutory system' (Wolfendon, 1978, pp.26-27). During the following years of Conservative government, 'enthusiasm for a minimum state led to a resurgence of interest in the voluntary sector and other alternatives' (Gill and Mawby, 1990, p.7). A change of government in 1997 shifted the emphasis more towards the development and promotion of the concept of active citizenship, so for quite different ideological and political reasons, the significance of the voluntary sector remained, and indeed its role has been enhanced.

Until recently, there was no formal umbrella or collective grouping that supported or represented the whole of the penal voluntary sector, and in particular the service providers. The Penal Affairs Consortium, founded in 1989, was the first body that gave any collective voice to the penal voluntary sector. However, its primary function is as a national lobbying organization 'providing a mechanism whereby its member organizations can work together for penal reform by presenting our joint views to Government, Parliament, the media and the public' (Penal Affairs Consortium Manifesto, 2000, p.20). The consortium is not exclusively for the voluntary sector, having a number of statutory and professional bodies represented. Furthermore, its membership is restricted and not open to all penal groups. It therefore is not a forum for voluntary sector service providers, though many are members and value its contribution to wider issues. An attempt to give the penal voluntary sector collective representation came in 1966 when Bishop Hardy, the Bishop of Lincoln and also the prisons Bishop, formed the Voluntary Sector Consortium. Its aim was to encourage good practice, to further knowledge and to provide a channel of communication between the Prison Service and the voluntary sector. However there was no staff or funds so therefore its impact was limited, and not extensively known about even within the voluntary sector. To all intents and purposes its activities have effectively ceased. However, its formation was symbolic and its pioneering work has now been handed over to CLINKS, formed in 1998, specifically to support and develop the work of the penal voluntary sector.

History shows a direct line from the early charities and the pioneering work of John Howard, Elizabeth Fry and Sarah Martin to the present day. The penal voluntary sector and charities enter the twenty-first century in a healthy and robust state. The significance of the role within prisons of a voluntary sector organization, for example the Samaritans, lies not just in the undoubted quality and impact of its service provision, but the concept that the Prison Service need not be the sole provider of all services to prisoners and their families.

CHAPTER 4

Recent Progress in Community-based Voluntary Sector Work with the Prison Service

Clive Martin

The purpose of this chapter is to give an overview of how the relationship between the Prison Service and the voluntary and community-based sector has developed in recent years. Readers will be aware from earlier chapters that there are now a number of terms used to describe the array of non-statutory organizations that exist within the UK—for example the voluntary sector, the not for profit sector, non-government organizations and social firms. In this chapter the term 'community-based' or 'community-based sector' has been chosen to describe the range of external agencies, usually voluntary but not always, who provide services to prisoners. The reason for this is that it is an inclusive term—covering paid and non-paid professional and volunteer staff from a range of organizations. Where the term 'voluntary sector' is used it is because it is a quote.

BACKGROUND TO THE COMMUNITY-BASED SECTOR IN PRISONS

Community-based organizations have played an important role in prisons and in the resettlement of ex-prisoners for almost as long as prisons have been part of the criminal justice process. The development of that role is traced in *Chapter 3*. The community-based sector today contributes considerably to the quality and effectiveness of prison regimes. Also, ex-prisoners, striving for a successful re-integration into their home communities, need to engage with a range of community-based service providers who could assist in this process.

There is substantial anecdotal evidence from prisoners, prisoners' families, victims of crime, prison staff, Her Majesty's Chief Inspector of Prisons, probation staff, the courts and the external agencies themselves that reinforces the importance of this sector within prisons. Services offered by the sector tackle some of the well-documented factors likely to be significant in the success of the rehabilitative process.

In addition to providing vital services to prisoners, community-based organizations also present additional benefits to prisons. They are organizations that have diverse community roots and who can offer flexibility of service delivery as well as a history of listening to the views of service users at the planning stage of provision. The community-based sector is also able to respond to need in a way that, while often being supportive of statutory organizations, is very different.

In the prison context, many community-based organizations will be familiar names—NACRO, the Prince's Trust and the Prison Reform Trust to name a few. But these are large national organizations. There are many more organizations that provide local services related to health, education, housing, addiction, relationships, spiritual welfare and so on that will be familiar to the readers of this book. It is hard to imagine a credible prison system and resettlement structure that does not include the contribution made by these community-based organizations.

However, the complexity of prisoners' needs and the way in which the provision of services has become more fragmented in recent years is no longer effective. Prisoners—and the wider society—are not well served by this current laissez-faire situation.

Many people who know prisons agree that the resources of both the community-based sector and the Prison Service are not being employed to their full partnership potential. Both could be better supported in meeting their social and moral responsibility, namely the reduction of risk and the rehabilitation and resettlement of ex-offenders. Local groups (even where they may be supported by a national initiative such as that involving the Samaritans) have to develop their own unique relationship with a prison or prison governor. These endeavours take place in the context of strong cultural differences between the community-based sector and the Prison Service. Different traditions, resources, and practice often give the appearance that the two sectors have different goals. Sometimes, different goals between the community-based sector and the state may be legitimate but organizations working in partnership also need to be very clear about their common goals and how they intend to meet them.

There have been some positives to this unstructured situation particularly where prison governors and organizations responding to the needs of prisoners have been able to build their own independent relationships with each other. But this has almost always been based on the personal relationships that existed between the staff of respective organizations. While these personal relationships often make partnerships between organizations more effective they can seldom provide the framework that long-term, and potentially difficult relationships, need in order that they may develop and thrive. Also, the fact that the Prison Service frequently transfers senior prison managers at regular intervals means that relationships will always be short-term.

The need to constantly restart and develop new relationships may outweigh any of the benefits that this unstructured approach may have brought.

THE INFLUENCE OF GOVERNMENT POLICY

The Prison Service as an executive agency of government in a democratic society needs to follow and reflect the policies and principles of government. Prison Service headquarters, area managers and all prison staff are therefore duty bound to reflect the principles of the government that they serve. Given that for many years there was not a clear government lead on the role of the community-based sector in prisons it should not surprise us to find a malaise in this particular area of statutory/voluntary agency relationships. The legacy of previous administrations created a stereotype about the community-based sector that often left it to be seen as a cut-price alternative to statutory provision. This was principally reflected in the letting of contracts to community-based agencies to provide services in a number of different contexts at a price that was usually lower than the statutory provision.

The General Election of 1997 saw New Labour come to power accompanied by a different vision and many hopes about the 'third sector' and the 'third way'. This new political initiative saw the voluntary sector as an important partner in the achievement of government objectives and meant that the need to define and explain the relationship between the voluntary sector and the state was of great importance. The groundwork for this had already been done by way of the Commission on the Future of the Voluntary Sector, chaired by Professor Nicholas Deakin. This set out an agenda for the voluntary sector into the new millennium.

As part of the 'post-Deakin Agenda' the home secretary and Sir Kenneth Stowe, chair of the English Voluntary and Community Sector's Working Group on Government Relations, signed the *Compact on Relations between Government and the Voluntary and Community Sector in England* (Home Office, 1998). The COMPACT states in its foreword:

> The Compact is aimed at creating a new approach to partnership between Government and the voluntary and community sector. It provides a framework to enable relations to be carried out differently and better than before. Government and voluntary and community organizations share many aspirations—the pursuit of inclusiveness, dedication to public life and support for the development of healthy communities. The Compact is a starting point for developing our partnership, based on shared values and mutual respects.

66 *Historical Development*

While the COMPACT has still to be fully implemented by all statutory providers, it has enabled significant progress to be made. The true meanings of some of the concepts that the COMPACT talks about, such as 'partnerships', will be long debated but it has helped move the relationship between the community-based sector and the Prison Service forward. This progress is evidenced in a number of ways, not least of all the appointment of a voluntary sector co-ordinator at Prison Service HQ.

The contracting culture still exists. It is often embraced by the community-based sector as a reliable, if often pitiful, source of funding. It is not obvious that the current government will, or should, seek to bring this contracting culture to an end but this new political impetus has sought to bring an additional dimension to the relationship between the voluntary and statutory sector. This political impetus, strengthening the concept of partnership rather than purchaser/provider, was demonstrated in the signing of the COMPACT.

CLINKS AND THE GROWTH OF RELATED RESEARCH

In was an early report that sowed the initial seeds of CLINKS and this in turn made it easier to undertake and facilitate other research activities in this field.

Silvia Casale and Paulette Haughton, who undertook a review of the criminal justice system, reported the following as part of their conclusions:

> The criminal justice system needs a multi-agency collaborative forum parallel to the Criminal Justice Consultative Council which includes organizations from the voluntary sector, academics and practitioners with experience of both the statutory and voluntary sectors.
>
> Casale and Houghton 1997, p.15

The need to facilitate a multi-agency dialogue was evident. There had of course been multi-agency work between a number of different parties, such as the then local probation services and certain community-based organizations, but there was clearly a need for an agency whose sole function would be to focus on collaborative work, and importantly, work that involved the community-based sector in prisons. Elaborating the conclusions of the same report the authors write:

> From the experience of the projects it is apparent that a valuable input can be made by the voluntary sector in partnership with statutory agencies in the penal system. The input has been relevant and cost effective in both financial and other terms has had a positive impact on the system at several levels.
>
> Casale and Houghton 1997, p.14

So, while not necessarily being a forum as promoted in the report and quoted above, CLINKS was established in 1998 specifically to support the role of the voluntary and community-based sector working in prisons and with ex-offenders. It was formed with a management committee that consisted of individuals working in the prison-related community-based sector, other practitioners and academics. This committee decided that the first task that CLINKS should undertake would be an evidence-based piece of research to illustrate the experience of the community-based sector working in prisons.

CLINKS pilot project report

The small but pioneering study started with a study of the work of the voluntary and community-based sector in four prisons in England during 1999.

The original proposal for this pilot study was made in 1998 when CLINKS approached the Prison Service (who subsequently financed the study) proposing a pilot study that would inform future policy and practice in this field. The original plan was to take a sample of eight prisons and to examine the relationship between them and the external organizations with which they worked. The resources available were limited and the community-based sector was still suffering from the 'cheap alternative' stereotype that had been foisted upon it. It had not yet, at this stage, been embraced (via the COMPACT) as a key partner vital in the securing of government objectives within the criminal justice system. Because of this it was decided that the pilot should be limited to four prisons—one prison from each of the major areas of the prison estate—women, young offenders, adult male and a male Category C training prison.

All external organizations, rather than just those who fitted the 'voluntary sector' definition, were included in the pilot project because it seemed very likely that all external agencies faced similar problems when working in prisons. It was also probable that prisons would not be able to distinguish voluntary sector organizations from other organizations such as a local health trust that come through the gate. What was needed was a greater understanding of which organizations were going in and out of prisons, what sort of experience this was for them and how prisoners obtained access to the services offered.

In addition, there was no sense in merely arguing for prisons to get it right for voluntary sector agencies working in prisons. It was important that *all* agencies involved in the delivery of services to prisoners should have clearly defined access to prisons, prisoners and prison managers.[1]

At the planning stage of the pilot study it was intended that one outcome would be for prisons and community-based organizations to gain a better understanding of their respective roles in building effective partnerships. So while the role of CLINKS is to primarily support and develop the activities of the *voluntary sector* in prisons it was decided that for the purpose of the pilot study all external agencies would be included. It is for this reason that the term *community-based* or *external* organizations is used in relationship to prisons.

It became clear very early on that the relationship between prisons and the community-based sector lacked both a philosophical and practical framework. Staff from both the Prison Service and the community-based sector stated this. Individuals in both sectors were left to act on the basis of their personal conviction rather than of policy. Both sides, prisons and community-based organizations, were asking the same questions—'What are the community-based agencies doing in prisons?', 'Why are they doing it?, 'Should they be doing it?' and 'Who should be paying for it?'

Where there was a positive relationship it was a nervous one. For example, pro-active governors took individual and personal action for their particular prisons but this lacked any direction that could have come from Prison Service HQ. Under these circumstances community-based organizations were often just very pleased to be allowed access to prisoners, albeit under difficult circumstances at times.

It was also very difficult to establish which organizations were working in which prisons. But this was only one issue—there was often a lack of clarity about how these organizations came to be working there, how they worked within a particular prison, how their work was evaluated and reviewed and so on. It many cases, the lack of importance attached to the work of the sector meant that it remained 'the secret garden' of much prison activity and because it was secret it was often underused.

The way the community-based sector is structured and the devolved authority that many prisons now have produces a complex local situation. Under these circumstances, producing a grand plan to be implemented in each prison seemed completely impractical. A consequence of this situation was that the recommendations of the pilot focused on establishing a national set of guidelines that would enable individual prisons and organizations to develop their relationship. In

---

[1] In this context, services should be broadly interpreted to include direct services as well as the activities undertaken by such groups as prison visitors who develop important relationships with prisoners.

essence this is also what the COMPACT had done and is the reason why it was so important to this work. It set out a national set of principles that should underpin the relationship between the voluntary and statutory sectors. It was important that the recommendations of the report mirror the national aspirations of the two sectors presented in the COMPACT.

Because of these findings and the way the COMPACT was developing nationally it seemed much more sensible to draw out the fundamentals of a good partnership whose legitimacy was endorsed by Prison Service Headquarters, and leave it to each establishment to decide how best to implement and manage these partnerships. For example the need to have the work of community-based agencies managed within a prison is undeniable. What is debatable and will vary in each prison is the exact nature of this management. In some it will be appropriate to appoint a specific person with responsibility to manage and develop the work of the community-based sector, as has happened at Huntercombe, Bristol and Aylesbury. In others it will make sense to incorporate the management of the community-based sector into the already existing functional management structure, with a clear management line to the governor, such as has happened at Holloway and Wandsworth. What is clear is that the work needs active and on-going management.

A key feature of the Prison Service management structure is the role of area managers. The important role that they could play in supporting the voluntary sector is outlined in *Chapter 6*. The role of area managers was not a specific part of the pilot project but how this work will be managed and developed at an area level is an important aspect that remains relatively undeveloped. While setting up an area-based structure for the community-based sector paralleling that of the Prison Service structure could be fairly straightforward it may prove limited in the long run. A more productive long-term approach may be one that incorporates new regional arrangements that are taking place as part of devolved government, particularly with Regional Development Agencies and the Government Offices for the Regions. This will ensure that prisons/community-based work is incorporated into the regional agenda, including new funding arrangements, as they develop.

What the CLINKS pilot did not do!

What the CLINKS pilot did not attempt to do was to measure the extent to which the community-based sector contributes to the work of prisons (for example the number of hours put into working with the Prison Service). Deciding how to measure such activity is not an easy task. There are, for example, no records held by prisons of the number of hours that community-based organizations involve prisoners in 'purposeful activity'. As our pilot report illustrated there is also no clear information about the organizations that offer services in prison, let alone the extent of the services they offer. Some community-based organizations keep detailed records of the time their staff and volunteers spend engaged with prisons, some keep more informal records that do not include this sort of detail. Other organizations only have lists of people who go into prison but have no record about the amount of time they contribute. In addition, the extent of individual volunteering, where individuals arrange matters with prisons directly rather than as a member of an organization, is unknown.

It was with this in mind that the Active Community Unit (the Home Office Unit responsible for promoting active citizenship) began work in 2000 on a wider survey. This sought to establish the extent of the contribution made by both the community-based sector and volunteers within prisons.

The research evidence is growing—the CLINKS pilot study shows the nature of the problems that are encountered in the relationship between the voluntary and statutory sector. Some of these problems are evident in any partnership relationship (see for example, Wilson and Charlton, 1997) and will disappear as we become more skilled at managing statutory/voluntary sector relationships. The Active Community Unit study will indicate the extent of the relationship and the size of the partnership nationally and local. This growing information base will enable us to draw out more effectively 'what works' in terms of building effective partnership relationships between these two sectors.

THE VOLUNTARY SECTOR CONSORTIUM

Community-based organizations have long expressed the wish to enter into a mutually supportive and beneficial relationship with each other. The Bishop of Lincoln, as the Anglican Bishop for Prisons, has provided a focus for this and a group that is referred to as either the Voluntary Sector Consortium, or the Bishop of Lincoln's Group, was formed. The first meeting of the group was held in Church House, Westminster on the 27 February 1996 and 46 organizations sent representatives. Although many Christian groups were present the meeting attracted interest from a wide range of secular groups as well. Well-known prison organizations such as the Inside Out Trust, Federation of Prisoners Families Support Groups and the Suzy Lamplugh Trust were all present. The Statement of Intent that was drawn up as a result of this meeting reflects common aims and desires:

1. The Voluntary Groups Consortium exists to promote good practice and high standards amongst those voluntary organizations working with prisoners and their families.

2. It provides an informal network between its members and through its meetings to enable them to keep abreast of developments in penal affairs and in the voluntary sector.

3. It provides a voice and channel of communication for Voluntary Groups with the Prison Service and with the Prison Governors Association.

In many ways the voluntary sector consortium was a forerunner to CLINKS and was close co-operation and support between the two organizations. The consortium continues to meet although the co-ordinating function has passed to CLINKS.

The Bishop of Lincoln's Group and the development of CLINKS has led to renewed thoughts about the development of a membership organization that would reflect and offer a focus for the aspirations of the community-based sector working in prisons. Organizations who currently attend the Bishop of Lincoln's Group will clearly want to make their own decisions about how they develop their future relationship with CLINKS. However, CLINKS is now a membership organization open to all community-based organizations providing services in this field. The *Good Practice Guide* (published by the Prison Service in 2001) and the pilot report are two examples of what can be achieved by an organization with this sort of role.

A key consideration about CLINKS as an organization is that it does not become a service organization delivering services to prisoners. Every organization, however, needs to provide some form of service; otherwise it would have no reason to exist. Fundamental to the development of CLINKS would be the notion that it provides services for the community-based sector working in prisons rather than prisoners themselves. Sometimes, like the production of the *Good Practice Guide*, the focus may need to be Prison Service HQ but the ultimate outcome of this has to be a more effective structure for the benefit of the community-based sector.

Recent developments have also meant that CLINKS is now in a strategic position to support prisons, prisoners and the voluntary sector. The 'Working with Prisoners Directory' (a database of service providers) is an invaluable resource. A development project has now begun that will establish 'Voluntary Sector Forums' within prisons. Regional networks of community-based organizations and prisons have started to emerge and these will be crucial to effective resettlement.

TOWARDS A PARTNERSHIP-BASED APPROACH

It would be naive to think that the involvement of community-based agencies within prisons would be some sort of panacea. However, positive and fruitful partnerships are one way of ensuring that prisons reflect the values of the communities that they serve. For example, anecdotal evidence seems to show that race relations teams work better and are more effective in prisons where the involvement of the black and minority ethnic community is actively sought and, importantly, incorporated into prison management structures.

Any prison or community-based organization with the vision to become more open and diverse should ensure that its vision, and the management structures to nurture it, is central to its overall structure. Organizations should know who they want to form relationships with, how they intend to form them, nurture and resource them, and measure their success. They should also know how they would be ended or expanded, whichever is appropriate at the time. Prisons and the voluntary sector potentially offer each other a diversity of culture that could enrich them both.

The current shift in Prison Service practice to incorporate the whole process of resettlement and the need of the National Probation Service to focus on risk assessments means that there is confusion around the co-ordination of many areas of service provision. It is the community-based sector that provides many of the services, for example employment services, housing, family support, health etc, which are essential to resettlement. However, the current Prison Service focus to look more holistically at imprisonment and resettlement does provide us with the opportunity to develop effective partnerships in these and other areas.

Additional partnership potential can be found in the area of accredited offending behaviour courses. David Thornton, head of the Prison Service Offending Behaviour Unit, highlighted the importance of the community-based sector:

> Other factors enhancing responsiveness [to offending behaviour programmes] include ... the attitude of participant's home community (the supervising probation officer and other agencies providing supporting services, outside family and friends, etc.) to the programmes—support and involvement rather than hostility, indifference or ignorance.
>
> Thornton, 1996

However, to keep this in proportion we need to remember that even the most optimistic projections are that the number of prisoners completing accredited offending behaviour programmes will grow from the current total of 6,000 to 8,900 in 2003-4. This leaves many thousands of prisoners untouched by the accredited offending behaviour programmes. The need to provide effective, relevant and high quality services that support the development of 'healthy prisons', the resettlement of offenders, and therefore safer communities, remains.

The community-based sector has a long history of involvement in prisons. However, it must not be forgotten that the relationship as a constructive partnership is still at an early stage of development. The collection of evidence by the Active Community Unit and CLINKS is a start. This should not be underestimated as an important first step but it should not be seen as more than that—a first step on the long road of constructive and positive partnerships in the difficult area of prisoner rehabilitation. To this end this chapter has given some consideration as to how partnerships could develop and this theme will be continued in the last section of this book.

Prisons are a part of the community. Prisoners are from our communities and the vast majority of prisoners will return to our communities—to our cities, neighbourhoods and so on. The services and resources that support our prisons, prison staff, prisoners, and victims of crime nearly all lie within the community. Prison Service HQ, prisons and the voluntary and community-based sector need to develop the opportunities offered by the COMPACT. Successful partnership will ensure that services are effective, relevant and offered at the right time and in the right place in an environment that supports and values them.

CHAPTER 5

Prison Service Policy on Voluntary and Community Sector Partnerships

Nick Sanderson and Jo Gordon

It is the nature of government that, year-by-year, it accumulates, or has thrust upon it, responsibility for a growing number of issues. Fifteen years ago, for example, most people would have been surprised at the idea of the government taking responsibility for rough sleeping. Thirty years ago we would not have expected to have a policy unit in the Home Office responsible for religious cults.

In small ways this process of accretion goes on in all government departments and agencies. As a new issue emerges we see the same pattern. First, there is a period of turning a blind eye. Then, when this becomes unsustainable, a period of attempting to fend it off. This is followed by a grudging recognition that something must be done, but preferably by someone else. The final stage is the full-hearted bureaucratic embrace, with a 'unit' created, committees appointed and a budget set.

In recognising its responsibilities towards the voluntary and community sector, the Prison Service is just entering the final phase. Why has it taken so long? And what will it mean for the future?

As noted in *Chapter 3*, historically the voluntary and community sector has been involved with prisons from their earliest days. Until recent times this was often in the form of individual volunteers, albeit sometimes members of organized groupings, such as the Women's Royal Voluntary Service or the National Association of Prison Visitors.

In the last 30 years we have seen a growth of non-governmental organizations (NGOs) in all areas of government work, and the Prison Service has been no exception to that trend. Many government agencies have learnt to value, and then depend upon, the input of NGOs and voluntary and community sector organizations, and so has the Prison Service.

Devolution of funding to prison governors in 1992 gave them greater flexibility to bring in outside organizations and gave the voluntary and community sector itself the opportunity to form alliances with governors at a local level. Many governors welcomed the innovation and responsiveness to new situations, which is a key strength of the voluntary and community sector.

But devolution also brought with it the seeds of the discontent which has characterised the relationship in more recent years. Voluntary and community sector agencies often became frustrated that the work which they were doing in one prison was rejected in another; or that there was no mechanism to pick up good ideas and spread them nationally. The sheer volume of voluntary and community sector agencies working in some prisons led to confusion. Furthermore, the voluntary and community sector did not feel that the importance of their work was recognised by the Prison Service at large.

These are all genuine concerns. They became a more serious handicap when, at the end of the 1990s the service began to draw in voluntary and community sector organizations, not just on the margins of its activities but also in helping it to deliver its main programmes. The role of the voluntary and community sector in prisons is a growing one. They are responsible for the delivery of the Prison Service's drug strategy; they run the majority of visitor centres; they co-ordinate the listener programme; they provide services in areas such as employment and training, education, housing, health and mental health; they provide counselling in areas such as sexual abuse, bereavement and family relationships.

LAUNCHING A MORE PARTNERSHIP APPROACH

A key step came in January 2000, when the then prisons minister, Paul Boateng, met the voluntary and community sector umbrella group CLINKS. At that meeting were Una Padel, the former director of CLINKS and current director of the Centre for Crime and Justice Studies, and CLINKS present director, Clive Martin. They outlined the recent history of voluntary and community sector groups' involvement in prisons and the frustrations and difficulties which they faced. This was reinforced by research by CLINKS, in 1999, on the work of the penal voluntary sector (CLINKS, 1999).

Following that meeting Paul Boateng asked the Prison Service, in partnership with CLINKS, to bring together governors and area managers with the voluntary sector and grant making trusts in a series of 'roadshows'. The purpose of these events was to discuss the sector's needs and aspirations, and to explore how it could help governors to deliver their objectives. Among the remits of the roadshows was that they should consider funding issues.

Two roadshows were held, at Styal Prison and at Leyhill Prison, in the summer of 2000. All governors were invited to one or other, and each was invited to bring a representative of a voluntary sector organization working in his or her prison. This was to ensure that, as well as the organizations with national representation, there should be representation from the smaller local groups.

In advance of the workshops the Prison Service had produced a new draft chapter for its *Prison Service Finance Manual*, setting out a more constructive framework, including the vexed question of funding in advance. This was widely welcomed at the roadshows, and is now a part of that manual.

The roadshows were significant not just because they promoted new initiatives supporting the work of the penal voluntary sector, but because they were a very public statement of the ministerial priority placed upon closer co-operation between the Prison Service and the voluntary and community sector. A clear message was sent out to governing governors and Area Managers to embrace the voluntary and community sector.

> The voluntary sector in prisons has been the engine for much beneficial improvement and change. The service cannot afford to miss the opportunity to make wider society see prisons, not as somewhere people are locked away and forgotten about but as places for change and hope for something better inside and out
>
> Paul Boateng, prisons minister, Voluntary Sector Roadshow, HMP Leyhill
> 11 July 2000

STRATEGIC DEVELOPMENTS

Two further decisions were made by the Prison Service Management Board in the course of the summer of 2000. The first of these was to co-operate with the Active Community Unit (ACU) of the Home Office in issuing a survey to all prisons to find out more about their involvement with voluntary and community groups and individual volunteers. Voluntary and community sector agencies were similarly being surveyed by the ACU in order to establish the range and extent of their involvement in prisons. Because of the devolved way in which the Prison Service operates, neither the use of outside organizations, nor their funding, is centrally collated.

The second decision was to recognise that the Prison Service could not continue developing its relationship with the voluntary sector in an *ad hoc* fashion. It needed a strategy, and that it would be a full-time job to develop and implement one. The decision was therefore taken to appoint a headquarters voluntary sector co-ordinator, with experience of working with the voluntary sector. Jo Gordon took up this post in January 2001. Her first task was to develop a strategy that strengthens the relationship between the Prison Service and voluntary and community sector organizations and volunteers at HQ, area and establishment level, in order that:

- community resources are mobilised to strengthen the support provided to prisoners and their families during imprisonment and on release;
- voluntary organizations and volunteers form an integral part of the delivery of constructive work in establishments and the community; and
- full use is made of the strengths and diversity of the voluntary and community organizations and prison staff in providing innovative programmes, and as a bridge to the wider community.

The HQ voluntary sector co-ordinator will then oversee the implementation of the strategy following agreement by the Prison Service Management Board, which it is hoped will be achieved by September 2001.

The voluntary sector co-ordinator is advised and supported in her work by a Voluntary and Community Sector Strategy Group drawn from the voluntary and community sector and Prison Service operational staff. This is chaired by Peter Kilgarriff from the Lankelly Foundation. The group reports to and meets regularly with the prisons' minister.

Individual prisons need effective partnerships with their local voluntary sector. For a local prison based in a city centre, this will be an easier prospect than for a high security prison in a green-field site. But in both cases it is a relationship which needs to be managed consciously. There must be clarity of contractual arrangements, consistency in funding, and a properly worked out policy over matters such as security clearance and access to keys. Above all there needs to be a recognition of the importance of the relationship by both sides.

These issues, and many others, have been identified within a draft strategy document which has been widely circulated and which provided a focus for a series of consultative events that were held between April and July 2001. These were launched in London by the then prisons minister Paul Boateng who said

> We are undertaking to extend and improve our partnership with the voluntary sector and to do this in a more strategic way. We want to avoid the problems that have frustrated relationships in the past and ensure greater consistency in the approach taken in prisons. It is important that we have better systems. But I think a bigger challenge is to ensure that we have in place the mechanisms and protocols, which establish an understanding so that everybody knows the basis upon which they will be

able to deal with each other. As we move from sentiment to strategy it is important that the protocols and mechanisms we put in place are not stifling. They shouldn't be so rigid that they prevent inspirational and innovative activity from happening and it is important that we are able to protect relationships that are informal and local. By creating common ground we are developing something that is better, something that can deliver change in individuals, institutions and society.

The consultation events brought together over 540 people and have included Prison Service staff at all levels and representatives from national, regional and local voluntary and community organizations. Each event included speakers and workshop leaders from both the Prison Service and voluntary and community groups and there were workshops covering general issues such as funding, resettlement, training, assessment of prisoner needs, contact and communication and co-ordinating work with the voluntary and community sector at an area level and issues for specific groups and/or groups working with specific groups of prisoners such as faith groups, black and minority ethnic groups, women prisoners, young prisoners, families, and healthcare.

Ideas and suggestions from the events and individuals commenting on the draft strategy were used to inform the final strategy to be presented to the Prison Service Management Board and Operational Planning Group in September 2001

The events also saw the launch of the *Good Practice Guide* for prisons working with the voluntary and community sector which was produced by CLINKS for the Prison Service. The guide will help to ensure that both prison governors and voluntary and community sector organizations know what is expected of them and know how to deal properly and professionally with each other.

A REGIONALISED STRUCTURE

In April 2000 the Prison Service adopted a new regional structure designed to mesh with police areas and the nine government regions for England and Wales. Within the Government regional offices there is a regional point of co-ordination for voluntary sector activity. This will be a resource which the Prison Service will be able to use to help it in developing local partnerships with the voluntary sector, particularly for those prisons which do not have an immediate hinterland. The Prison Service Area Manager for Yorkshire has posted a prison service representative at the local government office in Leeds. This person has been able to build effective links between regional voluntary and community sector organizations, the area and the prisons within the region. It is a model that others are adopting including Eastern Area, the South West and the Manchester, Merseyside and Cheshire Area.

It will also help the Prison Service, at a regional level, to tap into regional funding initiatives, including access to European funding. This is something which has already begun to be used, for example in supporting initiatives for foreign national prisoners in prisons in Kent, the Headstart programme in the North-west and the JADE project in Bristol. With management at the regional level, there is scope for making greater use of new funding sources of this kind in support of voluntary sector partnerships.

EFFECTIVE POLICY DEVELOPMENT AT A NATIONAL LEVEL

At Prison Service HQ in London there are some 2000 staff, grouped by policy responsibilities, whose job it is to respond to the world beyond the Prison Service and to develop new policies and guidance to meet the needs of the service.

There is a continual bringing up-to-date of guidance on familiar issues—such as family ties, prisoners' property, parole procedures, catering etc.—in order to meet the needs of a changing world. Other parts of the work involve developing entirely new policies—for example the agenda of issues to do with offender treatment, drugs and basic skills learning, which are grouped together under the heading 'what works'.

In both maintaining existing policies and developing new ones, the Prison Service, should, and does, consult with the voluntary sector. But there is unquestionably scope for improving and strengthening this consultative process. In some areas of work, for example, there are standing consultative committees bringing together members of the Prison Service and the voluntary and community sector. The Family Ties Consultative Group is a forum that meets quarterly and brings together prisoners' families support groups and other special interest groups to discuss and develop policy with the Prison Service. The group's main role is the fine-tuning of policy and its application by establishments. In terms of more tangible end-products, the group has also been closely involved in the production of the leaflet entitled *A Guide for Visitors to Prisons* which was co-ordinated by the Prison Service, the Federation of Prisoners' Families Support Groups (FPFSG) and the Prison Reform Trust, to provide information for prisoners' families.

There are other similar consultative groups. For example, the Women's Policy Group Liaison Forum. This meets twice yearly and provides an opportunity for discussion between representatives from individual establishments and voluntary and statutory organizations working with women prisoners. The meetings allows members to hear about the latest developments in the women's prison estate, to report on their work and to raise any issues or concerns.

The Prison Service has gradually been recognising the scale of its responsibilities towards the voluntary and community sector. At the same time a related, but separate set of responsibilities has been emerging, namely the Labour Government's initiative on the 'active community', which is intended to achieve substantial progress towards involving one million more members of the public in voluntary work by 2004

ACTIVE COMMUNITY INVOLVEMENT

Like all parts of government the Prison Service is required to play its part in meeting this objective. Superficially it seems as though it could be swept up in better co-ordination of the voluntary sector. But, on examination, many of the issues are different. Generally, volunteers working in prisons tend not to be recruited directly by the prison, but by the voluntary or community organization with which an individual prison has established a relationship or a contract. Because at present very few prisons have voluntary services managers, there is no-one within the prisons to play the role of a volunteer recruiter or supervisor. Different voluntary sector organizations providing similar services may have different policies towards the use of volunteers. Prisons are not volunteer friendly places: security checks, searches, and the difficulty of moving easily within a prison can all be off-putting to would-be volunteers. Additionally, because of the need for close supervision, volunteers may not always be as economically attractive a proposition as they might be in other environments such as schools or hospitals.

Given all these hurdles, it is encouraging that there are, in fact, many thousands of volunteers already working in prisons. The Prison Service believes that volunteers have a place in prisons and that they are an important part of the strengthening of links with the community, which the Prison Service wishes to achieve. Increased volunteer input through existing voluntary sector agencies would require additional funding for the agencies, as supporting the work of volunteers always involves costs. Volunteers are not a free resource.

Volunteers are already active helping in visitors centres, in prison visiting, and in Boards of Visitors. The Prison Service would like to see more volunteers in these areas, and particularly to widen the diversity of the skills and backgrounds from which the volunteers traditionally come. There is, for example, a desperate need for volunteers from foreign national communities to visit their compatriots in prison, who may be isolated because of language and lack of family in the United Kingdom. As part of the programme being promoted by the Active Community Unit of the Home Office to attract more volunteers to support statutory services, the Prison Service has co-ordinated a number of bids from prisons which lead to a large increase in the numbers of volunteers in prisons. These bids have attracted about £350,000 in matched funding and have created a number of voluntary sector and resettlement co-ordinators posts, peer group and mentoring support, support to prisoner's families and the numbers of listener schemes run with the Samaritans that help to prevent suicides in custody.

The Prison Service is committed to improving the way in which it deals with the voluntary and community sector and with volunteers. It will not be a task which will be achieved in months, or even in a year or two. It will require a shift in perceptions on both sides which will take time to achieve. The role of the voluntary sector co-ordinator will be to set this process in motion and to map out the track along which it will run. The Prison Service is now determined to embrace this new responsibility. The trick will be to ensure that the embrace is not so bureaucratic that it stifles the creativity and quick-footedness of the voluntary sector which is the key to its strength.

CHAPTER 6

Voluntary Sector Provision in the Penal System

Una Padel

This book is about the relationship between the voluntary sector and prisons and, as previous chapters have shown, the sector is extraordinarily diverse. Some voluntary sector organizations hold drug treatment contracts in a number of prisons. These contracts with the Prison Service are worth hundreds of thousands of pounds and large numbers of staff are employed to carry out the work. At the other extreme are very small organizations with no paid staff, and no Prison Service funding, undertaking specific tasks such as sending spiritual texts to prisoners or writing them letters at Christmas time. Between are many groups of varying sizes employing the services of paid staff and volunteers in different proportions and carrying out a very wide variety of functions. Some receive Prison Service funding, others rely entirely on charitable funds.

DEFINING THE VOLUNTARY SECTOR

Characteristics and organization

The majority of voluntary sector organizations working with prisons are registered charities or organizations which are exempt from registration because they are church-based. Information about the structure of the organization can be useful to help voluntary sector bodies to demonstrate their integrity and for governors who wish to check the credentials of an organization working, or wishing to work in the prison. The Charity Commission requires an annual return notifying any changes of trustee, and charities' accounts have to be submitted to the commission each year. The commission's website[1] has details of all registered charities, their registered charity numbers, contact points or correspondents and 'objects'. Registered charities are legally required to publish an annual report and accounts each year and this should contain information about the organization's trustees, sources of funding, expenditure and activities. An important caveat is that registration with the Charity Commission provides no guarantee about the quality of

---

[1] www.charity-commission.gov.uk

work the charity undertakes. The processes for governing voluntary sector organizations are usually set out in their constitutions, or sets of rules. They define where trustees are to be drawn from and what procedures are to be followed when decisions are made.

The primary purpose of voluntary sector organizations is to provide for whatever need they were established to meet. The sector is sometimes dubbed 'the not for profit sector' because, unlike the business sector, profit is not an aim. The trustees of voluntary organizations are forbidden from gaining financially from the organization. This does not mean that voluntary sector organizations never make a profit (or 'surplus' as it tends to be described), but that if they do it is ploughed back into the organization's work rather than distributed between shareholders as it would be in a business where profit was the goal.

The term 'voluntary sector' derives from the idea of voluntary activity. In many organizations all, or a majority, of those carrying out the main tasks do so on an entirely voluntary basis. In others the voluntary element is confined to the trustees who offer their time to govern the organization while professionals are employed to undertake the organization's work.

Unfortunately the misconception that the term 'voluntary sector' describes organizations staffed only by volunteers has led to many misunderstandings among Prison Service staff at all levels. This creates problems in a number of ways. Professional staff, trained to undertake specialist tasks often feel aggrieved if it is assumed that they are 'amateurs'. Prison staff may feel that resources are being channelled into something that should have no cost if their assumption is that the organization is staffed by volunteers when in fact the staff are paid. Sadly even the most senior managers within the Prison Service have been heard to use 'volunteers' as the generic term to describe the staff of voluntary sector agencies, indicating that this misconception is very deep-rooted indeed. Volunteer staff, who give their time without payment, can feel unhappy about being grouped together with paid staff—it can mean that they do not receive the credit they deserve for giving up their time. A more detailed exploration of the work and problems associated with volunteering in prison appears in *Chapter 7*.

Another common misconception is that where volunteers are used they have no cost. In order to offer a good quality of service volunteers need to be trained, supported and supervised. This is just as important with unpaid staff as with anyone else. It is likely to be even more difficult for someone who works a few hours per week or month to get to grips with the prison culture, understand the parameters of their role etc. Volunteers are an extremely valuable resource to prisons. They can offer services which would be impossible to resource if the full costs of their time had to be met, but under-investment in their training and support can result in poor quality work or even in difficult and dangerous situations developing for volunteers, staff and prisoners.

Range of organizations
The main difficulty in defining the voluntary sector, both generally and as it works in prisons, is its enormous diversity. That breadth applies not only to the way in which the organizations are constituted, but also to the variety of functions they serve and the manner in which they carry them out. A clearer picture of which organizations are offering what services and where may be gained from the Centre for Crime and Justice Studies website.[2] CLINKS has set up a website which will provide a comprehensive database of penal voluntary sector organizations.

As mentioned above, the range of agencies includes those using professional staff to provide services under contract to the Prison Service. Examples are the drug agencies such as RAPt, Compass and Cranstoun, each of which works in a number of prisons offering both treatment and CARATS services as defined by the Prison Service's drug strategy. There are also organizations which have a major presence in the community but have adapted their working methods to provide a service to prisoners. An example of this type is the Samaritans which has a presence in almost every prison and uses volunteers to train prisoners to take on some of the role as listeners. Some agencies operate only in one prison. For example, a number of the prison visitors centres are small organizations in their own right and use a few paid staff and volunteers to provide services including information, support, children's play and refreshments for visitors at a particular prison. Volunteers from some organizations befriend prisoners and maintain contact through letters and visits. These volunteers spend a considerable amount of their time working alone rather than with others and this sort of work can be particularly difficult. The importance of selecting, training and supporting volunteers adequately is discussed in *Chapter 7*. Staff and/or volunteers from some voluntary sector agencies work closely with particular prison staff to support and enhance their work. Chaplains often use voluntary sector agencies to broaden the range of their activities and to provide contact between faith groups in prison and in the community.

Some voluntary sector organizations work with very specific groups of prisoners defined usually by their faith or ethnic or national origin. Among these groups are prisoners who are particularly isolated in prison as they may have no families or friends in this country and may be unable to communicate in English. Prison staff are often frustrated by the language barriers, but unable to overcome them. The use of voluntary organizations to assist by helping these prisoners to have their

---

[2] www.kcl.ac.uk/ccjs

needs met, and possibly to link with communities from the same background outside prison, is very important.

Arts organizations also make an important contribution to the quality of life in many prisons. Some (such as Pimlico Opera) work with a particular prison in a concentrated fashion to stage a production, others offer a longer-term input. They can provide prisoners with important opportunities to experiment with new ways of expressing themselves and develop self-esteem.

Penal reform organizations such as the Prison Reform Trust, the Howard League for Penal Reform, Women in Prison and, internationally, Penal Reform International, exist primarily to press for change in the way prisons, and the broader criminal justice system, operate. They do this by gathering information, monitoring developments and sometimes publicising situations which concern them. Often the most effective way to press for change is to work closely with the Prison Service while retaining an independent and critical view. Inevitably the line between penal reform and service provision sometimes becomes blurred. Because of the lack of information available to prisoners in the mid-1980s the Prison Reform Trust started producing a *Prisoners' Information Pack*, funded entirely independently of the Prison Service, and distributed it to as many prisoners as possible. It was impossible to produce enough, or to ensure their efficient distribution. The Prison Service, recognising that its own information was poor, negotiated with the Prison Reform Trust and the Information Books, as they have become, are now a joint venture.

Some penal reform groups offer direct services to prisoners as well as campaigning for change. Women In Prison, for example, ran a successful project with women on remand in Holloway and now has a project designed to help women prisoners gain access to training and employment on their release. Unlock, the organization for ex-offenders, is developing services for newly released prisoners as well as vociferously pressing for improved release arrangements.

NACRO, the largest and most widely known organization in the field, successfully manages a very wide range of services including crime prevention initiatives, community projects, housing for ex-offenders and advice services in prisons. It is not usually described as a penal reform pressure group, but does become involved in campaigning for change. Because of its size, reputation and, above all, experience as a service provider it is frequently consulted by the Home Office and Prison Service on issues such as enabling ex-prisoners to become more employable. Without the pressure group label NACRO nevertheless exerts great influence.

Umbrella organizations, such as the Federation of Prisoners' Families Support Groups, the National Body of Black Prisoners Support Groups and the Unit for the Arts and Offenders play an important role in supporting the many small organizations active in their specific fields. While individuals and small groups may be working in different areas of the country they share many concerns. These umbrella organizations play a vital role in offering them support, organizing meetings which bring them together, defining good practice, offering resources and training which might otherwise be beyond their means, and providing a voice for them at a policy level within the Prison Service and with other significant policy makers.

Developing relationships with prisons
Earlier chapters in this book charting the development of voluntary sector involvement in prisons demonstrate that the large scale of this work is a comparatively recent phenomenon. The growth in the work of voluntary sector organizations in prisons has been largely at the voluntary sector's initiative. Typically an existing voluntary sector organization would identify a need in the nearest prison, possibly because they were seeing a number of newly released prisoners among their clientele in the community or because of publicity about the prison. They would then approach a member staff based in the prison (often the throughcare manager, education manager, chaplain or governor) to offer a service.

Initial discussions with the member of prison staff approached would then take place. Funding may or may not have been mentioned at this point—the overwhelming majority of voluntary sector work in prisons is not funded by the Prison Service. The next stage in the process has often been a security check, undertaken by the prison's security department and liaison police officer, on the voluntary sector staff (paid or volunteer) who will be working in the prison to find out if they have previous convictions. As long as no difficulties emerged at that stage the voluntary sector agency has then been able to start work with prisoners.

The result of this *ad hoc* method has often been a range of voluntary sector provision which has not been related to prisoner need in any planned manner; has not been co-ordinated in any way, so that no individual in the prison could provide details of every agency offering services in the prison; has not required agencies to demonstrate that they offer a high quality service; and has not required the prison to provide any firm commitment to support the work, whether through funding or simply through regular provision of space, escorts etc.

Many of these problems have arisen because of the inequalities in the relationships between often small voluntary sector agencies and prisons. The very fact that it has so often been the voluntary sector agency that has initiated contact creates an obvious difficulty. This immediately puts the prison in the position of having to respond to an offer. Instead of identifying a need among prisoners and finding out which agencies might be able to provide the service required the prison is faced with a service offered. If that service is being offered at no cost to the prison (in terms of additional outlay, obviously every service has a cost in officer time) the relationship balance is further skewed.

On the other hand prisons have, in may cases, been slow to see themselves as part of the communities in which they are based or to which the prisoners will return (though they may be geographically removed it is important nonetheless). Because of this, 'outsiders' (i.e. people who do not work for the Prison Service) were and sometimes, sadly, still are, regarded with considerable suspicion, sometimes verging on hostility. Prison staff at all levels can, if they so choose, make the delivery of services by voluntary sector agencies very difficult. This hostility has not been entirely one-sided and voluntary sector staff have also sometimes acted in a very negative manner towards uniformed prison staff, stereotyping and minimising their role.

Of course there are differences in the primary goals of prisons and voluntary sector agencies, but without the opportunity to understand one another's priorities it is inevitable that relationships have sometimes been difficult. Prisons sometimes provide voluntary sector staff working in prisons with a session designed to highlight the role of security in the prison providing guidance on avoiding security gaffes. Offered in isolation from any other information about aspects of the population, regime etc. this can be a negative and alienating experience. Voluntary sector agencies, for their part, often have no opportunity at all to provide prison staff with information about what they do both in the prison and in the community.

Many of these difficulties will be avoided in future if the use of local voluntary sector co-ordinators is developed. They will be able to take the initiative, find suitable agencies to provide services, co-ordinate provision to ensure that some needs are not overlooked while other services are duplicated, and develop a more systematic approach to the planning and review of work.

A very basic tool which can be used to help this process is the development of written agreements about what the work will consist of, how it will be conducted, what the voluntary sector agency can expect from the prison and vice-versa and how and when the work will be reviewed. Prisons have to be staffed 24 hours per day, seven days per week and prison staff work shifts. A written agreement is helpful because it can be used to inform all the staff who may come into contact with a particular voluntary sector agency about what has been agreed. The other characteristic of prisons (and one which is endlessly frustrating to voluntary sector staff) is the speed with which staff at all levels move between responsibilities in a prison, or even between prisons. A written agreement obviates the need to renegotiate every time the personnel change on either side.

Prison visitors

Not to be confused with the BoV, the Prison Visitors' Association was established in 1924 and now has over 1,400 volunteers working in prisons in the UK and Wales. It is an independent association and is not affiliated to any other organization, although it has the full support of the Home Office. The role of the prison visitor is unique in many ways as success is not so much about achieving goals or quantifiable outcomes but rather gaining a special and informal relationship with a prisoner whilst he or she is inside prison. Such an important befriending role within prison can benefit a prisoner through the regaining of self respect and self-esteem whilst at the same time easing tensions which in turn can reduce the risks to security and control. As with the role of other volunteers such as the Samaritans, prison visitors can also anticipate self-harm and potential suicides and the association is establishing suicide awareness courses.

Unlike many of the volunteers attached to voluntary organizations working within the penal system, training is less formal, usually achieved through the 'shadowing' of another prison visitor and with further support being gained through annual conferences and in-house training. But, like any other volunteer visiting prisoners inside, it is essential to develop strong and enduring relationships with staff, for without their recognition of this valuable work, access to offenders can be difficult. In stressing the uniqueness of volunteers in the penal system, recruitment and ongoing training must feature as one of the keys to success. Many prisoners feel that they have been let down by those around them, so prison visitors can help them regain trust by being reliable, compassionate, resilient (bearing in mind the need to be aware of one's own gullibility) and above all a good listener whilst acknowledging the limitations of the help they can give. However, prison visitors must guard against the desire to impose their spiritual and religious values on prisoners when this may be wholly inappropriate and the co-ordinator (ironically, very often the chaplaincy) must remain vigilant to ensure that prison visitors are fully aware that, despite being supported by the chaplaincy, it is not their role to 'convert' the prisoner.

Despite clear advantages of engaging prison visitors, some prisons are nervous about establishing prison visitor schemes often because of concerns about security. Volunteering in prisons is potentially fraught with conflicting cultures, with the voluntary sector's bias towards voluntarism, privacy and client-centredness, and the Prison Service's responsibility to combine security and the development of constructive regimes for its inmates. Communication and understanding from both

Accreditation

Until the end of the 1990s there was no systematic approach to work with prisoners designed to tackle their offending behaviour. There was little evidence about the effectiveness of the initiatives which were then in place. The primary reason for this was that few programmes of a large enough scale to create a reasonable size sample of programme 'graduates' existed. Following up ex-prisoners and looking at their rates of re-conviction during the two years after release is a long-term and costly process. Until very recently the cost of undertaking such research would have been disproportionate as most of the programmes available to prisoners were short-term, and there were few that were available on any more than a local basis.

This lack of a systematic approach meant that although some prisoners gained access to the few options available the majority did not. Offending behaviour work undertaken was extremely variable in quality and ranged from excellent to very poor. Although there was plenty of opportunity for creativity there was also scope for some fairly unsatisfactory ideas to flourish.

Over the last three years there has been enormous progress towards the development of a far more systematic approach to dealing with offending behaviour in both prisons and probation. There is now an accreditation panel for England and Wales charged with assessing possible programmes and accrediting those suitable. Accredited programmes tend to be long and have to be delivered consistently (there is no scope for those delivering them to 'personalise' the style of their delivery in any way). Staff delivering them have to be specifically trained to do so.

The relevance of this to the voluntary sector is that there seems to be diminishing scope for good ideas and new initiatives to be 'tried out' with prisoners. Governors are tied to very clear targets which include the number of prisoners who attend accredited offending behaviour programmes. However, the size and structure of the existing accredited programmes and the criteria for accreditation of new ones mean that voluntary sector agencies are unlikely to be able to become involved in this work on a large scale.

Of course much of the work undertaken with prisoners by voluntary sector organizations is not directly related to offending behaviour. Accreditation, as a means of demonstrating the validity of work, has already been in place in other fields for some time, and voluntary sector agencies have been involved in delivering parenting courses and some educational inputs which are accredited through the Open College Network.

The fact remains though that governors are under pressure to demonstrate that they are achieving value for money and that they are spending their resources on work which will reduce re-offending—a Key

Performance Indicator for the Prison Service. Although most voluntary sector organizations may not be able or willing to deliver programmes with the size and integrity requirement of accredited offending behaviour programmes, much of the work they undertake is indirectly designed to improve prisoners' quality of life after release and may impinge upon future offending. Activities or programmes directed at lifestyle, for example, may be extremely important if a prisoner wants to make changes. Interventions designed to improve prisoners' use of leisure time in the community may help individuals to stay away from situations or friendship groups likely to draw them back into offending. Help with practical and social skills may enable them to cope with everyday situations and demands (budgeting, cooking etc.) and prevent the 'need' to offend from arising.

There is a danger that the demand to provide ever more places on accredited programmes might 'squeeze out' smaller scale, more localised and less directly offence-focused interventions. In Scotland, the Accreditation Panel has recognised the need for work which is not solely directed towards offending and now has a range of approved activities—programmes which have been approved by the accreditation panel but which are designed to tackle a wider range of issues. These programmes tend to be shorter than accredited offending behaviour programmes. Although the requirements are still very exacting they would, if this idea were adopted in England and Wales, provide some voluntary sector organizations with a means of developing their work with prisoners and bringing it into the mainstream of prison activities.

Although accredited programmes have received considerable attention recently the fact remains that the overwhelming majority of prisoners will not have the opportunity to attend a programme. Over the next five years there is to be an expansion to 10,000 accredited offending behaviour programme completions per year, but at present the number is half that and the daily prison population is around 68,000. Voluntary sector agencies, together with prison education and training, will continue to provide an important range of opportunities to prepare for release for many prisoners ineligible, unsuitable for or simply unable to get on to accredited courses as long as they continue to be resourced to do so.

THE LAMING REPORT AND COMMUNITY PARTNERSHIPS

In January 2000, following a number of negative reports on prisons from HM Chief Inspector of Prisons, a small working group was established by the Home Office minister. Its remit was to examine how 'failing' prisons could be identified more effectively, and how they could be managed in such a way that their performance improves. The group was specifically asked to examine the role of community partnerships in accomplishing such improvements.

This was the first time that a working group of this sort had specifically been asked to look at the role of community organizations, although the Woolf inquiry had emphasised the importance of community links in its 1991 report. It came at a time when CLINKS was developing a presence as the organization pulling together the diversity of voluntary sector provision in prisons and highlighting areas of common concern. The Voluntary Sector Compact had already provided a framework for the relationship between statutory and voluntary sector agencies more generally at the behest of a government keen to forge strong partnerships with the sector.

Members of the Laming Committee visited a number of prisons and sought evidence from a range of voluntary sector and other community-based organizations working in prisons. The committee concluded that 'Community-based organizations offer an important resource to prisons, but one that is not efficiently used at present. Many prisons have no centralised information about which agencies are active in the prison, let alone what they do and how' (Laming, 2000). They recommended that every prison should have a named member of staff, either employed specifically for the task or a member of prison staff with facility time to undertake the role, to act as the main contact point for community-based agencies and take responsibility for finding agencies to work with the prison to meet identified needs.

The committee also highlighted the difficulties caused by the lack of formal agreements between prisons and community-based service providers in terms of the lack of clarity about what service was to be delivered and to what standards. Where standards or quality indicators were set they could sometimes not be met because of difficulties on the part of the prison. One major task of the Laming Committee was to formulate a strategy for identifying prisons at risk of failure. Where a prison is unable to meet its obligations to voluntary sector agencies in terms of service level agreements or contracts these failures can be measured and used to contribute to an overall picture of the performance of the prison. They may provide early warning of potential problems since small deteriorations in the regime often seem to precede more serious problems.

The Laming Committee concluded that:

> Links between prisons and community-based agencies should be strengthened and co-ordinated more effectively. Prison and community-based agency staff should be provided with training to enable them to work together more effectively. Community-based agency staff should be able to

convey any concerns they have about the prison to the Governor or Area Manager.

Laming 2000, pp.31-32

The recommendations of the committee on the role of the community can be found at the end of the book in *Appendix 3*.

A KEY TIME FOR THE ROLE OF THE VOLUNTARY SECTOR

The voluntary sector has a long history of involvement with prisons, but the year 2000 stands out as a time when the sector's role was recognised as never before and significant steps were taken to formalise it. These have included not only the specification that the Laming Committee look at the role of community-based agencies as part of its remit, but also specific mention of the importance of the continuing development of partnerships with the voluntary sector in the Prison Service's business plan, the involvement of the Active Community Unit looking at the role of volunteers in prisons and the appointment of a voluntary sector co-ordinator at Prison Service HQ. Many prisons are now appointing local co-ordinators or delegating the task to a member of staff. The challenge now will be to sustain this level of commitment. There is always a danger that this welcome level of attention to the work of the voluntary sector will be supplanted by another priority before the structures are adequately in place to ensure that the sector is able to continue to develop its role. The very diversity of the sector may be helpful here, because as its partnership with the Prison Service becomes more secure, and dialogue on a shared agenda concerning both develops, voluntary sector organizations should continue to be seen as allies on a wide range of issues.

CHAPTER 7

The Contribution of Volunteers in the Penal System

Roma Hooper

This chapter outlines the specialised area of volunteering in the penal system. The need to recognise such volunteering as *specialised* is crucial if one is to identify the uniqueness of the role of people who choose to work with prisoners or ex-prisoners, whether it is inside or outside the complex and closed institutional setting of the prison. Much of the general research and discussion surrounding the field of volunteering remains applicable to all those working as a volunteer or managing volunteers in the penal system. However, it is important to identify key areas which separate these particular volunteers from those working in the wider fields of social responsibility, particularly on issues of security and confidentiality. The chapter can in no way give credit to the great breadth of support provided by volunteers. However, it will highlight key organizations whose skill and experience of working with volunteers provides examples of good practice, whilst at the same time identifying many of the fundamental difficulties experienced by voluntary agencies and volunteers working within the penal system.

UNDERSTANDING THE TERM 'VOLUNTEER'

It is essential to understand what exactly a volunteer is. Much confusion lies within the terminology and the media often confuses 'volunteers' with 'the voluntary sector'. A succinct summary in *Introduction to the Voluntary Sector* (Hedley, 2000, p.12) clarifies the position:

> For my own working definition, I would extract the four elements which in my view are essential to volunteering. Each of these is important, not only for what it says that volunteering is, but also for what it says it is not. Thus:
>
> Volunteering is: unpaid (except for out-of-pocket expenses); freely chosen; done through the medium of an organization or agency, and for the benefit of others or the environment as well as oneself.

Volunteering is not: paid work (including low or semi-paid work, e.g. employment training); compulsory or coerced (e.g. community punishment and rehabilitation orders); informal help between friends, family or neighbours, or self-help, religious and leisure activities.

Most volunteers are attached to voluntary sector organizations and these *unpaid* volunteers are usually offered training, monitoring and support by *paid* members of staff within those organizations. However, not all voluntary sector organizations necessarily involve volunteers in their service provision. The organizations highlighted in this chapter recognise that volunteers are either their key resource or represent a fundamental element of their work.

VOLUNTEERING TO BE IN PRISON

With several hundred voluntary sector agencies involved in penal affairs (Bryans and Walker, 2000, p.18) there are many opportunities open to volunteer within the penal system. For example a volunteer may chose to work with a vulnerable young offender on remand, a teenage mother, a foreign national convicted of a drugs charge, someone on a life sentence or a sex offender. A volunteer may chose to do prison visiting, become a member of a Board of Visitors, a Samaritan, a mentor, a charity trustee, a member of a management committee or help run a helpline providing support and information to families and friends. There are schemes which enable prisoners themselves to become volunteers (such as community service volunteers) and organizations which involve ex-prisoners as volunteers (such as Unlock and Women in Prison).

However, such diverse areas of volunteering opportunities do not exist without problems, not only relating to appropriate training and support, but also of acceptance within a statutory system. The Howard League reminds us that 'the introduction of volunteers into the penal system has not been easy. Secrecy and hostility and indifference in penal systems all hamper work by volunteers' (Whitfield, 1980, p.2).

Twenty years on this remains a core issue and continues to generate debate. Establishing a foothold within a prison is often problematic for voluntary agencies. After agreed terms have been established at management level, there are often many obstacles that can hinder the delivery of the service at the practical level by volunteers or agencies; for example, many volunteers comment that prison officers can resist their efforts and actively make it complicated for them to have access to prisoners. Equally, prison officers may feel that volunteers are not aware of the complexities of staffing and security restrictions and fail to appreciate the circumstances in which they work. Volunteers can find themselves in the position of filling a gap when statutory provision is not available, and being used as unpaid auxiliaries or reserves (Gill and Mawby, 1990, p.14). This can itself cause hostility from prison staff who may see their positions threatened, or resent volunteers taking on some of the more interesting or rewarding roles. Increased voluntary activity can also potentially lead to a further erosion or even curtailment of statutory provision. This is a situation which grant-making trusts that fund the voluntary sector have understandable concerns about (*ibid*, p.26). Whether there is an ambivalence towards volunteers or not, there is no doubt that they have become an integral, if not necessarily acknowledged, part of the penal system and provide a valuable service.

BENEFITS OF INVOLVING VOLUNTEERS IN THE PENAL SYSTEM

Using volunteers in the world of the prisoner can offer a wide range of benefits to both the Prison Service itself, the prisoner and the family. They may:

- widen the range of skills, abilities and resources available to prisoners such as the work being undertaken by the Society of Voluntary Associates' (SOVA's) basic education scheme at Feltham Young Offender Institution and the Inside Out Trust;
- offer the special element of community involvement with community service volunteers;
- provide offenders with befriending opportunities through organizations such as New Bridge, plus offer more specialised long-term relationships through mentoring, for example Trail-Blazers, the mentoring scheme at Feltham Young Offender Institution and the Dalton Youth Project
- provide training and employment opportunities through organizations like Youth at Risk;
- in many instances, provide the prison with a virtually cost-free (that is cost-free to the prison, but not to the voluntary agency to which the volunteers may be attached) support system for both prisoners and their families, for example, prison visitors and the Prison Fellowship;
- strengthen multi-cultural and ethnic programmes with the support of organizations such as Uplift and the Black Prisoners Support Group;
- provide a non-institutionalised support network for prisoners and their families which can have a positive knock-on effect for staff morale;

- provide a crucial counselling ear to vulnerable prisoners, for instance through the Samaritans and Alcoholics Anonymous;
- keep the offender in touch with the outside world, and help guide him or her back into their community—Dependency2Work; and
- offer interim support for remand prisoners who often fall through the net—YMCA and The Children's Society.

For those volunteers working *in the community*, their skills and knowledge can:

- provide badly needed support for prisoners' families, through visitors centres (the Bourne Trust, the Ormiston Trust and independent centres), the Prisoners' Families and Friends Service, POPS (Partners of Prisoners and Families Support Group) and SOVA;
- help released prisoners re-adjust to life back in the community, for example by taking on ex-prisoners as volunteers in those voluntary agencies which have supported them;
- provide added staff for running helplines such as ADFAM's drug helpline;
- act as mentors for such schemes as the Dalston Youth Project, Islington Mentoring Plus and youth offending teams (YOTs);
- provide valuable administrative support, for example Women in Prison and Unlock have a number of ex-prisoners working as volunteers in key project areas;
- influence the community in breaking down barriers surrounding prison life and prisoners as well as working with schools and other key social institutions in creating awareness surrounding the issues of, for example, drugs and alcohol and the potential for criminal activity (The Howard League runs the Citizenship and Crime Project);
- provide support for victims and witnesses of crime through agencies such as Victim Support; and
- support community-based projects particularly those focussed on people at risk of offending.

KEY AREAS INVOLVING VOLUNTEERS

There are a number of statutory and other organizations which make use of volunteers and who are vitally important to the running of a humane and just prison system. Four of these areas of work are discussed below: the Board of Visitors; Samaritans; prison visitors and mentoring.

The Board of Visitors (BoV)

Over the centuries there have always been people ready to help the prisoner or ex-prisoner but the evolution of such support into a voluntary movement must be attributed to Elizabeth Fry. Volunteers became an integral part of the prison system after she first visited Newgate Prison in 1813 (Zedner, 1997, p.299). Appalled by the degrading and unsanitary conditions which both women and children experienced in Newgate, Elizabeth Fry was motivated to visit the prison regularly, supplying prisoners with clothes and even establishing a chapel and school. She set up the pioneering Ladies Association for the Reformation of Female Prisoners (Zedner, 1997, p.299). Her team of visitors were the forerunners for the development of the modern prison visitors and voluntary associates, and the Board of Visitors (BoV). Crucially, Elizabeth Fry sowed the seeds of the penal support system as it is seen today by highlighting the importance of improving standards within prisons, establishing special regimes for women, and promoting programmes for moral treatment (*ibid.*). As independent observers, these visitors were able to represent the prisoners who experienced a wide range of injustices within the penal system. It is the criteria of independence which is reflected today in the work of the BoV.

The Prison Act 1877 established a Prison Commission to take control of all the local prisons and unpaid Visiting Committees were appointed who were to have free access to every part of a prison, and to every prisoner (Draycott, 1998, p.4). The governor's report from HM Convict Prison Aylesbury commented in March 1899:

> With reference to the Prison Act of 1898, the chief change in administration brought thereby, which has chiefly affected this prison, is the appointment of a Board of Visitors. At first I inclined to the belief that the appointment of a Board of independent members who would only be responsible to the Secretary of State would prove to be a source of embarrassment rather than a benefit ... I am glad to find that my forebodings have not been realised, and I cannot now speak too highly of the advantages derived from the appointment of the board.
>
> Draycott, 1998, p.8.

Over 100 years later, BoV remains an independent watchdog of prison establishments, reporting to the secretary of state. Funded by the Prison Service centrally, a BoV is a body created by statute and there are currently about 135 boards with an average of 15 members each. Board members are lay people appointed by the secretary of state on an unpaid voluntary basis but their role is fundamental to the protection of prisoners' human rights. Unlike any other institution in Britain, the prison is a *closed* institution, therefore requiring close and sensitive scrutiny. To this end, the members must visit regularly, often unannounced, hear all complaints by prisoners whilst making time to listen to prison staff and any issues of concern they may wish to voice. Yet, whilst the role of members embodies much the same ethos as it did a hundred years ago, the penal landscape has changed significantly. With the continuing extension of the prison system, a board member now holds a position of greater responsibility and to support the work being undertaken by the BoV, the need for independent overviews has been reflected in the creation of the offices of Chief Inspector of Prisons (1981) and Prisons Ombudsman[1] (1994). Both of offices encompass areas of work where, originally, the only independent intervention was provided by the BoV.

Yet, despite these significant developments, BoV members continue to play a critical role in their day-to-day observances which can highlight any evidence of a reduction in standards of fairness and humanity within the prison system, whilst ensuring that the prison premises and administration are running satisfactorily. BoVs and their reports can potentially impact on certain aspects of prison practice. Such a unique function must, therefore, adhere to a quality of recruitment and training together with a support system which reflects the importance of their role. BoV members are not befrienders but should have very good interpersonal skills, and the ability to maintain an independent position free of prejudice and bias. Working full-time elsewhere need not be a hindrance as much of the visiting can be done in the evening and at weekends. Yet, they are volunteers and are often required to deal with extremely sensitive and difficult situations. As Delbert Sandiford, the national director for BoVs, highlighted in his speech to the Boards of Visitors Centenary Conference in 1998:

> It is difficult to recruit and train volunteers. The traditional means of word of mouth and networking does not provide enough people or a sufficiently diverse group of members . . . More generally the long hours worked in the United Kingdom impose their own restriction on time available for voluntary duties.
>
> Sandiford, 1998, p.1

As with many voluntary sector agencies, innovative solutions need to be found to provide volunteers with a deserved status such as the introduction of the accreditation of voluntary work. Equally the whole area of training and support needs to be revisited as often BoV members have to shoulder an unacceptably stressful workload, whilst some are criticised for not being vigilant or critical enough. It was with this in mind that a working group was established to review the legal context in which BoVs operate, the effectiveness of the existing structure, and to develop proposals for enhancing the performance of the system.[2]

---

[1] Now the Prisons and Probation Ombudsman.
[2] *Review of the Board of Visitors Working Group Terms of Reference*, June 2001.

prison staff and volunteers is essential to maintain the regime which is required. Volunteers can only be truly effective with the support of staff.

Samaritans

The need for staff support is particularly the case with the Samaritans whose presence within prisons can impact on the threshold between life and death. Founded in 1953, the Samaritans has nearly 20,000 volunteers spread over 203 branches. Most of their workforce, 98.8 per cent, is unpaid (*Annual Review 1999-2000*, p.8). Samaritans work in 160 prisons across Britain and Ireland involving 1,000 volunteers. The organization's vision represents its core function: 'Samaritan befriending is always available at any hour of the day or night for everyone passing through personal crisis and at risk of dying by suicide' (Waghorn, 2000, p.34).

There has been an increased awareness of the valuable work achieved by the Samaritans in prisons in their support of prisoners who are suicidal or in distress. They have also been influential in spreading suicide awareness and it is the skills and knowledge which they can bring that has lead to their increased involvement in prisons—the organization is now represented in virtually every establishment's Suicide Awareness Team and in some prisons each wing has a direct phone line to the local branches. The need for such support is clearly evidenced by recent statistics: one young person in the UK attempts suicide every 20 minutes (*Annual Review 1999-2000: Facing the Future*, p.6). In 1998, 571 young men and 159 young women between the ages of 15 and 24 succeeded (Official Government Statistics, 1998). However, the number of suicides in prisons fell from 91 in 1999 to 72 in 2001. Self-inflicted deaths in prisons fell by 11 per cent in 2000 and by a further 11 per cent in 2001.

Whilst the role of the Samaritans in prisons can be life-saving, on a more day-to-day basis the volunteer can be readily available to talk to prisoners, reducing stress and anxiety before crisis point is reached. One particular development which is being increasingly adopted by prisons is the Listeners' Scheme. Prisoners are selected to act as volunteers, with training and support by the local branch of the Samaritans, to work with those prisoners who would benefit from a range of extra support such as actually sleeping in the same cell to offer added support and help during the first night in custody. As Waghorn comments: 'for every shift spent supporting a Listener Scheme, each Samaritan volunteer is able to double the number of depressed, despairing or suicidal contacts that will use Samaritan befriending' (Waghorn, 2000, p.34).

A core principle for the Samaritans is, of course, confidentiality and their success in prisons is guided by this fundamental principle which enables vulnerable prisoners to express their anxieties and concerns in confidence. Confidentiality cannot be abandoned or jeopardised which can lead to difficulties between volunteers and prison staff who understandably often have real concerns when information received by the volunteer cannot always be made available to them. But as Waghorn goes on to comment: 'relationships require a shared vision, an understanding of the differences between you, a respect for each other's values and methods' (Waghorn, 2000, p.35).

The Samaritan volunteer represents the organization's key resource—a resource recognised by the organization itself:

> ... our hard-working volunteers need all-round support and this year we took new steps to help keep them motivated and informed. Our training 'package' included courses on how to plan and run in-service training more effectively, sessions on motivating volunteers and support materials which act as a 'how to' guide for volunteers responsible for selecting new team members.
>
> *The Samaritans Annual Review 1999-2000*, p.8

Mentoring

The increased interest and investment in the role of mentoring in society today has infiltrated the penal system and is fast becoming a popular form of intervention with vulnerable prisoners or young people 'at risk'. A modern definition of mentoring is:

> Mentoring is a term that is used to describe the relationship and arrangements whereby an individual provides support, advice and/or guidance to another. Other similar terms are buddying or befriending. The type and level of support will depend on the individual's needs and can include emotional, practical or general support.
>
> Dependancy2Work *Information Leaflet*, 2000

The Youth Justice Board issued draft guidelines for mentoring with young offenders in 1998 believing that there would be an increase in expanding mentoring programmes following on from the Crime and Disorder Act 1998 (Skinner and May, p.3, 1999). Youth offending teams (YOTs) are now establishing mentoring schemes as an 'arms length' voluntary sector service to ensure young people are not stigmatised when using this service.[3]

Teeside Probation Service has around 40 volunteers (who must apply to the service and receive basic training) and these people act as befrienders to prisoners in need of positive role models as well as providing very basic advice and support on employment and training. The government's Connexion Service links statutory agencies, the voluntary sector and specialist private sector businesses to offer every young person a personal advisor. However, these advisors will be paid (DfEE Publications). This scheme is being piloted at Huntercombe Young

---

[3] www.youthjusticeboard.gov.uk/policy/mentoring/

Offender Institution and there will be considerable focus on the outcomes of this two-year pilot.

Using mentoring in work with young people at risk and young offenders is a fairly recent innovation. SOVA, DIVERT Trust, Crime Concern and RPS Rainer have developed projects over the last few years which address the needs of young people with a more demanding range of problems (Skinner and Fleming, 1999, p.3).

With the growth in this particular area of volunteering, mentor training is becoming more structured and needs based. For example, a mentor may need specific training as he or she has agreed to support through letter writing, another mentor may require more substantial training if the role entails visiting the offender on a regular basis and maintaining a relationship on release. Mentoring a prisoner or ex-prisoner provides opportunities to realise the mentored person's (mentee's) potential, independent and non-institutional support and advice and a link from the inside world of prison to the outside world of reality. Yet, mentor expectations of mentees must be embedded in realism. It is unlikely that mentoring can effect major change but a mentor can present their mentee with an alternative to the way they are living and can be there to reinforce any such alternative view. Indeed,

> mentoring interventions may address several risk factors, including alienation, academic failure, low commitment to school and association with delinquent and violent peers, as well as the protective factors of opportunities for pro-social involvement, bonding to pro-social adults and healthy beliefs and clear standards for behaviour.
>
> Joseph Rowntree Foundation, *Sourcebook of Juvenile Offenders*, p.95

THE REWARDS OF VOLUNTEERING

Volunteering, by definition, is done for reasons other than financial reward, though expenses are usually covered. For the prisoner, volunteering can have a real resonance and open doors to employment opportunities. Community service volunteers have gained a reputation in placing pre-release volunteers into social care settings. The benefits gained by both the volunteer and the recipient are well recognised. Some volunteers have achieved so much on placement that they have been offered the chance to return after release and continue the work started during sentence.

There have been volunteers working inside prisons who have gone on to gain employment via the Prison Service, for example, in education departments, the Probation Service or the voluntary sector.

Recognition for the work of volunteers may come in the form of Butler Trust awards. The trust was launched in July 1985 to recognise and reward excellence among people working in the three prison services in the UK. Many volunteers in the system, including prison staff who give up their time, have received Butler Trust awards since the trust's inception and have contributed to the development and dissemination of best practice. Volunteers in the penal system, particularly prison visitors and mentors, can be vulnerable to stress, particularly when there is a high degree of dedication and commitment. Acknowledging anxieties may compound any feeling of inability to cope. Therefore, recognition and reward, topped up with good training and a support network, can often prevent volunteers devaluing themselves. Voluntary agencies working within the penal system have a major responsibility to ensure that this very valuable resource does not 'burn out' (*Volunteering*, 2000).

TODAY'S VOLUNTEERS IN THE PENAL SYSTEM—LOOKING TO THE FUTURE

The importance of community involvement was highlighted in 1999 by the publication of a strategy report by the Working Group on the Active Community, which outlined that 'volunteering and community activities are central to the concept of citizenship and are the key to restoring our communities. They can help with social inclusion, life-long learning, healthy living and active ageing'. With this increased focus on public involvement in community life it is crucial that the closed institution of the prison is not forgotten.

Whilst there is as yet little evidence-based research into the value of volunteers working with prisoners, there is anecdotal evidence that the informal support network offered by visitors centres, prison visitors, the BoV, mentoring schemes and many other schemes provide a life-line and can have a significant impact on the prisoner's time in custody and on release. For example, Radio Feltham, Britain's only prison radio station run by young prisoners, continually reports an increase in confidence and self-esteem experienced by the young offenders, who are supported in the main by volunteers who help with the radio station: 'Radio Feltham has helped me prove to myself and prove to my mum that I am actually doing something with my life'. With the pressure on prisons to deliver constructive regimes, volunteers can provide added value to any educational or vocational activity.

Recent studies involving the statutory sector have indicated the added value provided by volunteers in improving literacy and numeracy rates and in reducing crime levels. This is evidenced by the work of the SOVA Literacy and Numeracy Project. Trained volunteers work one-to-one with prisoners providing additional educational support. Research undertaken by SOVA highlights that 90 per cent of the students commented that the style of tutoring had made a significant difference to their learning process (Deverson, 2000, p.13). With between 60 and 70 per cent of prisoners falling well below the level needed to be functional in the work place, the lowest levels being those of young prisoners, trained volunteers working in this area can have a major impact on the future of many young prisoners.

As a result of the 2000 Spending Review, the Home Office Public Service Agreement includes a national target of volunteering. The spending review outcome, to ensure that this target is achieved, included added support such as extra investment by the Home Office in developing the national and volunteering infrastructure. Extra funds have been made available (over £120 million in 2001-2 to 2003-4) ('News', *Volunteering, the Magazine*, Aug/Sept 2000).

But how will the Prison Service and the voluntary agencies working with prisoners access such funds? Few governors know how many volunteers they have working inside their prison. A recent questionnaire from the Active Community Unit in the Home Office to governors and voluntary agencies may well provide the answer but there needs to be considerable discussion around how to develop the role of the volunteer within the penal system. The creation of a new position, that of voluntary sector co-ordinator at Prison Service HQ will also facilitate voluntary involvement. Support undoubtedly came from the CLINKS' *Good Practice Guide* which was made available to all Governors and voluntary agencies in 2001, but a greater cohesive strategy needs to be established.

Considerable effort needs to be made to increase the number of black volunteers. This would make sense in the light of the increasing number of young black people entering the criminal justice system, and criticisms of the prison service as being 'institutionally racist'. In a recent report on a survey by the National Coalition for Black Volunteers, David Obaze, director, comments:

> . . . in the light of the Stephen Lawrence enquiry it is disappointing to find that charities are not in the forefront of good equal opportunities practice. Given that black people are disproportionately affected by unemployment, it is shameful that volunteering, which can bring so many benefits, is seemingly not on offer to them. The prime minister talks of inclusion but black people are excluded from the mainstream and there are precious little resources for the black voluntary sector.

Noticeable by their Absence: Black Volunteers in Charities, June 2000

These issues are explored more fully in *Chapter 8*.

The lack of empirical research to evaluate the benefits or otherwise of involving volunteers with prisoners and their families may be one reason why there has been a lack of any structured support system coming from the Prison Service for volunteers and their voluntary agencies. The lack of overt support from the Prison Service in the past suggests a certain ambivalence in recognising the work undertaken by volunteers. Yet, despite this, most voluntary agencies retain the loyalty and support of their volunteers, and continue to be invited into prisons.

Considerable time and resources are expended by voluntary agencies upon the recruitment and selection, training, co-ordination and support of their volunteers. Most agencies offer training schemes which are professional and satisfactory. However there is an argument that there would be advantages in a more cohesive approach towards training. For example there could be more joint training initiatives as between the various agencies, either at the geographical level or establishment level. There could be benefits from including voluntary agencies and their volunteers in joint training initiatives with the Prison Service, in addition to that provided by the voluntary agencies themselves. Joint initiatives would help break down barriers and reduce mutual stereotypical attitudes, and offer opportunities for increased awareness and understanding of the very diverse cultures of the Prison Service and voluntary sector. Training for volunteers on issues such as suicide awareness within individual establishments might be particularly useful. This is not to suggest that volunteers and voluntary agencies should be inculcated into prison culture or integrated into their methods. On the contrary, it is vital that they retain their independent culture and alternative perspective, as this is their quality and strength. Indeed, there has been debate as to whether volunteers in general should be trained at all (Aves, 1969; Banton, 1973; Barr, 1971; Fielding, 1988), as this could blur the distinction between their voluntary status and the paid employees alongside whom they work, and with volunteers thereby 'losing the quality of being distinctly different' (Aves, 1969 in Gill and Mawby, 1990, p.114). Certainly, there are a number of issues surrounding the training of penal volunteers, particularly if their numbers are likely to increase following government initiatives, and as such these issues warrant research.

As policies and initiatives are established to increase the number of those people volunteering, key issues will arise. Volunteers in the penal system are, in general, an unusually autonomous group. To over-managerialise them could not only be demotivating, but deny them the most important quality they have—a non-statutory, experienced, confidential and caring listening ear which transcends the institutional setting and enables the prisoners and their families to benefit from services and support which they may not be able to access elsewhere.

Yet, at the same time, to be accepted into such a complex institutional setting as a prison can be very problematic. Prison staff may view volunteers with caution, uncertain about their skills and appropriate experience. Often seen as lacking professionalism, a volunteer may quickly be 'written off' as simply a do-gooder with no understanding of working inside a prison. It would be irresponsible to encourage more volunteers to enter the penal system without proper preparation. Induction and security training should be automatically offered to all voluntary agencies and their volunteers and joint training initiatives established (shared by voluntary agencies and prison service staff). There are very many examples of models of good practice established between voluntary agencies, volunteers and the prison service, where barriers have been broken down and bridges built. Such co-operation is for the mutual benefit of all involved.

CHAPTER 8

The Faith-based and Minority Ethnic Voluntary Sector

Yousif al-Khoei, Robert Green, Richie Dell and The Venerable William Noblett

The historical development of the penal voluntary sector is outlined in *Chapter 3*. That chapter highlights the fact that many of the early charities and aid societies were either faith-based or targeted at specific groups of people. Over the years the tendency has been for agencies to amalgamate and to focus less upon specific faith groups but instead to be far more generalist, ecumenical or secular in their approach. The Bourne Trust is typical in that, whilst it retains links with its Catholic heritage, its service provision and ethos reflects and embraces cultural and religious diversity.

However, increased immigration and the evolution of a multi-faith and diverse Britain means that the specific needs of some groups of prisoners have not been met by the traditional agencies. One example of this is the needs of prisoners from the Black and Minority Ethnic community and another is the needs of Muslim prisoners.

In response to this there has developed a new wave of penal voluntary sector organizations and the necessity for other agencies to critically review their practice to ensure that they meet the needs of a diverse prison population. This chapter considers some of the issues raised by these changes. It firstly covers the response of the Muslim community to the increasing numbers of Muslims in prison, and then there are two personal reflections from different perspectives. Finally, there is a contribution that acknowledges the historic role played by the chaplaincy, but which also recognises that this may need to change in order to address the key challenges and opportunities that diversity presents to both the voluntary sector and the Prison Service.

MUSLIMS IN PRISON Yousif al-Khoei

HM Prison Service's experience in addressing the issue of Muslim prisoners is relatively new. When the Prison Act 1952 was passed there was no significant Muslim presence in prisons in the UK. As a consequence of post-war immigration and particularly from around the 1970s onwards, a Muslim presence began to be felt within the prison population. At this time, however, numbers were low and, accordingly, basic arrangements were put in place for small groups of Muslim prisoners on an *ad hoc* basis.

In this period, imams of local mosques or lay volunteers would act as visiting imams and generally confine their activities to conducting Friday prayers. Many such visiting imams would have a weak command of English and unsatisfactory communication skills. On the national level, two organizations were concerned with the welfare of Muslim prisoners: the Islamic Cultural Centre, followed later in the 1980s by the IQRA Trust.

Muslims now constitute approximately seven per cent of the total UK prison population of around 68,000. In the 1990s, the Muslim prison population had increased markedly—more than doubling in ten years. It was clear that the existing arrangements would not be adequate to deal with this change. What was needed was a major overhaul of the way in which the needs of Muslim prisoners was addressed.

This increase can be seen as a result of two more recent developments: the rise in numbers of second and third generation Muslim youths often living in socially deprived environments more prone to crime; and the rise in the number of Muslim asylum seekers who were sometimes kept in mainstream prisons. Moreover, around 25 per cent of the current Muslim prison population are either white or black (Caribbean) as opposed to Asian or North African origin. This is disproportionate to their numbers within the Muslim population at large and it is not clear whether they convert after entering prison or before.

The government recognised the problem this increase brought and in 1999 appointed the first Muslim Advisor to HM Prison Service, Maqsood Ahmed.

National Council for the Welfare of Muslim Prisoners
The Islamic Cultural Centre and IQRA Trust together with the Al-Khoei Foundation, who have been sending visiting imams for a relatively small number of Shi'a Muslim prisoners since 1994, recognised the need for better coordination and cooperation and in 1989 set up the National Council for the Welfare of Muslim Prisoners (NCWMP). Other national Muslim organizations were also invited to join as well as imams from different ethnic backgrounds and a wide range of geographical locations across the country. These organizations included: the Union of Muslim Organizations, Imams and Mosques Council and the Muslim Council of Britain among others. Two female colleagues were also invited to join to ensure that the concerns of the small number of female Muslim prisoners were adequately addressed within the NCWMP.

At its inception, the NCWMP inherited the dual problems of managerial incoherence and meagre resources. This was mainly a consequence of the fact that the coordination of welfare for Muslim prisoners had depended largely on voluntary work and commitments from individual members. It set out to work towards the welfare of Muslim prisoners under a more coherent and rational organizational structure and to locate and respond to the needs of Muslim prisoners more effectively.

Visits and reports

A regime of regular and comprehensive prison visits was put in place, arranged by the office of the Muslim advisor. These visits were in addition to the visits the Muslim advisor himself conducts and entail a thorough inspection of all aspects of the quality of religious life from a Muslim prisoner's perspective. Their central results are individual and detailed reports following each visit. These have been an effective tool in increasing the pressure for reform of certain aspects of the system. Problems encountered were, typically:

- *position of imams:* This relates to issues concerning employment status and includes: the question of whether or not the imam is an integral part of the system or is regarded as a visitor; lack of hours and the resources available to the imams to meet the spiritual and pastoral needs of Muslim prisoners; the holding of prison keys; and lack of participation of imams in the Prison Services' training programmes.
- *Halal diet:* This concerns the procurement, handling, storage and preparation of Halal diet, the avoidance of cross contamination, and the availability of choices on the menu and its clarity and inadequate arrangements during the fasting month of Ramadan. The Prison Service Order (PSO 5000) did not address the requirement of the Halal diet.
- *places of worship:* Arrangements for Friday prayers vary considerably and are often conducted in 'multi-faith rooms' or even in corridors with no carpets or ablution facilities. Some prisons have allowed the use of chapels during Friday prayers.
- *racial and religious discrimination:* As a consequence of the specific and visible needs of Muslim prisoners, many of them feel vulnerable to discrimination on the grounds of difference. This is particularly acute among immigration detainees who often do not speak English. Moreover, owing to their short hours and marginal position within the system, imams rarely participate in race relations and parole meetings. Most Muslim prisoners feel that

Islamophobia is a phenomenon which exists in different parts of the prison establishment.
- *observance of religious festivals:* These include Ramadan and Eid.

To date, the NCWMP have visited over 30 prisons and the reports arising from these visits have been extremely useful in complementing those of the muslim advisor in highlighting the above issues. The NCWMP visits also provide a direct and independent channel between Muslim prisoners and Muslim civil society representatives.

Other work
The NCWMP is also a member of the Religious Consultative Services and the Advisory Group on Religion in Prisons established by HM Prison Service. These give an opportunity to raise points of concern and to maintain a constructive working relationship with senior civil servants and representatives of the Christian faith, including the chaplain general, as well as other minority religions such as the Jewish, Buddhist, Hindu and Sikh representatives to discuss issues of common and individual concern to minority faiths.

The NCWMP has had meetings with the director general of the Prison Service, in the presence of the muslim advisor and other senior staff. These discussions have been very frank and constructive and are contributing considerably to addressing the concerns raised above.

The NCWMP also works with other institutions and academics in organizing training seminars for imams and staff and has cooperated with the Runnymede Trust's Commission on Muslims and Islamophobia and Forum Against Islamophobia and Racism (FAIR) in organizing seminars.

NCWMP liases with the Muslim advisor in his area imams' meetings, nomination of imams and consultation on various documents (PSI and PSO publications). The Muslim advisor also consults the NCWMP on the various Islamic festivals, their timing and observance as well as questions on Islamic jurisprudence. NCWMP newsletters have also been produced, but have experienced some teething problems due to lack of resources.

The appointment of the muslim advisor and establishment of the NCWMP, signalled important recognition of the specific needs of Muslim prisoners. The NCWMP also reflects the possibilities for cooperation and co-ordination between Muslim organizations and the potential for them to affect positive change. One full-time imam has been appointed and a number of other prisons with a large Muslim population are considering employing full-time imams. There has been some improvement in the provision of the Halal diet and prayer facilities in certain prisons. The new PSO 5000 on the Halal diet addresses the requirement but this needs to be coupled with action at the operational level.

One of the challenges for the future, however, remains for prison legislation to reflect more accurately religious diversity so that all prisoners' rights are enshrined in law. This is a wider challenge facing multi-cultural, multi-religious society in the UK and beyond.

PERSONAL PERSPECTIVE: THE ROLE OF BLACK PRISONER SUPPORT GROUPS Robert Green

A question I am often asked is, 'Why isn't there a white prisoners' support group?' Through gritted teeth, I politely reply that there is. It currently has around 40,000 employees, is answerable to its own government minister and is located in every major town or city in the United Kingdom. I am reliably informed that its annual budget is a whopping £1.7 billion. Its name? Her Majesty's Prison Service. The sad fact, as we enter this supposed new and enlightened millennium, is that if you go to prison and you fit all of the three following categories, white, male and Christian, then your needs are pretty much well met, however inadequately. Prisons, by and large, remain a monochromatic monolith, and in practical terms have struggled like every other social, private and public institution to put race-related policies fully into practice. Academically sanctioned and socially 'included' middle-classes dominate the morality and social mores that provide the yardstick by which the 'excluded' are measured. All this against a backdrop of political and social rhetoric that replaces racism with 'socially excluded'. It is in this context that Black Prisoner Support Groups (BPSGs) have steadily grown over the last few years.

Origin of Black Prisoner Support Groups
The history of early groups is patchy. Many began their lives as front room support groups led by women, either partners or mothers, who realised that sons and lovers had now entered a revolving door of crime and punishment. Other groups, for example Hibiscus, provide support to a highly over-represented and often overlooked group of women foreign nationals. Black Prisoner Support Groups are currently located in London, Coventry, Birmingham, Wolverhampton, Leicester, Nottingham and Manchester. Some groups only serve a specific ethnic group, as in a South Asian Offenders Project in Manchester, or a certain age range, like Cariba in Coventry, which primarily works with young offenders. Many provide similar services on a very skeletal workforce, and all but Nottingham are dependent on funds provided through partnership arrangements with local probation areas. This in itself is very limiting as funding comes with a condition of no campaigning. Some or all run

drop-in sessions; one-to-one counselling and befriending; culturally appropriate group work; history classes and cultural or spiritual events such as Diwali, Black History Month and Rastafarian celebrations. Black Prisoner Support Groups may also sit on various Race Relations Management Teams, engage in prison officer training or provide transport service for families to far flung prisons.

Management of race relations in prisons
With groups so overstretched and working in tacit isolation, the formation of an overarching National Body of Black Prisoners Support Groups (the 'National Body') was imperative. Comprised of individuals from varying disciplines and background it can legitimately campaign and collectively voice major social and political concerns on behalf of Black prisoners and the groups that represent them. Formed in 1998 and constituted in 1999 its aims are:

- to encourage and promote the development of a nationwide network of support groups and services for Black prisoners;
- to act as a voice for Black prisoners and represent their views and concerns to the Prison Service and other agencies;
- to publicise issues affecting Black prisoners;
- to promote the just treatment of Black prisoners by the criminal justice system and by society.

There is an irony that its target, the Prison Service, can legitimately claim to be one of the first criminal justice public bodies to introduce a comprehensive manual for the management of race relations. Prison Service Order 2800 was introduced in June 1997, yet much of the criteria for its implementation rests on satisfying quantitative measures. For example, a tick box for the existence of a multi-faith room does not elicit whether or not that room is suitable; is exclusive for religious services; is clean; has access to washing facilities for Muslim prisoners conducting ablutions, or is maximised by the varying religious groups. For many prisoners it is the basics that remain the priority: the availability of the appropriate hair care, skin care, food, information in appropriate first languages that should be available in every prison across the country as a right, and not in some cases, as a grudging privilege.

It is on these issues that the National Body has sought to bring some influence to bear on Prison Service senior management. The inclusion of the Body onto the Director General's Race Advisory Group has made the exchange of ideas, information and priorities easier. And whilst one of its few successes has been the nationwide availability of culturally appropriate hair care and skin care, it remains an inconsistent corporate commitment, despite some prisons being located near communities with a very large Black population.

Whilst the National Body's seat on the Race Advisory Group has given it a degree of legitimacy and credibility, bolstered in no small way by the Lawrence Inquiry Report and the Human Rights Act 1998, the experience of groups working in their locality is very different. Groups are often treated with a degree of suspicion by staff and prisoners. The word 'Black' seems to raise the hackles of many people, and 'support' conjures up the image of a vegetarian do-gooder who sees prisons as oppressive nineteenth century relics. The National Body does not see prisons as an anachronistic tool. But, it is the effective *use* of prisons and how Black prisoners are *treated* within them that remain the primary concerns of the National Body.

Working with Black prisoners
For the National Body, the question of what to do with prisoners once they are inside remains a bone of contention. Whether white or black, conflicting arguments continue to rage between psychologists, probation officers, prison reformists and the public. Imported remedies from North America often herald a new dawn. Cognitive behaviour work is currently in its ascendancy. Yet a probation inspectors' thematic report acknowledged that what works with women and Black offenders remained a mystery. Even with that knowledge, Black prisoners, whether male or female, are still being measured on a euro-centric one-size-fits-all basis.

Specialist work with Black prisoners remains thin on the ground. Much of it is conducted, by and large, by support groups or individuals who recognise that familial constructs, culture, value systems, religion, ethnicity and subsequent experience has a direct impact on offending behaviour. Whilst some of the work is currently being evaluated by the Home Office, the National Body would like to see more prisons open up their doors to innovative work such as that conducted at Moorland and Glen Parva. The success of these two initiatives is due in part to the Race Relations Liaison Officers (RRLOs). In fact, the status of the Race Relations Management Teams (RRMTs) and the role of the Race Relations Liaison Officer remain the key components to successful transference of policy to practice. Whilst the National Body recognises a number of dedicated and hard working RRMTs and RRLOs, the converse is also sadly true. RRMTs, by and large, have a tendency to monitor statistics and fail to take remedial action where necessary.

The following is a prime example of this inertia. The subject of the under-representation of Black prisoners gaining Cat D status has been a rolling agenda item since the mid-1990s. Although there has been talk of 'a plan', to date one has yet to be brought to the table. This is from a prison that prides itself on having prisoner representative at its meetings. Eager, participating, articulate and patient inmates (white and Black) eventually become totally disillusioned and leave what they consider to be a mere 'talking shop'. The same is experienced by Black Prisoners' Support Groups which tend, as a consequence, to only sit on those RRMTs that they feel they can have an impact on.

Minority ethnic staff

There is a great deal that the Prison Service needs to do to raise the Black experience of prison to that of its white counterpart, and its current strategies are long overdue. The RESPOND programme, launched in February 1999, led by the Prison Service's first race advisor, looking at the recruitment, retention and promotion of staff, as well as equality in the treatment of prisoners, is a step in the right direction. Backed up by the home secretary's own targets for public bodies this will hopefully make a small but significant impact. The Body has been encouraging and supportive of this change, despite the fact that Black prisoners have often complained that Black officers have tended to be harsher than their white colleagues in order to fit into the prevailing canteen culture. Merely having an increased number of Black faces within an organization will not drastically change that organization if their knowledge and experience is not embraced and used to significantly influence management understanding of working with diversity. Having Black and white governors who are encouraged to think out of the norm would be a truly progressive step. The *Good Practice Guide* developed by CLINKS, if used effectively, should bring in Black groups into prisons' mainstream thinking.

Local initiatives

The 1999 Race Relations Revue conducted at Glen Parva, under a partnership team comprised of prison staff, an outside consultant and led by the Black Prisoner Support Project (BPSP Leicester), was an initiative first mooted at the National Race Advisory Group. It provided a much more qualitative view on prison life and incorporated the views of staff and prisoners alike, irrespective of ethnicity. The findings proved illuminating and challenging and Glen Parva responded by incorporating the recommendations into its subsequent RRMT action plan.

The rolling series of workshops/groups at Moorland prison, run by Partners of Prisoners continues because of the tenacity and belief of the RRLO. If a culture is to change then these small steps need to be celebrated, encouraged and rewarded. Other initiatives where Black organizations are absorbed into the fabric of the prison remain thin on the ground. Funding is often the main stumbling block. As yet no BPSP has been put on mainstream funding priorities of local probation areas, and only the Moorland programme, to my knowledge, is part of the funding mainstream of the prison. However, the Body, like all reform groups pressing for change remains a tiny voice echoing in a vast dull chasm.

The Body has hosted two very successful conferences to date and will continue to host more. It is hopeful that the death of Zahid Mubarek at HMYOI Feltham and the continuing furore over the death of Alton Manning will promote rapid change and is not a sign of more of the same.

Future role
Whilst historians would have us believe that Black people, whether from the Caribbean, Africa or South Asia, have only been in this country a short time, the reality is that we've been here 2,000 years. There is documentation of young African Caribbean males in London entering prison in 1750. Significantly, a proclamation banning them from gaining a trade precipitated a rapid increase in their imprisonment. Two hundred and fifty years on, the discrimination in education, training, and employment has been on an equally dramatic rise. Yet today we claim to live in enlightened times. However with the prison population growing as it is and the trend to imprison disproportionately more Black men and women here than even in America, the Prison Service cannot afford to keep the work of the BPSP marginalised. The National Body will continue to exist only as long as inequality remains. We wait with optimism, but history has told us not to hold our breath.

A DUAL PERSPECTIVE Richie Dell

Minorities and the voluntary sector
I joined NACRO from the Prison Service in 1999 and remember being inducted into the organization, which included a visit to the head office in London. Having come from a rural community in the South West, it was striking the numbers of Black and Asian faces working in the building. Was it just because there was a large minority ethnic population living in the area, or was there more to it than that? Enquiring of some of my minority ethnic colleagues why they had chosen to work in the voluntary sector, some stated it was just an opportunity that had arisen; others said NACRO offered them necessary social work experience, but most indicated that it gave them 'the opportunity to give something back to the communities from which they came'. It would appear that a significant proportion of the Black and ethnic minority people working in the voluntary sector feel they have a chance to contribute to their communities based on empathy for the service users circumstances in relation to exclusion and racism.

An example of this could be seen in the case of a female colleague, an ex-offender who spoke passionately of her desire to help other Black women in prisons, giving hope to all in re-building their lives. In the early 1990s she had received a lengthy prison sentence for a drugs offence and whilst in prison she had developed quite a reputation for being non-conformist and disruptive. On the day of her release from prison she found herself with nowhere to live, without employment and, having become institutionalised, was not used to coping with such major problems in her life. Remembering a Black NACRO worker who used to visit her prison she decided to contact her. Help was forthcoming and emergency accommodation found. This proved to be the start of a remarkable transformation in this woman's life. She decided that she might like to help women in a similar position by showing them that being a Black female ex-offender did not mean there was no hope for the future. Her experiences with those working in the statutory sector left her feeling that that was not the way she would like to help, and she chose instead to join the voluntary sector. Some years later she continues to try and help others and describes this continued desire with overwhelming passion.

Prior to joining NACRO, I had been a prison officer for the previous eleven years. Having grown up facing severe racism and social deprivation, I was drawn to help others in a similar position right from the start of my time in the Prison Service. The first two years were spent 'learning the ropes' in a remand centre where staff from all over the country had been posted. Very little racism was encountered there. However, racism increased dramatically upon transfer to a prison in a rural community. If a prison officer (in a position of relative power) faced racism, how would it be for Black and Asian prisoners? As a consequence, in an attempt to help those who faced social and/or racial injustice, the ensuing years were spent taking on such roles as race relations liaison officer, equal opportunities officer, pre-release tutor (resettlement help) and offending behaviour tutor. At times over that eight-year period it felt that the Prison Service was not always truly committed to those issues. Indeed it sometimes seemed as though only 'lip service' was being paid and these issues were no more than 'flavour of the month'.

Progress and lessons

In recent years the Prison Service has begun to take both race issues and its joint working with the voluntary sector more seriously. It has employed a voluntary sector co-ordinator and a race advisor and this could possibly point to a new direction for the service, tackling both these issues in a more positive and sustainable manner. Most areas of good practice are the same for any organization. There are a number of strategies that *both* the Prison Service and penal voluntary sector agencies can employ to enhance the working relationship with the Black and ethnic minorities.

First, having meaningful an equal opportunities policy and strategy helps Black and minority people to feel that an organization takes notice of relevant issues. These policies must not be paper exercises that sit gathering dust on shelves; but instead an integral part of the way an organization conducts its business. Every aspect of training, recruitment, promotion, retention and service provision should be considered in any race strategy. This would help Black people feel their concerns are taken seriously. This is especially true of service provision. Black people want to feel they can help their own communities as well as others and a sound, working equal opportunity strategy gives them the security to do so.

Targeted recruitment of Black and ethnic minorities is also a strategy to be employed as is the explanation of the equal opportunity policy in the community. Offering secondments to staff could help improve the flow of relevant information between different organizations and therefore increase the areas of good practice. Black staff support groups can be useful in offering a voice to Black people working in organizations. A recent debate within one of the NACRO directorates asked if they should continue with the Black staff support network and it was heartening to hear the debate centred around 'Do staff still need it?' and not 'Why should they have it?' Training should be conducted in a safe environment where staff can explore their prejudices in a respectful manner, learning how other people feel whilst being told what is and is not acceptable behaviour.

Also a strategy for developing systematic links with the Black and minority ethnic community could prove advantageous in two ways. Firstly, firm links could lead to a better spread of good practice and an increased understanding of diversity. Secondly, more contact with that community is likely to increase the number of volunteers an organization can recruit from. Finally, the use of minority ethnic volunteers can (if used wisely) enhance the level of service provision offered by an organization. Black staff and volunteers can help build the trust of the minority ethnic community in the service offered by any such organization. Pro-active race strategies need to be in place and implemented so volunteers and service users alike can maintain their faith in organizations. Statutory organizations should seek to use voluntary organizations and their skills in trying to build their relationships with communities by developing long-term partnerships. Above all, the issue of racial equality should run through the veins of an organizations body—not just for now, but also for its entire existence.

THE CHAPLAINCY AND THE VOLUNTARY SECTOR The Venerable William Noblett

The context and understanding of chaplaincy is changing. A developing chaplaincy, reflecting prisoner needs from all faith traditions, and none, is seeking to work in a collaborative, multi-faith way. It will bring together chaplains of all faith traditions in a way that enables them to serve the needs of prisoners, staff, and faith communities, within and without the prison. As this multi-faith approach to chaplaincy develops within the Prison Service, the voluntary sector, and volunteers will have increased opportunity to work as 'partners not substitutes' (David Blunkett, home secretary). People of faith, and faith-based groups, will have more opportunity to represent the diversity that is part of our culture and to celebrate it; to help fight racism and religious discrimination, and to signal an inclusive approach whilst recognising the distinctiveness of each faith tradition.

Whilst this chapter is written from a primarily Christian perspective, it is also written in the belief that the contribution from faith-based community groups of all traditions will grow in the future, bringing a new, and enriching dimension.

Lord, what would become of the prisoner if Christian society, that is, the Church, were to reject him or her as civil society rejects him or her? There could not be a greater despair than that for the prisoner.

Fyodor Dostoevsky, the Russian novelist, knew what it meant to be a prisoner. He knew the depth of human failing, serving his time with those who had committed incredible violence and acts of deprivation. But he did not lose sight of the responsibility of Christians to respond to the needs of those in prison. A responsibility placed on us by Jesus, whose words, 'I was in prison and you visited me' have come to form the basis of so much that has been done, and is being done, in our prisons: prisons that are part of the community and belong to the community.

The involvement of Christian volunteers in the penal system is long and honourable, working in partnership with prison staff and chaplains over many centuries, going back much further than John Howard and Elizabeth Fry. A recent survey I conducted through chaplaincy teams, suggests there are currently over 6,000 active Christian volunteers in English and Welsh prisons, some of whom may visit on a regular, though infrequent basis. Many are members of faith-based voluntary sector groups. A further 1,000 offer prayerful support on a regular, and committed basis. In one prison I visited recently, chaplaincy volunteer hours over the course of a year equated to nine full-time members of the team. A large number of groups are involved, including: the Catholic Agency for Social Concern, Prison Fellowship, the Mother's Union,

Alpha, the Salvation Army, and the New Testament Church of God of Prophecy.

The range of activities with which Christian volunteers are involved covers a broad spectrum, and it may be helpful to draw them together under loose headings:

- *prayerful support:* many Christians throughout the country regularly pray for all who live and work in prison. Almost half of the 2000 people involved in Prison Fellowship are dedicated to praying for their nearest prison, with every prison in England and Wales supported by a prayer group.
- *involvement with worship:* a feature of so many Christian worshipping communities in prison is the link with people from the wider communities of the Church, joining together in the regular worship being offered within the walls of prisons. A symbol of the Churches commitment to be with the imprisoned, to bring some sense of normality that ensures prisoners are not abandoned by society, but are seen as part of that wider community of Church and society. An example of this would be the recent annual celebration of the Mother's Union in Wakefield Diocese. It brought together branches from all over the Diocese, including that of New Hall Women's prison, with the service being held in the prison chapel. The interaction provided by individuals and groups through gathering for worship, can provide a dimension to prison life otherwise in short supply. Individuals and groups bring diversity, social contact and the expression of care centred on the needs of the individual. Participation in worship with those from the wider community also helps to transcend the prison environment.
- *leading and supporting chaplaincy group work:* volunteers are involved in a significant way in much of the group work that takes place within chaplaincies, such as Bible study, and specific courses that include Alpha, Sycamore Tree, Skills for Living and Can Marriage Work? Theological study, and formation in faith also takes place. All of these varied activities are closely related to the pastoral care offered by volunteers; through befriending, and listening to prisoners with a wide range of particular needs, and often complementing the work of staff members; in helping with literacy projects and letter writing; through bereavement counselling, with individuals, and in groups; in the staffing of visitors centres; in Alpha groups, and in prison visiting, through the chaplaincy, or through the National Association of Prison Visitors (a group with members from all faiths and none).

In all of the above ways, chaplaincy volunteers make a significant contribution to the resettlement and rehabilitation of prisoners, the decency agenda, and the concept of a 'healthy prison'. The concept of a 'healthy prison' needs to acknowledge all aspects of what it means to be a person, for Christians, created in the image of God, with intrinsic worth and value. Faith-based groups celebrate those aspects of people that are essential for their self-esteem, personal growth and well-being within the 'total institution' (Irving Goffman) of the prison, and which help them to prepare for release.

In bringing 'the outside in', the voluntary sector contributes a sense of the normality of life in its representation of the wider community, interacting with prisoners and staff in ways that can help alleviate such things as isolation, anxiety, and low self-esteem. The very act of listening, of support, of positive role models of breaking down a 'them and us' stereotyping, challenging assumptions, expressing care and demonstrating the love of God, can all help a prisoner's self-understanding, assisting in the aim of rehabilitation and resettlement, whilst again contributing to the decency agenda, and the expression of the respect due to all people.

Such a vision of the contribution of chaplaincy volunteers and the voluntary sector is not without difficulties, however, and individuals and groups face a number of issues, some positive, some negative. In an environment where primacy is given to the measurable, the verifiable, to the 'what works' agenda, it is sometimes hard for voluntary groups, and volunteers, to see that what they have to offer is of value, is of significance, and is worth offering. Whilst, rightly, there is emphasis on that which is measurable and verifiably proven to work, we need to remind ourselves that there is more to the person than just the programmes he or she can participate in during a sentence. Martin Narey, director general of HM Prison Service, has reminded us about the need for prisoners to be treated with humanity, and this is part of the Prison Service Statement of Purpose. Treating people in prison with humanity, means looking at the whole person, and responding to him or her in an holistic way, remembering that 'prisoners are always more than the sum of their deeds' (Sr Helen Prejean, *Dead Man Walking*). In-cell television may contribute to that humanity, but it must go further, and cannot be the only one way to cater for prisoner needs when not at work or participating in programmes.

To enable volunteers to undertake their necessary role, involves not just chaplaincy staff, but the willingness of all staff to see that chaplaincy volunteers are more than misguided 'do-gooders', but with a complementary role to their own. Whilst some staff recognise this, and utilise such an understanding for the benefit of prisoners and the prison, some will need help. The introduction of a voluntary sector strategy, with local and area co-ordinators, will go some way to raising understanding of the role of volunteers. The *Good Practice Guide* produced by the Prison Service Voluntary Sector Co-ordinator, Jo Gordon, and CLINKS, will help groups and individuals to forge good relationships with prisons in a structured and realistic way. With adaptation for faith groups it may also provide a guard against prosleytism and create realistic and workable partnership that encourages mature and positive relationships.

Chaplains, of all traditions, will still have an important role to play in ensuring effective and professional systems for the recruitment, welcoming, induction and training of volunteers in many places. They will continue to offer a link between the prison and the faith communities, ensuring that the involvement of individuals, and groups, is in line with the vision of the chaplaincy team. This in turn must link with that of the Prison Service as it seeks to hold prisoners in a 'safe, decent and healthy environment' (Prison Service Mission Statement). Chaplaincy also has a role to play in the resettlement of offenders, through links with faith communities, hostels (e.g. Langley House and the Stepping Stones Trust) and community chaplaincy. Community chaplaincy, a model from Canada, seeks to help 'bridge the gap' between prison life and community life in a professional and practical way. It is also an area for multi-faith working.

People of faith can seek the common values necessary in an 'active community' that wants 'progress and decency' (David Blunkett, home secretary). Chaplaincy volunteers, and members of the voluntary sector, can make a difference to the lives of some of those people in our prisons, working in partnership as they seek the common good.

CHAPTER 9

A Governor's Perspective

Katie Nutley and Stephen Rimmer

A survey of prisoners (NACRO, March 2000) found that they reported the following areas of need:

- 56.2 per cent were unemployed before entering prison, and a further 34.1 per cent said that they had lost their job as a result of imprisonment;
- 37.9 per cent reported losing their home as a result of their imprisonment;
- 42.9 per cent stated that they had lost contact with their families whilst in prison;
- 40.4 per cent had been excluded from school and 38.2 per cent had no qualifications; and
- 22.7 per cent reported mental health problems.

Numerous studies have found that prisoners face disproportionate levels of substance misuse, physical and mental health problems, physical and sexual abuse as children, low self-esteem and poor educational attainment. These factors contribute both to a large pool of human unhappiness and also to a raised risk of reoffending on release, with all of the consequences which flow from that.

Faced with this level of need and close scrutiny of the finances of his or her prison, a governor is right to look to partners with whom to tackle this tide of work. Voluntary sector organizations bring with them a raft of skills, and an enthusiasm to work with their client group during a time of crisis.

BENEFITS TO PRISONERS, PRISONS AND PARTNER ORGANIZATIONS

In considering a joint approach with the voluntary sector prisons can benefit from the values and skills which many organizations will bring with them. Voluntary sector organizations challenge prisons to look at the needs of prisoners in a new light: for example they may be more able to see prisoners as the key to addressing their own problems. This has been demonstrated through the Listeners scheme which now operates in most prisons in the country. The Samaritans have trained prisoners to offer a 'listening' service at any time of day or night to those who request it. This approach, whilst radical at the time of its inception is accepted by prison staff and managers as an ideal way of both supporting prisoners and developing the skills of those who have the capacity to support their peers. A study is being carried out at the time of writing, supported by the Cropwood Fellowship scheme, to establish whether or not the approach can be shown to reduce the rates of reoffending of listeners after release.

Voluntary sector organizations can also offer a service to those prisoners who, for whatever reason, feel unable to engage with Prison Service staff in addressing their problems. Voluntary sector staff inevitably develop different relationships with prisoners from those of directly employed staff, although the issues of security and confidentiality must be clearly agreed and this is explored more fully later in this chapter. Voluntary sector staff can also offer a personal example to prisoners, informed by their own experience. For example, drug rehabilitation schemes include those who are themselves in recovery working as counsellors.

Over ten years ago the Woolf Report into the disturbances at Strangeways identified that prisons should become a more integrated part of their communities, and this is a goal towards which many prison governors are still working (Woolf, 1991). Voluntary sector organizations are often rooted in their local communities because they have developed from a locally identified need, make use of local facilities and have links with local authorities and umbrella groups which many prisons have yet to develop. In the case of those organizations that employ volunteers, they have a special connection through local people themselves. This relationship can be particularly important for local prisons, which hold for a short time many people who live and offend in the local area. Such groups can help prisoners to establish links with their communities in preparation for their release, and a seamless service. It has been established through many studies and anecdotal experience, that the time of release from prison is a crucial point in a prisoner's rehabilitation and the support of a service from a familiar worker can make it much more likely that resettlement plans become a reality. Most prisoners are released with no statutory support, and where this is provided through the National Probation Service, pre-release contact can be severely restricted.

A further benefit of voluntary sector work within prison is the challenge to those from both sectors to learn from the best of what is offered by each. The Prison Service has well-developed risk assessment tools and deals with security questions in relation to staff and service recipients in all aspects of its work. It has also developed a range of programmes which have been demonstrated to reduce offending. Links between prisons and other statutory bodies are developing rapidly to provide much more effective management of dangerous prisoners on their release. Many voluntary sector organizations are much more successful in developing staff ideas, changing quickly to meet new demands, and rewarding the commitment and loyalty of staff in innovative ways. Prisons can become a centre where a group of organizations come together to provide a net of services for the huge range of needs identified in the population before, during and after their time in custody.

As links are established and projects develop within the prison, individual staff learn from the values and working practices of each organization. All governors engaged in this work will have experienced the new skills which prison officers develop in providing information and help to prisoners, and the incremental growth of projects as staff work together to increase their scope and the efficiency of delivery.

A less tangible, but arguably more important result of partnership working with voluntary sector organizations is the challenge which is offered to the culture of the institution. Staff and volunteers from partner agencies bring with them a wealth of experience which demands that a prison questions the system and practices which have often prevailed over many years in a closed environment. They also bring a diversity of approach which can quietly influence the establishment in unquantifiable but important measure. The greater the extent to which partnerships develop the greater this benefit will become to all those living and working within it.

There can be a temptation to see voluntary sector organizations as a cheap or free alternative to paying prison staff to carry out core work in an environment of continual efficiency savings from a tight budget. There are many local organizations which are willing to give the time of volunteers to carry out demanding work, for example in the fields of befriending isolated prisoners, counselling, pastoral care or developing experience which will enable the volunteers to move on to professional training. However, there is an increasing group of organizations which operate on a professional basis and which seek to offer highly skilled services for a fee. The Prison Service has responded to this for example through the development of its CARATS drug misuse services in all prisons, which are provided by voluntary sector organizations. As a result, each Prison Service area has a drug co-ordinator who is employed full-time to manage contracts. This demonstrates that governors must look to the specific need which has been identified and the nature of the service which is required to meet it. Whilst partnerships with the voluntary sector may be less expensive than alternatives provided directly by prison staff, they also represent a large and increasingly important section of the overall prison budget which is scrutinised closely through the management of ring-fenced allocation, and is tied closely through contracts to the outcomes which must be delivered by partner organizations.

Both voluntary sector organizations and prisons can benefit from jointly bidding for funds in order to meet the needs of prisoners. This approach enables the voluntary sector organization to expand into a new area of work and for the prison to secure additional funds in order to meet an identified need within the prison. Funding of these initiatives is covered more fully in *Chapter 11* of this book.

POTENTIAL PITFALLS

Whilst the aforementioned advantages of partnership working are significant the prison governor must approach it with care in order to avoid the many pitfalls which can be experienced. Whilst there are few managers who would still regard non-uniformed workers in prison as inevitably a risk to security it is important that security remains a concern at all stages of the relationship. Governors must ensure that potential partner organizations are reputable bodies which truly reflect their stated values and methods of working with prisoners. In this regard liaison with Prison Service HQ is vital to ensure that unsuitable organizations are filtered out. Individual staff and volunteers must be security checked and given security training before they commence work in the prison, and this should be repeated at intervals. Clear protocols must be developed in relation to issues including disclosure of information which constitutes a risk to security or harm to self or others, and this involves more than simply writing an agreement. Voluntary sector staff and volunteers must understand how such information will be treated and have the confidence to come forward if such agreements are to be acted on, and this involves managers addressing mutual trust, respectful working practices and monitoring of working relationships on both sides.

Contact between workers and family members can be damaging, and can undermine painstaking public protection work carried out over a long period of time. Training to make sure that staff and volunteers are aware of this must be frequently updated, and proper channels of communication must be established to ensure that it is carried out on every occasion.

Important work can be disrupted or endangered if it is not allowed to proceed on a predictable basis. This can be caused either by the unreliability of the partner organization or by operational pressures constantly interfering with the work of the project. Whilst operational emergencies are a fact of prison life, partnerships must be entered into on the basis of facilities and staff time being allocated and given an appropriate level of priority. Many partnerships have foundered after an initial period of enthusiasm due to the most basic facilities not being provided on a regular basis. This can make it difficult to re-establish services due to the cynicism that has been engendered as a result of ill-planned ventures in the past.

Whilst stereotypes and poor practice can often be eroded by positive contact with a partner organization, these problems can be exacerbated by inadequate preparation for a new project. Prison staff who are to work with a new organization need to be properly prepared, and minimum standards agreed with all parties, so that each organization gives respect to the other. Before the introduction of such work, issues need to be anticipated and properly dealt with. Will prison officers see the new service as erosion of their professionalism, or a threat to their jobs? Will the incoming organization realise the requirements of the unit on which they are working, such as times at which prisoners are not available, and what to do in the event of an incident? Will the responsible manager allocate sufficient time to dealing with any problems which arise in the delivery of the project, and does this person know that they are to take on such responsibility in addition to their existing work? Whilst these are all obvious questions, a single issue can endanger the future of a project, and others which follow in its wake.

The potential value of partnership working in challenging cultural problems has already been discussed, but failure to manage the process properly can have the opposite effect. It can be a difficult experience for both parties to accept and work with the values of the other. The Prison Service has a quasi-military structure in which a great deal of importance is attached to rank and procedure. In times of emergency this is vital for the effective management of serious incidents. Many voluntary sector organizations have much looser organizational structures, and this in turn has often enabled them to carry out their work with little formal support or financial security. Staff and volunteers from the sector can find it frustrating to work within a tight rank structure where decisions are made through reference up the line, and procedures may appear to be implemented with mindless adherence to bureaucratic principles. Change is not so easy to achieve as in a small and flexible organization, and the roles of individual staff can seem to prevent the achievement of an important piece of work.

The organization of a prison can also feel exclusive to the voluntary sector organization working to establish a project. Prison staff may present an unapproachable façade to the worker, both visually, through uniform, and in less obvious ways through the use of incomprehensible jargon and working practices which may not be understood by the worker who is new to the environment. It can demand time and patience for the worker to understand, even less accept or endorse, these issues. Such differences are easily magnified into insuperable barriers if they are not acknowledged and discussed by those in both organizations, to create understanding and tolerance.

UNDERSTANDING SECURITY ISSUES

Practical problems can also arise due to the many security procedures which are necessary to the day-to-day running of a prison, and these will depend on the security category of the institution. There are restrictions on items which may be brought into the prison, and those items which are allowed must be approved in advance and subjected to searching as they enter the gate. It is equally important to be aware of the rules regarding items leaving a prison. It is a criminal offence for any person to convey a letter or other item outside the prison for a prisoner. Posting a birthday card may seem like an easy way of assisting a prisoner to maintain family ties, but it may contain a threat to the prisoner's victim, or information which is or discloses a threat to the security of the establishment. It may well not, but it poses a risk to staff and other prisoners. As well as this obvious risk, such breaches can also lead to the withdrawal of the project due to concerns about the risk it represents.

Compliance with, and contributing to, security procedures, can be the most difficult area for an establishment and a voluntary sector organization to tackle together. Achieving this can be the cornerstone or the breaking point of the partnership. Staff and volunteers need to understand the methods of reporting security issues, and have the confidence to use them. Some may feel that by doing this they are contributing to a system which has treated an individual or group unfairly, or that an important piece of work may be jeopardised by the consequences of exposing an incident which has occurred in the prison, however hazardous that activity may be. For those who have decided to give their time freely to correct what they perceive as failings within the prison system, participation in security reporting, or the adjudication system, may seem the opposite of what they wanted to achieve. Nevertheless, if a working agreement cannot be reached and adhered to it is not possible for the partnership to continue, and the project will not succeed.

Voluntary sector workers and the Prison Service must also reach agreement on protocols which protect the volunteers and staff themselves. Whilst many of those from outside of the service bring valuable experience which is lacking within the prison, there are also opportunities for their independence to be manipulated by prisoners in order to blur or remove the boundaries of appropriate relationships and roles. Many voluntary sector organizations work in areas in which confidentiality is vital for the success of the work, for example in counselling survivors of abuse. Some prisoners may seek to cause doubt in the mind of the worker between information which is properly not disclosed elsewhere, and that which is a threat to themselves or another person. Of course, prison staff must also be constantly aware of this issue and the areas of potential conflict are increasing as prison officers become involved in more therapeutic work. Nevertheless, the voluntary sector worker may be considered more vulnerable to this approach by some prisoners, and appropriate supervision and confidence in the consequences of disclosure of sensitive information is vital for the project to work safely within the prison environment.

As work in the area of drug rehabilitation in particular increases, voluntary sector agencies in prison employ a growing number of staff who themselves have previous convictions and who have served prison sentences. In recent years the Prison Service has been more ready to approve those with previous convictions to work within prison establishments. Whilst the backgrounds of individuals must be treated in confidence, work is required in order to ensure that prison staff have confidence in their colleagues from other organizations, and that they understand the contribution that they can make. Those who have been prisoners themselves in the past may find it more difficult to accept the role of the Prison Service. The requirements of working in prison, and the importance of firm agreements which are adhered to in order to maintain security are only increased. Failure to address all of these issues correctly can have extremely damaging consequences for prisons, voluntary sector organizations, their work and individuals who are placed at risk.

MANAGING THE VOLUNTARY SECTOR CONTRIBUTION

There is a multitude of organizations which are in an excellent position to work effectively with prisons, and most large prisons will have significant numbers of people already working there, but at present there is little co-ordination or oversight of the work. This inevitably reduces the effectiveness of what is done, and can increase the risk of the problems which are discussed above. A proper system of managing organizations as a group should include the following elements:

- an audit of existing provision identifying the service being provided, the level of need, gaps, duplication and work which is not appropriate;
- needs of prisoners which are not being met, and a plan for exploring the most appropriate method of addressing this, from within the prison or with a partner. What are the assumptions which are being made during this process, and should they be tested against objective evidence?
- inclusion of partnership work in the prison's Service Delivery Agreement, with costs and outputs allocated;
- identification of a senior manager to assume overall responsibility for work with voluntary sector organizations, together with time allocated to the work;

- ensuring that there is a manager who is responsible for liaison with each organization in the prison, and who is aware of this and supportive of the work that is being carried out. Liaison managers should have regular contact with the responsible senior manager and each other to ensure a consistent approach to this aspect of their work;
- service level agreements (SLAs) between liaison managers, on behalf of the governor, and each organization which is working in the prison. As well as the issues already discussed, the SLAs should include processes for regularly reviewing the work of the project, its delivery of agreed outputs, contribution to the prison's Service Delivery Agreement with the area manager, and the extent to which the prison has provided agreed support for the project. The SLA should also include procedures for dispute resolution, alteration or termination of the project, and the future of funding agreements and changes of funding after short-term grants have been exhausted;
- creation of a forum for voluntary sector organizations to ensure that information is passed on, prison staff can attend and communicate vital messages, support and awareness is raised, and issues are seen through once identified in the meetings. This forum should meet regularly and report to the governor;
- an accessible format for disseminating information on all voluntary sector organizations to all parts of the prison. A loose leaf, regularly updated format is ideal;
- development of a positive relationship between organizations and the security department, to ensure compliance with the requirements described above, and to smooth the flow of information and ensure that confidence exists as to the work that is being carried out on both sides;
- specific training for voluntary sector staff and volunteers, and their inclusion in most parts of the training which is offered by the prison to its staff; and
- incorporation of the work of the voluntary sector organizations into the self-audit and management review processes of the prison, and the involvement of prison managers in the wider reviews of the organization itself, such as membership of the management committee of the project, attendance at AGMs etc.

This list may appear to be an enormous amount of work for a prison to consume on top of what is perceived as its core work. However, an audit of services already provided by the voluntary sector in most prisons will reveal that this level of management attention would be supporting a great deal of time and effort on the part of workers from outside, prison staff and prisoners. Closer supervision will ensure that this is directed towards the prison's priorities rather than an historical and subjective perception of a few interested parties. The work will also be improving performance against key elements of the Service Delivery Agreement such as constructive activity, as well as achieving all of the less measurable benefits which are discussed in the first half of this chapter. This includes, crucially, the cultural gains made by opening up the closed institution to the external light of the voluntary sector.

Finally, as the prison governor returns to contemplate the depth and breadth of need which exists amongst those in his or her custody, he or she will conclude that not only are partnerships necessary to tackling the work which is required, but that managing them properly is essential.

CHAPTER 10

Principles and Pragmatism: Surviving Working with the Prison Service

Adam Sampson

OK so you've managed to persuade some gullible prison governor to let you in through the gates. You've recruited a few passionate lunatics who are prepared to carry out the work and raised some money to finance it. You've dealt with the initial hostility of the prison staff and negotiated the turf wars to win yourself acceptance in the prison. Everything looks set fair.

And indeed it might be. However, there are real challenges that you will have to face if you want your voluntary organization not merely to survive but to flourish in a prison environment. Some pull off the trick. Most, however, last only a few months and years before disappearing or finding themselves again struggling for access.

It is not simply the traditional vagaries of prison life which you will have to negotiate. A fundamental shift in the relationship between the Prison Service and the voluntary sector is currently underway. This poses a whole new set of difficulties.

Perhaps the most obvious demonstration of the challenges and potential minefields that face voluntary organizations seeking to work in prisons comes with the recent developments in work with drug addicts. In the mid 1990s, there were a large number of small voluntary agencies providing services to imprisoned drug users. Most were locally-based, employing a few drugs workers via local agreements with individual governors. Funding came from a variety of sources: charitable donations, health authorities, probation services, or, in a few cases, direct from the governors.

So far, so commonplace. That sketch describes the position of many, if not most, voluntary agencies providing services in prisons. Which makes what happened in the following few years so interesting.

Between 1996 and 1999, the Prison Service gradually began to regularise the involvement of outside drugs agencies in prisons. Formal contracts—albeit of a rudimentary nature—began to replace informal understandings between local agencies and individual governors. The beginnings of competitive tendering for contracts began to creep into the system. In some areas of the country—Kent is a good example—the service even began to take a strategic approach to the issue, specifying what sort of services it wanted to be provided and where.

This was a gradual process, affecting only a small number of prisons, mainly in the South East of the country. Most agencies therefore remained untouched by the developments. However, the government decision in 1998 to invest £76 million in drug services in prison over the next three years transformed the position. From 1 October 1999, all drug services were to be provided according to specifications laid down by the Prison Service Drugs Strategy Unit and all outside agencies wishing to be involved had to engage in a competitive tendering process. The old 20 page locally-produced service level agreements were replaced by inch-thick standard Home Office contracts, with providers having to undertake to collect over 100 pieces of management information each month.

The result was depressingly predictable. The contracting process favoured the larger and more commercial organizations, and those who were more willing to adapt their style to that demanded of them by the Prison Service. Local agencies, particularly those who were wedded to their particular conceptual approach, lost out. While it may be that practice overall improved, the concentration of the contracts in the hands of half a dozen larger agencies both reduced the range and diversity of provision and, crucially, significantly weakened the link between work done in prisons and the drugs agencies working in the local community outside.

This may be an extreme example. However, it matches the history of other, similar initiatives in the Prison Service over the past few years, such as the contracting-out of education services in prison. These stories pose real questions for anyone who wants to be involved in working in prison. No matter how good the work you are doing, no matter how entrenched in the prison you are, no matter your intentions or good will, your future may be at the mercy of developments outside your control.

DEMONSTRATING EFFECTIVENESS

If the history of what has happened in the drugs sector is a pointer to the future, voluntary agencies wishing to work within prisons have to prepare themselves for change. The relatively free, unregulated market will disappear. In its place will come a quasi-commercial, contract-driven relationship. How then can you ensure that your agency is one which survives in the world which is to come? And how can you resist the influence of such a huge corporate body as the Prison Service?

There are a number of strategies which voluntary sector agencies will need to adopt if they are to have any hope of surviving. First, it is essential that any agency which wishes to receive money for work in prisons is able to demonstrate that what it does is useful to the Prison Service. This is perhaps a simplistic statement. However, the requirement that they have a responsibility to demonstrate effectiveness is one which many agencies find difficult to accept.

There are a number of reasons for this. First, the notion of having to submit themselves to independent evaluation is contrary to the ethos of many agencies. In many cases, this is because organizations place a high degree of emphasis on principles of confidentiality and anonymity. RAPt, for example, is an agency which has its roots in the 12-step fellowships of Alcoholics Anonymous and Narcotics Anonymous. Despite the fact that 12-step treatment has been one of the most widely practiced interventions for addicts for more than half a century, the commitment of the fellowships towards anonymity of members means that 12-step remains relatively unresearched.

Second, some agencies find it difficult to identify demonstrable outcomes for their work. Organizations which specialise in alternative medicine or medication, for example, occasionally struggle to articulate exactly what the outcomes which their work aims at actually are. Holistic improvements in health and psychological functioning, for example, are almost impossible to quantify. Similarly, some providers of low-level drugs counselling and advice also struggle to specify what effect they expect their interventions to have on drug-users' behaviour.

The obvious mechanism for persuading the Prison Service that what you are doing is effective is obviously via independent research. However, there is sadly often a reluctance for agencies to take the risk of submitting their work to independent evaluation. When RAPt decided to commission independent research into the effectiveness of our 12-step treatment programme (Martin and Player, 2000), it was with our fingers crossed behind our backs. The fact that the results proved extremely positive did not lessen the level of stress attached to the exercise. The fact that we knew that independent evaluation more often than not revealed that programmes have little discernable impact weighed heavy on our minds.

Linked to this is the fact that any proper research is a costly exercise. The research which validated the effectiveness of the RAPt programme cost some £40,000. There are no funds available from statutory sources to pay for such research—RAPt had to rely on the generosity of a number of charitable trusts to secure the necessary finances. Few voluntary agencies will be in a similar position.

Even if these obstacles are overcome, there may be a disjunction between the Prison Service's agenda and that of the agency concerned. Voluntary agencies may be anxious to pursue very laudable aims. However, unless these accord with the priorities of the Prison Service— or the prejudices of an individual prison governor—the chances of the service allowing access, let alone providing funding, are minimal.

CONTRACTING WITH THE PRISON SERVICE

Second, agencies wanting to flourish in prisons must be prepared to recast themselves as sophisticated, professional commercial operators. As the Prison Service increasingly looks for contractual relationships with other agencies, organizations which want to access any financial recompense from the government for what they do will increasingly find themselves competing against other voluntary, statutory or even private agencies for it. However good your product, unless you can persuade the Prison Service to buy it, you will find yourself out in the cold. Few of us went into the charity world because we believed that we had an ability to answer tender specifications or construct marketing and pricing strategies. It is those skills as much as our ability to work with prisoners which will provide the key to our continued success.

The process of contracting with the Prison Service can be an uncomfortable one. The service is still learning how to let and manage contracts, and providers can often be at the mercy of disputes within the service itself about contract management. One example is the contracts for the new low-level drugs counselling service (CARATS), which were let in clusters covering three or four prisons within an individual Prison Service area. Soon after the contracts were let, however, the Prison Service decided to undertake a geographical reorganization of its management structure. Contract management was suddenly divided between two or three Prison Services areas, each of which often had its own priorities and expectations. In the case of one contract operated by RAPt, the arguments between the Prison Service staff about how the service should be structured are still continuing a year later. There is not even any agreement about what outcomes are to be monitored or how much sickness cover should be provided.

Such sudden changes tax the patience of anyone trying to do business with the Prison Service. All too often when working in prisons, one is left at the mercy of political manoeuvring and personal conflicts. Unless you have the skills, and frankly the sheer bloody-mindedness, to deal with these, your days working in prison are numbered.

Navigating the choppy waters of Prison Service politics is extraordinarily difficult. However, for some of the sadder individuals amongst us—including, to my shame, myself—it is also endlessly fascinating. Staying afloat amid the storms which habitually rage across the Prison Service seas is a challenge in itself. It is just worth warning anyone who is wanting to work in prisons to be aware of assuming that rank means authority or that authority equates with power. If you are going to look for allies in prison to protect you when times get tough or even just to sort out the minor irritations which bedevil any attempts to do any constructive work (disappearing desks and chairs, prisoners who suddenly cannot be unlocked, security clearances which are withdrawn overnight, invoices which remain stubbornly unpaid), do not automatically assume that you will do best by cultivating the governor or other senior manager. Power all too often resides elsewhere.

ACHIEVING AGREED STANDARDS AND DELIVERING OUTCOMES

Any voluntary organization which wishes to have a lasting future within the prison system will also increasingly have to conform to the formal quality control mechanisms and standards being introduced by the Prison Service to govern work done with prisoners. The most obvious of these is the Home Office system of accreditation for programmes run with prisoners. Accreditation has a huge level of political support and one of the requirements attached by the Prison Service to the letting of drug treatment contracts is that providers have gained official Home Office accreditation for their programmes.

Gaining accreditation is an immensely complex and time-consuming task. At a minimum, the journey from first submission to full accreditation usually takes some two years; in RAPt's case, our first bid was submitted in March 1998 and we were finally accredited in October 2000. The process also requires a high level of academic skill: the panel who will judge whether or not an individual programme is effective is made up largely of academic psychologists and researchers, rather than practitioners.

Achieving accreditation is also impossible unless one has assembled good quality research evidence that what you are doing works. Not only does the accreditation process demand that programmes provide empirical evidence of effectiveness. It also assesses programmes on a very narrow set of criteria, which centre on their impact on criminogenic risk factors. No programme which does not put achieving a reduction in reoffending as its primary purpose stands any realistic chance of gaining accreditation.

The importance of accreditation for agencies which want to do intensive work with prisoners cannot be overstated. It might be thought that accreditation is an obscure intellectual exercise with which the voluntary sector need not engage. However, accreditation is part of the wider political push of the past two decades to require the public sector to demonstrate that its is spending the public funds entrusted to it cost-effectively. Just as the increasing cost of the NHS has produced a greater emphasis on targeting funding on interventions of proven effectiveness, so the cost of the criminal justice system has led politicians from both sides to attempt to introduce systems for eliminating waste. Those who are tempted to hope that accreditation is a passing fancy should note the moves to extend its use to programmes run by the National Probation Service and the impending creation of the National Treatment Agency, which looks likely to be required to perform a similar function for all work with drug and alcohol misusers.

It is therefore vital that any voluntary agency which wants to be in a position to work with prisoners in any significant way be prepared to engage with some Prison Service quality control mechanisms. In the short-term, only a small number of agencies will probably need to seek full accreditation. The accreditation system as it is currently set up only seeks to audit programmes which seek to do intensive or significant work with prisoners. Low level counselling work or advice-giving and other, similar types of intervention will almost certainly not be required to submit themselves to the full accreditation process. However, the push towards agreed standards and auditable outcomes will undoubtedly extend over the next few years to encompass all aspects of work with prisoners.

REGULATING VOLUNTARY SECTOR STAFF

Along with responding to the moves towards quality control, agencies also have to deal with increasing regulation of work undertaken by the voluntary sector in prisons. One of the side issues which bedevilled the extension of drugs work in prison was an attempt by the Prison Service to control the identity of the staff who would be delivering the new drugs services. For the first time, central standards were laid down to govern decisions about security clearance for voluntary agency staff. All staff who were to work in prisons had to have at least five years free from criminal convictions and imprisonment, and no staff who had convictions for offences against children, for drug dealing or importation would be allowed access. Those working in high security prisons had to pass even more stringent tests.

The attempt to standardise who should be allowed to work in prisons was welcome; previously individual governors had been able to decide. However, the formulation introduced caused—and continues to cause—considerable disquiet on the part of drugs agencies. The bar on people convicted of certain types of offences was considered by some to be wrong in principle: as a service which is attempting to rehabilitate drug addicts should accept that some people convicted of drug dealing may at some point in the future be trusted to work in prison. There was also a practical difficulty: many agencies have a proactive policy of seeking to employ ex-users, many of whom will have extensive histories of drug-related crime. The new regulations severely restrict the ability of voluntary agencies to recruit and deploy good quality staff.

Even more difficult was the decision by the Prison Service to require voluntary agency staff working in top security prisons to agree to submit to drug tests. Indeed, the original proposal—and the proposal still supported by some senior Prison Service staff—was to impose random drug testing on all voluntary agency staff working in prisons. This proposal caused considerable debate within the service itself.

BALANCING PRINCIPLES AND PRAGMATISM

The imposition of such policies by the Prison Service creates fundamental problems for agencies wanting to work in prisons. Agencies are left with a stark choice: are we prepared to compromise on our principles in order to be allowed to carry out our work? In the case of the drug testing proposals, the price for many was too high. However, there was little or no attempt by the agencies concerned to mount a co-ordinated campaign of opposition. One effect of the contracting process was that it had lessened the ability of drugs agencies to work together effectively to resist the service's policy.

It is this balance between a desire to take advantage of the new willingness to work with voluntary agencies on a formal and remunerated basis and the drive to remain true to their principles which represents the most difficult challenge. The temptations for agencies which have been able to establish their effectiveness and professionalism in the eyes of the Prison Service then to chase the cash can be almost overwhelming. In the drugs field, some agencies have grown very rapidly over the past few years, with every chance that more growth is possible.

It is a temptation which we would do well to resist. The processes by which we are expanding—competitive tendering, increasing profession-alisation, cost-effective management, recruitment of 'safe' staff—are driving us to become increasingly like commercial businesses. There are examples elsewhere of the gradual replacement of high ideals by strictly commercial considerations, for example the disappearance of mutual building societies and their replacement by commercial banks.

Voluntary agencies must therefore have strategies to deal with such temptations. Crucially, they must be clear at the outset about the extent to which they are willing to compromise their principles in pursuit of access to prisons and funding for their work. RAPt has been faced by a dilemma about the theoretical basis of our work. As already noted, the organization has its roots in the 12-step fellowships of Alcoholics Anonymous and Narcotics Anonymous and was created in order to offer abstinence-based treatment programmes to drug addicts and alcoholics in prison. However, 12-step is a theoretical approach of which many Prison Service psychologists are ignorant and dismissive, despite the clear evidence of the success of the RAPt programme over the past few years.

RAPt finds itself in a curious position. Whilst we appear to be regarded as an effective and professional agency, our theoretical approach is regarded as, at best, eccentric and at worst, thoroughly misguided. Unquestionably we would be in a far better position to compete for contracts if we abandoned or toned down our commitment to the 12-step approach. I cannot pretend that RAPt's response to this dilemma has been without flaw. However, in general, I believe that we have stayed true to our purpose. In some respects, we have extended the scope of our work, taking on some of the generalist, low-level counselling and advice role (CARATs) envisaged under the Prison Service drugs strategy. However, we have resolutely refused to compromise on the theoretical underpinnings of our treatment programmes.

This is not pious boasting. There is nothing particularly praiseworthy in a refusal to compromise. Nevertheless, it is essential that voluntary organizations cling onto the features which make them unique. If your agency is good at one particular thing, something in which you believe and which no-one else offers, the risks in diversification may outweigh the advantages. Moreover, although the Prison Service ultimately decides what work is done with prisoners, it is the voluntary sector which has the expertise in providing particular types of interventions or services. With drugs strategy, many external drugs agencies had considerable doubts as to the wisdom of some of the policies the service was pursuing. If however you ignore your doubts and agree to work to the service's agenda, you validate the approach the service is taking, and provide a service which may be less effective than it should be. So long as agencies allow themselves to be seduced into providing inadequate services, flawed policies will remain unchallenged.

Despite these difficulties, prisons are a challenging and rewarding setting for voluntary sector agencies. Indeed, in some respects they are ideal, providing a steady supply of needy, motivated and grateful clients. There is also much goodwill from prison staff, who are a resource which can contribute much to your work. You ignore their skills and commitment at your peril. Nevertheless, the move towards a more formalised relationship between the Prison Service and voluntary sector brings with it some real dangers. Reform of the hitherto chaotic nature of that relationship was long overdue and many of the innovations which the service has introduced are entirely laudable. However, the Prison Service's decision to adopt the identical mechanisms to control the work of the voluntary sector—competitive tendering, contracts, financial penalty clauses—as they use with profit-making firms will inevitably force charities to act increasingly like commercial businesses. And if we do that, we lose what makes us both valuable and unique.

CHAPTER 11

Funding the Penal Voluntary Sector

Peter Kilgarriff

I write this chapter with some hesitation for I do not speak on behalf of other independent funders nor with any great personal experience of working within prisons, apart from that gained in the course of my work for the Lankelly Foundation. But the Foundation's perspective on the way voluntary agencies interact with prisons and the Prison Service draws on a long and widespread involvement, which may prove useful when looking at questions of funding.

How do voluntary sector agencies manage to fund their work in prisons? Where do they get necessary financial resources? Who decides funding priorities and how are decisions taken? What role should independent funders play; should they be involved in this work at all?

FUNDRAISING: A NECESSARY EVIL?

Voluntary sector agencies survive on a jigsaw of funding that is often difficult to piece together. This results in a constant search for funds that distracts from the task in hand, consuming valuable time and skills for what some consider to be a secondary purpose, almost a necessary evil. But fundraising is about more than money. From the perspective of a voluntary agency whose task is to help fund other voluntary agencies, the funding jigsaw is not a complete picture but a process, which has an important dynamism of its own. An agency working in a local neighbourhood needs to win the backing of that neighbourhood if it is to succeed and it is usual to see this support translated into a healthy mix of funding, both in kind and cash. An agency working on a wider scene needs to get its message across to policy-makers and decision-takers and one of the effective ways of doing this is to submit funding bids.

This process of attracting support for an idea, of convincing possible funders or backers, is itself a central part of an agency's work and can achieve a number of things. It is an educative process for all concerned. It helps challenge contrary assumptions and gives valuable opportunities to explain aims and motivations. Most importantly, however, a funding jigsaw gives an agency an independence, which it would never have if it were assured of funding from one single source, whatever that might be. This assumes an even greater importance in the context of work in prisons. That a voluntary agency retains its independence is vital; without that the work could easily be compromised and its value diluted. If independence goes, so too does the necessary process of learning and challenging assumptions which takes place when small voluntary agencies work within large public institutions.

That said, it is evident that voluntary organizations face an uphill task in raising the necessary funds for work in prisons and it takes an unusual stubborn confidence underpinned by luck to succeed. The Prison Service and individual establishments can pass the buck to each other and voluntary organizations can be squeezed in the middle. Bidding for contracts with the Prison Service is possible in certain areas of work and other government or European funding programmes might be applicable if, say, the proposed work is focused on resettlement of short-term offenders or gaining employment on release. In general, this is not an area of work that attracts wide public sympathy and it is unlikely to benefit from public generosity. Finally, although it is true that this work falls within the priority areas of some grant-making trusts, it is a myth to think that independent funders are lining up to help.

INDEPENDENT FUNDING BODIES

Independent funding bodies are grant-making trusts and the Lottery boards, although amongst the latter only the National Charities Lottery Board (NLCB—since renamed the Community Fund) makes a significant contribution in this field of work.

Grant-making to support work in prisons is essentially different to supporting work in other settings and this, incidentally, is why independent funders need to be involved in the developing conversations between the Prison Service and the voluntary sector. Not only is the delivery of the service often more complex, but control of it is more quickly and absolutely dependent upon a third party than elsewhere. Normally, when a project is assessed for funding, the independent funders meet all the main players; management committee, senior staff, project workers and clients. They see where the work is to be done and examine the work plans and budgets; they consider the environment and the co-operative networks which underpin successful work. This investigative process gives them confidence that the plans are well thought through and that the agency has sufficient skills and resources to achieve what it is planning to do. With prison-based work, funders may not get a chance to see where the work is to be carried out and they may not be involved in planning discussions between the agency and the governor. Most significantly, funders are responsible for the proper use of public or charitable funds in an environment which is not controlled by the voluntary sector agency providing the service but by a third party with whom the funders may have minimal or no contact. Thus, they are unable to measure the level of mutual understanding and agreement which is vital to the success of the work.

The true extent of independent non-statutory funding in prisons is not known. From the published 1997/8 annual reports of 25 grant-making trusts, most of them members of the Association of Charitable Trusts (ACF) Penal Affairs Interest Group, it is established that roughly £5.5m was made available to support work in prison during 1999-2000. This is not a huge sum when set against the variety of work voluntary agencies undertake in prisons, and it is positively dwarfed when set against total giving of £655.7m by ACF members in 1999 (including NLCB, but excluding the Welcome Trust). Nevertheless, it is a significant funding programme (to which has to be added approximately £2m from NCLB: below) with which the Prison Service needs to be fully involved.

However, just as fundraising is not just about money, support from independent funders can be more than a cheque in the bank. Trusts are very keen to ensure that their grants achieve what was intended, but they are often willing to take a calculated risk or support an individual in a way which may not be appropriate with public funds. Their grants might come with fewer strings attached, increasing the independence and flexibility an organization needs when working in a prison inside a bureaucracy. They will come with a greater understanding of voluntary agencies and the parameters within which they have to work. They often take account of the perennial problem of core funding and do not simply target project costs. Nowadays, most trusts are willing to associate themselves in some way with the agencies they support, putting their mouths where their money is; encouraging and speaking up on behalf of grant-recipients, giving references, signing match-funding certificates and offering general support. In a prison setting, this kind of support is even more effective if trusts have been involved at an early stage in discussions between the prison and the voluntary agency.

The Charity Aid Foundation's much more comprehensive recent survey of where trust money goes (Vincent and Pharoah, 2000) shows that a quarter of all grants are targeted at social care. When broken down into specific socio-economic needs, work with offenders appears to receive eleven per cent of these grants, but not all of this will have gone to prison-based work. Much of it went in support of preventative work including schemes which offer an alternative to custodial sentences, as well as post-release and family support. This may suggest that trusts are willing to pay special attention to this field of work, but it is not at all clear that this extends to the support of voluntary agencies within the prison environment. It would appear that this remains an unpopular field of work even amongst grant-making trusts.

For the most part, those trusts that will consider this work are on the lookout for good ideas or work in progress, but homework is advised.

Information about grant-making trust's priorities and ways of working is easier to come by nowadays and poorly targeted applications are not appreciated. Be aware of a trust's grant-making potential. The larger trusts may look at both capital and revenue needs and there is more recognition of supporting work over a period of years. This is a difficult area because it can, in extreme cases, limit a trust's ability to support something new, but there is growing recognition of the importance of longer term funding. Finally, funding applications should be clear about costs and timing and whether there can be any flexibility in regard to the latter.

Appendix 2 lists some of those trusts that have already shown an interest in this field of work and they will be familiar names to many people who have tried to raise funds for their organization, but this list is not exhaustive. Nowadays, since annual reports and accounts are published by most trusts, it is not difficult to find out what a trust has funded. It is less easy to discover what they *will* fund, but the past is often a guide to the future. The Charities Aid Foundation and the Directory of Social Change have collected detailed information which makes fund-raising from trusts much easier than it used to be (Fitzherbert, Addison and Rahman, 1999). The variety of work trusts support in prisons reflects the spectrum of need existing outside the prison walls, within the community at large. This ranges from the individual needs of prisoners themselves to substantial pre-release services which have the ability to have a real impact on the regime as a whole. Many visitors' centres depend upon trust support to survive and applications for childcare support within prisons, gainful employment schemes, pre-release training, literacy and numeracy projects, mentoring schemes, resettlement work, and drug rehabilitation programmes are typical. The visual arts have long played an important role in prison life and there are also many examples of theatre, dance and music being used to improve self-knowledge and expression, most of which depend upon support from charitable trusts.

In recent years the NCLB has been the largest single independent funder of the voluntary sector but its work in prisons faces the same 'additionality' test as all its other work. In its first five years, NLCB has made 193 grants totalling £64.4m in a broad field of work encompassing prisoners, prisoners' families, people at risk of offending, crime prevention, penal reform and the rehabilitation of offenders. The bulk of this money went to the last four of these categories, but some of it funded resettlement work taking place within prisons towards the end of prisoner's sentence. In the 12 months to the end of September 2000 the NLCB made at least 20 grants totalling just over £2m to 19 different agencies working directly with offenders in custody.

Finally, churches and religious bodies provide yet another important group of independent funders. Although the extent of their contribution cannot easily be measured, many agencies and individual prisoners rely upon it. They provide volunteers as well as funds and they can be an especially effective bridge to the communities beyond the prison walls.

PRISON SERVICE FUNDING

The Prison Service is, according to many voluntary sector organizations, the chief beneficiary of voluntary activity within prisons and should, therefore, be its principal funder. Indeed, the Prison Service may take the view that this is the case but, although the service's input into funding the voluntary sector is likely to be significant, there are no figures to support this. It appears that there is no way of extrapolating either from the Prison Service's annual accounts or the accounts of a particular establishment, what money has been spent in support of voluntary agencies. It is accounted for under headings which do not reveal such detail and, it can be argued, is indicative of the service's approach to voluntary sector input. It is no wonder that there is such confusion between voluntary agencies and volunteers, but signs are now appearing that attempts to disprove the syllogism 'voluntary agencies equals volunteers equals free' are being listened to.

The Prison Service has devolved budgets to local establishments through its 13 areas, and there are many examples of good co-operation between individual prisons and voluntary agencies. A recently published addition to the Prison Service Order on finance included guidelines on the support of voluntary agencies and these, rightly, underline the need for value for money and accountability. In particular, they made clear that it is possible for agencies to receive prison funding at the beginning of a quarter, when warranted by the cash flow situation of the agency in question. But there remains a high level of discretion available to individual governors and as a result there are wide discrepancies between establishments. As in most spheres, success seems to depend upon individual vision and commitment rather than national policy, and the latter often lags behind the former.

Although the assumption is that individual prison establishments will be primarily responsible for funding voluntary agencies, occasionally the Prison Service supports voluntary agencies with a regional or national remit. It would help if voluntary agencies knew more about how these decisions were taken and the criteria used, be it innovation or capacity to be reproduced elsewhere, but these decisions, apparently, are taken on an *ad hoc* basis. There is no set procedure and no figures to report.

Government initiatives also have an effect on voluntary sector funding. The policy emphasis on contracts and evaluation is felt throughout the sector and prisons are no exception. On one level this should be welcomed. The award of contracts to voluntary agencies publicly underlines the understanding that there are some tasks which are best done within a prison setting by specialist voluntary agencies. However, these contracts need to be based upon a real partnership that recognises the strengths and weaknesses of the partners. Ideally, they should cover the full costs of the service being provided, but in the prison setting this does not always happen. Often it seems that the commitment of small voluntary agencies, for example to family or visitor support or childcare, appears something to be exploited by prison establishments. Much is expected when the level of resources provided by a prison is woefully inadequate. The resourcefulness of the voluntary sector should not be allowed to cloud the issue here and independent funders should work to ensure that their support does not simply make bad funding practice by the Prison Service (or individual prison establishments) appear acceptable.

The increasing emphasis on evaluation is generally welcomed. Prisons still offer an opportunity for independent funders to test out a model of working which the Prison Service itself then funds more widely throughout the prison estate. If there are regional or national implications, the Prison Service may prescribe the methodology of these evaluations, even if they do not pay for them, and independent funders look with interest to see if they are effective in persuading the service to agree further support.

These evaluations need to take account of any additional resources which voluntary agencies are so good at gathering together. For example, whilst it is good that NACRO's work in the resettlement of short-term offenders in Birmingham is supported by funds from the Home Office's Pathfinder programme, it is hoped that the evaluation of this scheme, which could lead to the work being duplicated elsewhere, recognises the impact of the second worker who is funded independently, in this case by the Lankelly Foundation. Similarly, following the Prison Service's swift response to the government's National Drug Strategy, a number of drug and addiction agencies have won contracts in prisons for the running of rehabilitation units and CARATS (Counselling, Assessment, Referral, Advice and Throughcare) programmes and these also are subject to strict reviews and evaluations. But they too seek extra support from charitable trusts, which is likely to increase their effectiveness, and, again, this needs to be taken into account when these schemes are evaluated. For their part, trusts need to be aware that their support for a contracted agency might do little more than make one voluntary sector provider more attractive to the purchaser than another.

FUNDING BY OTHER STATUTORY BODIES

No attempt will be made here to list all the sources of statutory funds which might support the voluntary sector's work in prisons. Instead, the chief ways government agencies support the work of voluntary agencies in prisons and some of the issues that surround that support, will be examined.

The amount of prison-based work funded by the European Union (EU) seems to be growing. Its focus is clearly on training, vocational guidance and job creation, but the bewildering variety of funding programmes and the bureaucracy which surrounds applications and reporting procedures puts many agencies off. Advice is necessary in order to submit funding applications, and it is available from specialist agencies and those Councils of Voluntary Service who have trained staff who can help. Also there are good examples which can be drawn upon from within the Prison Service's own experience. These are normally based upon a mixture of partnerships between individual prisons, the Probation Service (historically in its pre-nationwide form: see below) and voluntary agencies, e.g. Comeback's work within prisons in the South East of England, and the JADE Project at Bristol Prison.

European funding normally requires some matched funding and independent funders sometimes have a role to play here, as do other statutory funders. This seems to be an area ripe for partnership within the Prison Service, and between the Service and external agencies. One characteristic of EU funding which is not true of funding bids to charitable trusts or the NLCB is that the prison itself can take the initiative, e.g.: Headstart UK, an employment initiative which began at HMYOI Thorn Cross. EU funding is perhaps one of the very few sources of external funding available directly to governors. From the independent funder's perspective this makes it a very valuable source of funding, and some investment by the Prison Service in support for governors in their applications for EU funding, perhaps based in the area managers' offices, would surely pay dividends. Incidentally, it is a condition of European funding that recipients give information about their scheme and about how the funding operates, so that prior to applying for EU funds, it would be worthwhile to arrange a fact finding visit to an existing prison-based, EU-funded scheme.

Amongst other statutory agencies which fund voluntary groups to work in this field perhaps the most prominent is the Probation Service which has a long record of partnership with the sector. In the past this was underpinned by a requirement to allocate a percentage of available funds to support voluntary agencies, but with the advent of the National Probation Service and a shift of emphasis away from resettlement to enforcement, this requirement no longer exists. The National Probation Service's future partnership with the voluntary sector is unclear.

The Department of Health and health authorities may also be a source of funding for voluntary agencies which provide health care support, but, again, unless it is an extension of community-based work (e.g. the Revolving Doors agency's work with mentally disordered offenders) this support is less likely to be for work specifically within prisons.

ETHICAL ISSUES SURROUNDING FUNDING

Independent funders generally seek to fund things which are not the responsibility of the state. How these responsibilities are defined is open to debate but just as the NLCB insist upon 'additionality', so most grant-making trusts refuse to help fund mainstream services in health, education and personal social services. Over the last 20 years the boundary between statutory and voluntary services, between those things we expect to be paid for out of our taxes and those services which are properly provided by voluntary agencies, has been greatly eroded. The old clarity that informed the work of charitable trusts seems to have disappeared and some would argue that it should be re-discovered. There is a real debate to be had about whether it is the state's responsibility to find the resources that are needed to fund effective prison regimes and whether it is legitimate to expect non-statutory organizations and charities to provide core funding.

Society needs to look closely at prisons. The media sometimes present them as an answer to crime and they are not. For most prisoners they are a temporary home before returning to the area, the relationships and problems which nurtured offending behaviour in the first place. Society needs to be involved in the process, not just through elected representatives serving in government departments, but through the concerns and groupings which exist in every community. Everyone has a stake in what happens in our prisons.

The voluntary sector is a vital ingredient of our democracy. For many people it is the means through which they become involved in local and national issues. Prisons provide our society with a measure of its own health. But they are more than a thermometer; they are an opportunity to influence, train, educate and heal, important tasks which necessarily involve people outside the prison walls. Whether an individual's motivation is personal or professional, it is right for the wider public to be involved in their work.

Voluntary and community groups as well as local and national organizations may provide ways to become involved, but it is important that resources come from as many different strands as possible to support this process and maintain its independence. This way, strong bridges can be built between closed establishments and a society that does not care to look too closely at them.

This is important work. Voluntary sector organizations can bring new ideas, imagination and commitment. They can also bring resources which properly complement government funding and which help underpin the necessary partnership between the Prison Service and the kaleidoscope of communities and groups within which it has to operate.

CREATING 'JOINED-UP' PROVISION

There are signs that a better understanding is developing between the Prison Service and voluntary sector agencies. The director general of the Prison Service, has publicly stated his commitment to the continued and increasing involvement of the voluntary sector. The appointment of a voluntary sector co-ordinator at Prison Service headquarters should strengthen links between the voluntary sector and the service in general. This post has the support of a group of people drawn from the Prison Service and the voluntary sector and is responsible for developing a strategy to present to the Prison Service Management Board which should lead to a better understanding between agencies and prisons.

It has already been mentioned how prison-based work poses problems for funders. The CLINKS *Good Practice Guide*, which has been produced in conjunction with the Prison Service, is designed to help both prison staff and voluntary sector staff in the planning and delivery of a mix of services in prisons. The guide's emphasis that the involvement of funders in the drawing up of a project plan, which sets out each party's responsibilities, is very welcome. Funders will want to know how what is planned will be achieved. Is it included in the prison's own business plan? Will the work involve changes to the prison day? Where will it be housed? Does the work impact upon sentence planning? It would also be helpful to get a sense of the support a particular piece of work enjoys within a prison and how it involves staff at all levels. Indeed, the more there is evidence of co-operation between prison staff and voluntary agencies, the more attractive an application for funds is likely to be.

Of course, independent funders will want to be able to piece together the funding jigsaw and, if at all possible, to be clear about a prison's own financial contribution. Sometimes, trust funding is conditional upon Prison Service funding, either from HQ or from an individual establishment, but independent funders will need to explore the likelihood of this before imposing an impossible burden upon the voluntary agency itself.

Finally, funders will want to discuss how the work will be evaluated. Who will judge it a success and what happens after the temporary external funding expires? There is no easy answer to this last question.

How do we sustain what has been started? Funders can provide some security whilst future funding is being secured and they can sometimes play a useful part in those discussions, but this latter is much more likely to be of help if an effective partnership has already been established. It is very difficult if funders are only brought into discussions when there is a funding crisis.

The ministerial commitment to taking forward partnership between the Prison Service and the voluntary sector is clear. The prisons and probation minister speaking in the summer of 2000 acknowledged that the more voluntary and community agencies are involved in prisons, the more pressing it becomes that the issue of how they are funded is addressed. Some voluntary sector organizations have recommended that consideration be given to setting up a dedicated fund to help underpin new initiatives and sustain well-proven ones. There are various models. Such a fund might be similar to the Department of Health's 'Section 64' funding which gives voluntary agencies operating in the health and personal social services field the possibility of three to five years funding. The Probation Service has provided another model where local budgets contribute to voluntary sector funding. Yet another model might be the establishment by the government of a separate independent organization with a brief to attract sponsorship or match funding from the private sector, in a similar way to Crime Concern. Such a fund could draw upon the regional strengths of the Prison Service and promote a new pattern of co-operation between the Prison Service and voluntary sector agencies.

Independent funders are more likely to support work in prisons if they are clearer about the role that the Prison Service already plays in funding the prison-based work of voluntary and community sector agencies. There is, at present, some clarity where there is a formal contract between a voluntary sector agency and the Prison Service, but this is often after the event. The Prison Service has also reviewed the instructions and guidelines which they give to governors about how they might support voluntary agencies. However, although this helps to resolve the vexed question of funding in arrears, it does not help solve the sustainability problem, nor is it addressed to voluntary agencies. It is hoped that it will not be long before the Prison Service feels able to publish its own information, for the benefit both of its staff and the actual and potential voluntary sector partner agencies, about the voluntary sector funding budget it is working to, and the criteria and procedures which underpin its funding decisions.

New initiatives to find out what voluntary agencies and volunteers are actually doing in our prisons are to be welcomed. If any one thing is likely to discourage the long-term involvement of independent funders, it is the lack of information that surrounds what is already happening. Rarely does an individual governor know which voluntary agencies are working in his or her establishment and the Prison Service itself has long since dropped its attempt to keep track of which external agencies are operating where. The voluntary sector is no wiser and its networking in this field of work seems to depend more upon anecdote than fact. As a consequence, there is a real danger that any work in prisons is seen as innovative, that lessons learned are rarely passed on and that good practice is overlooked. The Active Community Unit's survey of volunteering and voluntary agency involvement in prisons, and the establishment of database of voluntary agencies by CLINKS 'The Working with Prisoners Directory'), will certainly be of interest to independent funders.

It is to be hoped that this involvement will grow. Voluntary agencies will certainly continue to develop their work and initiate new projects and with the active support of independent funders they will make an increasing impact upon prison regimes. This is a field of endeavour, rich in those qualities that independent funders look out for. The work is with some of the most disadvantaged people in our society, many of whom have a mighty struggle to move away from its margins. It is often innovative, its potential for creating change is considerable and its effects, although sometimes slow, are often long-lasting. It is work that challenges funders and we cannot afford to neglect it.

CHAPTER 12

Practical Steps for a Successful Partnership

Shane Bryans

Governors are increasingly being encouraged to enter into partnerships with a range of statutory, commercial, voluntary and community-based organizations. This chapter considers the rhetoric and reality of partnership working. In particular it looks at the shortcomings of the existing approach, considers why prisons should involve the voluntary sector in delivering services to prisoners; outlines the types of services which the voluntary sector can deliver; identifies some of the management issues which have to be considered when entering into an agreement with the voluntary sector and suggests how best to audit, monitor and evaluate the work of that sector.

WELL INTENTIONED CONFUSION

The use of the voluntary sector in prisons has been inconsistent, disjointed and *ad hoc*. Some prisons involve many voluntary sector organizations and others involve none. Many governors, if asked, would not know what voluntary sector organizations operate in their prison, as accurate records tend not to be kept. Furthermore, many staff still see voluntary sector groups as consisting of the stereotypical amateur 'do-gooders'. Prisons in which the sector is thriving tend to have a governor who is keen on partnership working, or where local organizations have taken the initiative.

This chaotic approach emerged for a number of reasons. Until recently, there has not been a clear strategic steer from Prison Service HQ on the role of the voluntary sector, or guidance on what services the sector should provide. The contribution of the voluntary sector has traditionally been viewed as being low key, peripheral and not contributing to the core activities of the prison. At establishment level there is often no one who takes responsibility for the co-ordination and development of links with the voluntary sector. There are also strong cultural differences between the Prison Service and the voluntary sector. Differing traditions and values often cause conflict and frustration. The approach to resources and practices has also created a division between the two sectors. The voluntary sector tends to be much less hierarchical and more inclusive in its approach, whereas the Prison Service remains authoritarian, highly structured and bureaucratic.

A lack of mutual understanding also exists. Voluntary sector agencies often fail to grasp the impact performance management has had on governors and the fact that Service Delivery Agreements between the governor and area manager dictate what services are delivered in each prison. The need to focus on the delivery of key performance indicators (KPIs) and key performance targets now dominates resource allocation in prisons. Resources are now primarily allocated to areas where positive outcomes can be obtained. There is also an increased tendency for 'short-termism' and a push to demonstrate outcomes within months rather than years. In return, governors have not understood the need of voluntary sector managers to account to their management committees, trustees and funders, and the impact that the 'contract culture' has had on smaller voluntary sector organizations. Governors also do not realise the pressure on voluntary sector organizations to raise and maintain funding in order to survive.

It must also be pointed out that some governors view the voluntary sector as posing a potential security risk and discourage them from working in their prison. The idea of voluntary sector staff and volunteers wandering around prisons, or setting up projects and services, would still be an anathema to a small number of governors. Whilst the concern may be based on a desire to protect voluntary sector personnel, it can also be the result of a lack of trust and understanding.

There is also some resistance to the expansion of voluntary sector involvement in prisons from prison officers and other staff who view the voluntary sector as taking their jobs. The running of workshops, visitors' centres and resettlement courses, for example, may well have been a matter for prison staff in the past. The introduction of a new service provided by a voluntary organization can lead to resentment and anger from existing staff. This in turn can lead to a lack of co-operation, and, on occasion, deliberate attempts to thwart the efforts of the voluntary sector organization.

Governors are able to develop their own differing approaches to involving external organization. Schemes are often started in response to a 'good idea' from a member of staff or approach from an organization. However, these schemes are rarely reviewed to see if they meet (or indeed ever did meet) the needs of the prisoner population. This *ad hoc* approach resulted in some needs not being met, a duplication of services in a few areas and poorly managed provision in others. Governors also often fail to properly establish the credibility and reliability of potential voluntary sector service providers. This has led to a variable quality and a poor reputation of service delivery in some instances.

Where a voluntary agency has begun a service in prison they can be often faced with a lack of support, a shortage of information and management inconsistency. Prison staff do not always understand the role of the voluntary sector and can put up barriers to effective working. Cultural differences often result in a lack of synergy and fragmented working. Well intentioned projects, if not properly structured and managed, can have a destructive impact on prison staff, prisoners, the voluntary agencies and on the order and security of the establishment.

THE GROWING IMPETUS FOR INCREASED PARTNERSHIP WORKING

A few years ago it would not have been conceivable that the Prison Service would contract out the provision of particular services, let alone whole prison establishments. Yet today we have a number of privately managed prisons, and all prisons contract out the delivery of education, drug services, library provision and probation work. Some prisons have gone further and have entered into commercial contracts for the delivery of healthcare, catering, prison shops, physical education, work provision and building repair and maintenance. Many of these arrangements are based on commercial contracts with private sector organizations. Increasingly, despite the problems identified above, partnerships are developing between prisons and the voluntary sector.

One of the main reasons for the growth of voluntary sector involvement has been the clear political commitment to closer cooperation between the statutory and voluntary sectors. As the prisons and probation minister pointed out at the Prison Service conference in February 2000:

> The use of the voluntary sector is rapidly increasing throughout government, and the potential for developing partnerships between prisons and voluntary organizations is enormous. The significance of these partnerships in helping us to deliver constructive regimes and meet targets cannot be over-emphasised. Voluntary organizations are an invaluable, and currently under-used, resource, and it is vital that we involve them in our work wherever they can make a contribution.
>
> (Home Office, 2000)

The Prison Service Business Plan for 2000-2001 reinforced the message by committing the Prison Service to 'developing a series of partnerships with the voluntary sector to reflect Government thinking on the "active community".' (Prison Service, 2000a, para 3.6). Indeed, the same theme was adopted by the Chief Inspector of Prisons in his annual report in which he commented 'working with and within existing community arrangements must be better than going it alone, which is what the Prison Service has tended to do in the past (HM Inspectorate of Prisons, 2000, p.10).

Involving voluntary agencies in the delivery of services in prisons also makes sense from a practical viewpoint. The provision of a service by the same organization inside the prison and in the community will often represent the 'normalisation' of services delivered in prisons. This is important, as it will ensure that prisoners get a similar type and quality of service that they would have obtained in the community. It can also promote continuity, as short-term and medium-term prisoners may be able to receive services from the groups with whom they dealt prior to their imprisonment and with whom they will deal on release.

Another reason for the growth in voluntary sector involvement in prisons has been that governors have seen the sector as a means of providing additional services which could not be provided from the prison's budget. The voluntary sector is able to obtain sponsorship, access funding, and make use of volunteers to provide services in prisons. This can lead to improvements in the regime provision which would not otherwise have been possible.

Governors also view voluntary sector work in prison as an opportunity to import interesting and creative projects which help to create a healthy environment. Prisoners and staff involved in such projects often tend to have the lowest sickness rates, are better motivated and have higher morale. Such schemes also help to make prisoners feel that they are 'active citizens' and are contributing something back to the community. This improves their sense of self-image and can help to ease their reintegration back into society.

PROFESSIONAL AND CONSISTENT PARTNERSHIPS

Partnerships with the voluntary sector already deliver services to prisoners in a myriad of areas including healthcare, family ties and responsibilities, education and personal development, employment and employment prospects, recreation, offending behaviour programmes and religious and cultural ties (including those of prisoner minority groups). The political commitment to the growth of voluntary sector involvement in prisons will lead to the number of partnerships greatly increasing. There is clearly therefore a need to put in place a strategic framework, and management arrangements, to ensure effective partnership working. This will help to overcome some of the shortfalls identified earlier in this book.

The *Good Practice Guide* referred to in *Chapter 4* will assist governors to formalise protocols with voluntary agencies, and adopt a more systematic approach to future partnerships (Prison Service, 2000b). A voluntary sector co-ordinator has also been appointed at Prison Service HQ. The main role of the co-ordinator will be to help create the appropriate framework for partnership working between the Prison Service and the voluntary and community-based sector.

The process which governors are encouraged to follow in establishing partnerships is covered in the following sections which have been informed by the contents of the *Good Practice Guide*. The themes identified will be of interest to both governors and voluntary agencies, so that both parties can approach joint-working from an informed viewpoint and a good level of mutual understanding.

CONTRIBUTING TO REDUCING CRIME AND 'ADDING VALUE'

All prisons have a Service Delivery Agreement (SDA) which outlines what it will deliver, what resources it will get and what key performance targets have to be achieved. In addition, most establishments have a vision or mission statement which tries to capture the ethos of what it is trying to achieve. Within the SDA or vision statement there should be a statement about how voluntary and community-based agencies can contribute to the work of the prison. Any proposals for a new service or partnership agreement must be judged against the statement and whether the proposed service will contribute to the achievement of the establishment's vision and 'add value' to the work of the establishment. If the voluntary agency is not mentioned in the SDA/vision then there is a need to agree what role it will perform and how it will contribute to delivering the establishment's plans.

The *Good Practice Guide* outlines a number of questions which Governors should ask themselves:

- **Evidence**—What evidence is there that the proposed activity is needed in the prison? If there is no factual evidence is there a widely held belief amongst staff that a need exists in the proposed area of activity?
- **Appropriateness**—How would the new activity fit into or complement the current range of activities within the prison?
- **Relevance**—How would it support a reduction in re-offending and/or contribute towards constructive and healthy prison regimes?
- **Effectiveness**—What may happen as a result of the activity being undertaken and how will you measure this?

Within any establishment there will be a range of unmet needs. Prisons are not sufficiently resourced to fully meet all the needs identified on prisoners' sentence plans or to address all the core areas shown in a 'needs' assessment of the prisoner population. Whilst additional resources of £226 million have been allocated to constructive regimes, prisons had to make efficiency savings of £36 million in 2000/1 and £55 million in 2001/2, often at the expense of purposeful activity. Around 53 per cent of adult male prisoners and 77 per cent of male young offenders are reconvicted within two years of discharge from custody (Home Office, 1999). The voluntary sector has a contribution to make in helping the Prison Service to reduce this reconviction figure.

The CLINKS pilot project in 1999 identified the following areas where needs were generally not met (CLINKS, 1999):

- housing and accommodation;
- employment and benefits advice;
- mental health issues;
- gambling addiction;
- minority ethnic groups where the need falls outside religious provision;
- education and support for people living with HIV and Hepatitis C;
- counselling and support in the case of relationship breakdown;
- trauma resulting from sexual abuse;
- language/interpretation services at short notice;
- specific support for foreign nationals;
- family mediation in a broad sense (that is, involving more than just maintaining contact); and
- mentoring (through release to effective resettlement).

Governors have to allocate the limited resources available to areas which will impact on reducing re-offending. The key areas which must be provided if offending is to be reduced are: offending behaviour programmes, vocational training, literacy and numeracy provision and employment related projects (Home Office, 1998, p.133). Proposals from voluntary and community-based agencies which require Prison Service resourcing (money, people or physical space) must therefore be prioritised.

It is likely that proposals which are not able to demonstrate outcomes which reduce re-offending or contribute to a 'healthy prison' will not be supported. The Prison Service is now only introducing schemes which are intended to reduce re-offending if they conform to the 'what works' literature. The Home Office made clear that 'implementation of initiatives more generally should be planned so as to ensure that the "what works" principles are adhered to and adequate and appropriate training and evaluation are included' (Home Office,

1998, p.3). Voluntary agencies are increasingly having to incorporate the 'what works' principles in their programmes and to develop ways of demonstrating outcomes. A guide has been produced by a charity to help organizations to develop outcome monitoring systems in order to demonstrate the effectiveness of their services (Alcohol Concern, 2000).

IDENTIFYING THE RIGHT PARTNER ORGANIZATION

Assuming that a need has been identified and resources are available, the governor will have to decide how best to meet the need. In some cases the service can best be provided 'in-house' by prison officers or by directly employed civilian staff. For example, a resettlement programme could be run by pre-release trained staff, the Employment Service, a voluntary sector provider or as a partnership between all three. The governor will need to consider the relative merits of using prison staff or a voluntary sector provider.

If the governor decides to use an external agency or organization they will need to go through a process for selecting that provider. In some cases the provider will be self-evident: such as Samaritans to train prisoner 'Listeners' or the National Association of Prison Visitors to set up a visiting scheme. However, in most cases the governor will need to search out an organization or respond to an approach by an organization. In both cases the governor will need to screen the organization to ensure that it is the most appropriate to deliver the proposed service, and is able to do this within the restrictions that prison environments impose; believes in and is committed to multi-agency work; works according to good equal opportunities practices; understands its role in delivering a service to a vulnerable group of people and that its motivation for doing this is clear and appropriate; and is a properly constituted and well-structure organization.

The *Good Practice Guide* provides a list of pointers to a healthy voluntary agency (Prison Service, 2000b).

- Does the agency have a recognised record of service delivery within a prison, a criminal justice agency or in the community? If so, is the service they are now proposing the same or similar to the service they deliver elsewhere?
- Have you seen their recent annual report? This will give you key information about the organization. Remember that prohibitive costs mean that the quality of reproduction of the report is not a reflection of the quality of the organization.

- Management committees are very important in voluntary organizations. They will be named in the annual report.
- Are the staff appropriately trained and supported to undertake the service they are providing? Do professionals delivering the same or similar services within the community hold comparable qualifications. There are ways of checking this via National Training Organizations, voluntary sector umbrella groups, professional associations, and so on.
- Registered charity status is one way of legally constituting a voluntary sector organization. While this ensures that the organization fulfils certain legal and structural requirements it does not guarantee quality of service delivery. Some organizations do not qualify or have chosen not to gain charitable status. You should ensure that you understand the reasons behind this choice.
- Many charities are also registered companies. This means that they have chosen to work within this legal framework, but this decision should not be interpreted as an indicator of quality provision.
- Does the organization openly advertise and recruit staff? An open recruitment policy, supported by an Equal Opportunities Policy, usually indicates that the organization recruits staff and volunteers openly and not on the basis of any other criteria or via any other network.
- Who are the funders of the organization and of the project? The funding for the project may be different to the main source of funding for the organization as a whole. Many funders are independent charitable trusts whose experience of project work can often be drawn on.
- Sources of funding are usually indicated in the annual report.
- Anonymous funding is also a legitimate source of funding for some organizations and this is normally recorded in the annual report.

FUNDING THE PARTNERSHIP

Voluntary sector work in prisons always has a cost. Salaries of paid staff, office accommodation costs and the prison element of their management costs must be met. Agencies using a majority of volunteers also often employ paid staff to train and support the volunteers. Volunteers' travel costs need to be reimbursed and these may be substantial given that prisons are often in isolated locations.

Many community-based agencies working in prison receive funding from the individual establishment or from Prison Service HQ. The Prison Service has recently issued a new chapter to the Prison Service Order on

Finance which outlines the funding issues surrounding charities and the voluntary and community sector. It clarifies arrangements for 'payments in advance', 'payments of grants-in-aid' and donations to charities.

Voluntary agencies often look appealing to governors because they can attract resources from a wide range of other sources including: grant-making charitable trusts; statutory bodies (healthcare trusts, local authorities, Employment Service); Community Fund (National Lottery); European Union through various social fund projects, and religious and spiritual organizations.

As Peter Kilgarriff points out in *Chapter 11*, these funding sources generally expect the voluntary agencies to apply or bid for money. These applications should include the methods to be used, the likely support for the work in the prison (rooms, materials etc.) and the expected outcomes. They may also have to describe how the work will be ended or closed, or sustained after the period of initial funding expires. Many grant-givers see their role as initiating new work and are sometimes reluctant to make grants for projects which are already under way. Once schemes have been set up there is often an expectation that the Prison Service or other statutory agency will provide the ongoing funding. These issues need exploring early on in the dialogue between the partner organizations, though this is usually not the case, and often leads to the abrupt cessation of successful projects when external funding dries up. The issue of funding is covered in more detail in *Chapter 11*.

REACHING AN AGREEMENT AND THE CONTRACTUAL PROCESS

Once the formal selection or procurement process has been completed an agreement or contract will need to be formulated and signed. Standard formats for contracts are produced by the Prison Service Contracts and Procurement group. The agreement will need to cover at a minimum the following:

- names and addresses of the two parties;
- outline of the service to be provided, including key deliverables and outputs;
- preparatory issues;
- management of the project;
- funding arrangements;
- training requirements;
- monitoring arrangements;
- evaluation process;
- dispute resolution mechanism;

- termination protocol;
- job descriptions for key workers; and
- Health and Safety and Equal Opportunities policies.

ENSURING EFFECTIVE DELIVERY

Once the needs have been identified, funding is secured to meet the need and the service provider has been appointed, the challenging task of delivering the service has to start.

At an early stage information has to be given to the senior management teams of both the prison and the voluntary sector organization about the partnership and the service to be provided. Bridges will need building, support will have to be generated for the project and decisions made about how the new activity will be managed within the prison. The staff and prisoners will need briefing about the project and referral system set up.

It is critical that issues such as confidentiality and child protection are addressed. An agreement of protocol will need to be reached on the way sensitive issues will be dealt with. Guidelines will need to be issued to the volunteers and paid staff of voluntary sector providers.

An issue that will come up if the community-based organization employs ex-offenders as staff or volunteers, is the issue of security clearance. This will need addressing early on in order to avoid delays and complications.

A range of other practical issues will need to be addressed, including the following which are identified in the *Good Practice Guide* (Prison Service, 2000b).

- Who will advertise the service in the prison and how will this be done?
- How will all staff know to include the possibility of the planned activity when writing sentence plans or other appropriate documentation?
- What selection criteria, if any, will be used for prisoners wanting to use the service?
- How will the use of the service by black and minority ethnic prisoners be monitored?
- Who will arrange rooms to house the service and where will these be situated?
- What officer support, if appropriate, will be available during the activity?
- What will the arrangements be in the case of cancellations either by the prison or service provider?

- Who will be responsible for arranging an induction and training programme?
- Are keys to be issued? If not, who will be responsible for escorting staff from the gate?
- What records of attendance will be kept? Who is responsible for keeping these and where will this information be held?
- Will reports be written about prisoners by the community-based agency staff? If yes, what will these reports be used for and what will their legal status be? What training will be available to external staff working in prison who may be asked to write these reports?
- Who will keep gate staff informed about the arrival and escorting arrangements? Are any identity documents to be issued to external staff?
- What support will be available to members of staff? What opportunities will be available for them to reflect on their experience of working within prison?

From both the prison's and the voluntary agency's points of view preparing voluntary sector staff to work in an institution is critical. Voluntary sector organizations often have their own training programmes for their staff and may issue written guidance to staff working in prisons. However, governors must satisfy themselves that everyone working in their institution has had sufficient prison-related training to operate effectively in the prison. Prison specific training, often known as 'jailcraft' should include: security awareness, hostage, breakaway techniques, and key and radio security. In addition, new staff should receive training in equal opportunities and race relations, suicide and self-harm, substance abuse and function specific matters (for example, the Trust for the Study of Adolescence training on working with young people in custody).

MONITORING AND EVALUATING THE SERVICE

Monitoring is an essential part of service delivery. It enables staff and managers to identify who uses the service, when it is being used, its effectiveness and the nature of any problems. There is a potential difference in monitoring requirements between funders, providers and governors. In order to overcome this the signed agreement should identify common monitoring procedures and specify what will be monitored, by whom, when and in what form will it be presented.

The evaluation of the project is important for all parties involved and will inform whether the project is worth disseminating and 'mainstreaming' (being reproduced elsewhere). The evaluation process itself will involve: collecting relevant information; assessing the information against agreed criteria and targets and reporting the results so that they can inform future planning. Both quantitative and qualitative outcomes of a project will need to be identified in order to conclude whether the purpose of the project was fulfilled and the identified needs of the prisoners met.

CO-ORDINATING THE WORK OF THE VOLUNTARY SECTOR

Experience indicates that dealing with one voluntary agency delivering one project is manageable. However, with the proliferation of projects, delivered by a multitude of providers, management becomes increasingly problematic. If voluntary agencies working in prison are to feel valued, and be informed and integrated into the prison community then time needs to be devoted to co-ordinating the activities of the various organizations. Effective communication systems need to be put in place, relationships built, and people kept up-to-date on the wider developments in the prison.

One approach to doing this vital, and inclusive piece of work, is to appoint a voluntary sector development co-ordinator. The potential key tasks and duties of a co-ordinator are shown below:

- to ensure a consistent and professional link between the voluntary agencies and Prison Service staff;
- to attend all voluntary sector service provider meetings, throughcare steering group and other appropriate meetings to ensure the highest level of co-operation and communication within the prison for the benefit of both staff and prisoners;
- to liaise with all voluntary sector organizations and volunteers on a regular basis, to brief them on developments within the institution and to identify any problems or issues which they are experiencing;
- to create a network and advice service within the prison in order to overcome the sense of isolation experienced by some members of the voluntary sector and volunteers and at the same time alleviate the difficulties experienced by prison staff in gaining accurate knowledge regarding the work being undertaken by voluntary agencies;
- to provide a forum for debate about issues of concern to both the voluntary sector agencies and prison staff;
- to advise and support the establishment of evaluation procedures for the work undertaken by the voluntary sector;

- to develop a database (and library) of potential volunteers, volunteer training opportunities, support services, voluntary sector agencies, conferences, literature and new voluntary sector initiatives being established in other prisons;
- to network with voluntary sector organizations in order to gather best practice;
- to seek out funding for voluntary sector projects and the funding for your post;
- to identify any potential gaps in the services provided by voluntary sector agencies;
- to contribute to the assessment of the suitability of voluntary sector organizations wishing to work with the prison;
- to be in regular dialogue with the Sentence Management Group, Resettlement Team, other staff and prisoners to ensure that their appropriate identified needs are being met by the voluntary sector agencies;
- to manage the drawing up of service level agreements and contracts with new providers;
- to provide public relations and media information on voluntary sector work in the establishment; and
- to offer a co-ordinating role for those organizations not working directly with young prisoners or inside the prison (e.g. Prisoners' Families Support Groups).

RHETORIC INTO REALITY

There has been a longstanding recognition of the value and role played by voluntary sector organizations and community agencies in prisons. They are an important resource, often under-utilised. Used effectively, voluntary sector agencies can complement and enhance the work carried out within prisons, and provide a bridge into the community. However, effective partnership requires dialogue, understanding, tolerance of differences and mutual respect, in order to achieve positive outcomes.

This chapter has hopefully identified some of the problems associated with the existing *ad hoc* arrangements and provided a clearer understanding of the management issues surrounding a partnership approach to delivering services in prisons. It is not intended to dissuade potential partners but to provide a realistic bedrock on which to base future joint working.

CHAPTER 13

The Road Ahead: Issues and Strategies for Future Joint Working

Shane Bryans, Clive Martin and Roma Walker

The voluntary sector now forms seven per cent of GDP, involves more than 16 million people and employs 530,000 paid staff.

There can be little doubt that the government is firmly committed to continuing the expansion of the sector and it has made clear that it wants to develop a strong, independent and diverse voluntary sector, which can make a significant contribution to the health and dynamism of the economy and society. As part of that commitment, the Performance and Innovation Unit in the Cabinet Office has been asked to undertake a broad ranging review of the legal and regulatory framework for charities and the voluntary sector. The review will make recommendations 'to better enable existing organizations to thrive and grow and encourage the development of new types of organization' (Cabinet Office, 2001). In addition, the Government announced grants of more than £18 million to 149 voluntary and community organizations in order to support their work (Home Office, 2001b).

This growth in the work of the voluntary sector has been reflected in the penal sector, as earlier chapters in this book have shown. In the light of the Government's view of the role the voluntary sector, it is clear that the Prison Service and the voluntary sector will be working together in the future and we may well see a rapid expansion in the work of the voluntary sector in prisons. This last chapter seeks to pull together some of the key themes identified elsewhere in the book and to identify the main advantages to both the Prison Service and voluntary sector of working together effectively. It also sets out the potential problems which will need to be addressed if the aim of effective joint working is to be achieved. The book concludes by providing a map for the 'road ahead', if the relationship between the Prison Service and voluntary sector is to move from being one of 'co-operation' to a much more 'partnership'-based approach.

THE CONTRIBUTION OF THE PENAL VOLUNTARY SECTOR

The reasons why the voluntary sector should be involved in the penal system now appear very clear both in philosophical and practical terms. Given that, in general, the voluntary sector works with the vulnerable, the excluded and the disadvantaged, the penal system is an obvious arena for a concentration of their activity. Women, young people and the Black and Minority Ethnic community are all over-represented within the prison population. The indicators of social exclusion are also higher in the prison population than in the population generally. Agencies may be driven by ideological, philanthropic, humanitarian and religious motives or a secular practicality to work towards a more inclusive and safer community.

Whatever the motivation, and despite differing cultures and ways of operating, the penal voluntary sector and the Prison Service overlap in their broad aims of seeking to aid resettlement and reduce re offending. For the voluntary sector, involvement may be to ameliorate against some of the worst excesses of the penal system, or as part of a 'normalisation' process (King and Morgan, 1980), or simply to supplement the inadequacies of state provision. These too may be some of the reasons, though not necessarily articulated, for the Prison Service and individual establishments to accommodate voluntary sector activity.

The literature points to a number benefits which the penal voluntary sector can bring to the work of the Prison Service. These benefits are explored below:

(a) Extended range of services
Some commentators suggest that the provision and variety of services are extended by voluntary and community involvement (Gill and Mawby, 1990). Certainly this claim can be substantiated in the case of the penal voluntary sector, where, in many establishments, services are provided for which there would be no or little statutory provision by the prison. For example, the provision of facilities for visitors and families has been extended greatly by the voluntary sector.

(b) Improvement in quality of service
The extended provision can lead to an overall improvement in the quality of service, as the statutory staff are 'provoked to increased commitment by the enthusiasm and vigour of volunteers' (Gill and Mawby, 1990, p.22). The variety of voluntary sector agencies and the wide ranging differences between individual establishments make such generalisations of limited value in the case of prisons. Nonetheless, many agencies could cite examples of enthusiastic cooperation with committed prison staff that

facilitates and enhances the service provision they are delivering. However, the prison staff may well be committed anyway, regardless of any voluntary sector involvement. The voluntary agency work may merely be a focus for their commitment and may give added interest to the more routine or unpleasant features of their jobs. One governor recently commented, in relation to voluntary agency involvement, that 'if you let prison staff work with creative and interesting projects, and creative and interesting people, you see the benefits in greatly reduced sick rates'. However, because prisons are large and complex organizations, many staff will not necessarily come into direct contact with voluntary sector agencies or volunteers

(c) Innovation

There is the notion that voluntary agencies are pioneers, innovative, flexible, proactive and creative, that they are 'trailblazers' (Brenton, 1985). It is certainly true that because they are smaller, less bureaucratic and less hierarchical, voluntary sector agencies can be dynamic, and can often respond more quickly than statutory organizations. Hugh Mellor suggests that 'because of its relative smallness of scale, the voluntary body is able to experiment, by doing old things in new ways, or trying out quite new services, and in doing so take the risks which might be more difficult for a large and essentially more bureaucratic state concern' (Mellor, quoted in Gill and Mawby, 1990, p.22). Many examples of such innovative activity could be cited, but a good example would be the provision of drug treatment programmes by small drug agencies that were the trailblazers during the 1980s.

(d) Ability to criticise

Gill and Mawby (1990) claim that voluntary bodies, being independent, can criticise both government policies and the practices of statutory bodies. Certainly some penal voluntary agencies (service providers as well as the pressure groups) are vocal, both in the media and on the various bodies upon which they sit as representatives, in expressing their opinions of certain aspects of penal policy and practice. Furthermore, being in receipt of direct or indirect government funding appears to be of little constraint to their criticisms, despite suggestions to the contrary by Lewis (1988). Indeed, the right of voluntary sector agencies to criticise government policies and statutory practices whilst in receipt of state funding is a principle endorsed by the Compact on Relations between Government and the Voluntary and Community Sector in England (1998). The effectiveness of such lobbying is the subject of ongoing research by Roma Walker, but it is clear that pressure groups can make claims to highlighting issues and altering practices (Ryan, 1996).

(e) Watchdog function

Linked to the ability to criticise is the suggestion that the voluntary sector can perform an independent watchdog function, in addition to HM Chief Inspector of Prisons, and Boards of Visitors, the latter of which are themselves made up of volunteer members. Clear distinction should be made here between the pressure groups and service provider agencies. For the pressure groups it is one of their primary functions to expose and to report to the proper authority any abuses they discover. Indeed Stephen Shaw, the Prisons Ombudsman and formerly director of the Prison Reform Trust, says that 'one of the roles of the pressure groups, unelected and largely unaccountable though they may be, it to act as whistle-blowers.' (Shaw, in Bryans and Jones, 2001, p.355). This will undoubtedly at times lead to tensions in the relationship between these groups and the Prison Service, but will not threaten the core campaigning activities or the existence of such groups.

Whistleblowing is a sensitive area and if the voluntary sector were to adopt the role as 'public spies' there is a likelihood that they could be excluded from prison establishments altogether. In common with other aspects of the relationship between the Prison Service and the voluntary sector, whistleblowing protocols remain underdeveloped and *ad hoc* and in need of clarification.

(f) Cost effectiveness

Voluntary agencies may provide a more cost effective service, particularly if they have less bureaucracy and rely upon volunteers (though volunteers never come without cost to the agency). Funding for additional voluntary agency services is borne largely by grant-making trusts and foundations, and voluntary sector agencies may be deemed attractive to prisons. Whilst volunteering is not cost free, particularly in terms of the employed voluntary sector staff who recruit, train and support volunteers it is recognised as being cost effective and provides a good return on investment (Haxby, 1978). Certainly for prisons there are significant financial benefits to supplement state provision with alternatives from the voluntary sector.

(g) Mechanisms for social cohesion

Finally, according to Mawby and Gill (1990, p.230) voluntary agencies, and particularly volunteering are a 'mechanism for increasing social cohesion'. This last claim as a benefit of voluntary sector involvement is more intangible and one that Gill and Mawby concede is practically impossible to test in any quantitative way. In terms of the penal voluntary sector activity, increased social cohesion may result, for example, from the training by the Samaritans of prisoners as volunteer counsellors. The listeners, as they are called, develop supportive relationships with fellow prisoners and thus build a more cohesive prison environment. Voluntary sector agencies represent a bridge into the community and normalisation of services particularly where they deliver similar services in the community.

WORDS OF CAUTION: POTENTIAL PROBLEMS

The previous section highlighted some of the benefits which have been observed since the voluntary sector became more involved in the work of the Prison Service. However, like any rapidly expanding and dynamic development a number of potential pitfalls have become apparent. These need to be borne in mind as voluntary sector work in prisons continues to grow. Some of these problems are set out below.

(a) The relationship between volunteers and paid employees

The relationship between volunteers and paid employees attains significance where employees see their jobs, status or overtime threatened by an increasing use of volunteers (Gill and Mawby, 1990 p.23-24). In the penal context, this has less significance *within* voluntary sector agencies, but more with the agency/prison staff relationship. Resentment at the role of voluntary sector personnel within prisons can sometimes manifest itself in deliberate obstruction of the delivery of voluntary agency service provision. Voluntary agencies can be at the mercy of a minority of prison officers in the pursuance of their own agenda (Douglas Hurd, Bourne Trust Annual Lecture, 1999). Resentment may be a result of a perception that the voluntary sector corners the more creative and interesting aspects of prison work, taking it way from prison staff who are left with more routine and mundane tasks.

(b) Area inequalities

There is an unequal geographical distribution of voluntary agency provision. Some prisons may have little voluntary sector input, and are not fulfilling a need, others may have a duplication of provision due to lack of co-ordination between the prison and individual agencies. The level of voluntary sector activity is not consistent throughout the prison estate. There is a very stark contrast between the Victorian inner city prisons and the many newer establishments located in more isolated areas. Inner city prisons tend to be able to access a wider voluntary sector input, as there is a greater concentration and variety of agencies nearby. The cost of voluntary sector engagement in isolated areas severely restricts their activity, as does the additional security measures imposed by the high security estate. Minority ethnic prisoners, in particular, when imprisoned in rural areas may consequently have less access to those agencies that are best able to meet their needs.

(c) Funding issues

Funding problems, which are covered extensively in *Chapter 11*, manifest themselves in several ways. For example, insecurity of funding from trusts may mean that voluntary agency projects cannot always be sustained even once established and proven to be successful. This can result in the closure of projects, often at short notice. These projects may have diminished previously existing in-house skills. The net result is that a prison can be left worse off when a project terminates due to the de-skilling of its staff. This is a direct result of the current funding arrangements.

According to Lewis (1988) funding from government 'contaminates' agencies and they can only be 'creative and critical' if they are financially independent (Lewis, quoted in Gill and Mawby, 1990, p.25). In the case of the penal voluntary sector, the funding arrangements are additionally and uniquely complex. Voluntary agencies are entirely dependant upon the goodwill and co-operation of a third party (in this case prison management and staff) in order to fulfil their service provision upon which their funding and any potential future funding is based.

(d) A question of balance

Where should statutory provision end and voluntary sector provision begin? As governors look to save money, their sights invariably fall on the voluntary sector which is perceived as a 'cheaper' alternative provider of many services. Certainly many funding trusts would be reluctant to support agency work that did anything other than complement and enhance, and not *replace* statutory provision. Gill and Mawby (1990) argue that it should not be the role of the voluntary sector to fill gaps caused by a curtailment of state provision. This issue often causes problems for both the Prison Service and the voluntary sector, but reflects concern in society generally about entitlement to state provision of core services. It is important that both parties to any agreement understand why the agreement has been reached and on what conditions.

(e) Limited choice of services

Whilst the range of service provision may be increased by the arrival of the voluntary sector, there is often a sharp contrast with the range and choice that is available in the community. Prisoners' access is usually restricted to the one single agency that provides that particular service within that establishment. No choice is available and in many instances the appropriate service may not be available at all, either limited by the voluntary sector's ability to provide or because of perceived lack of prisoner need by prison management. This lack of choice means that prisoners, unlike the general population, do not have the same ability to engage with the agency that is most targeted towards their needs. While others may move from one agency to another until they find the one most suited to help, prisoners have to work with the agency that has that remit within the prison. This makes the selection of agencies working within prisons a very specialist and sensitive issue, and of critical importance.

Many important social initiatives delivered by the voluntary sector also remain unrepresented within prisons. For example, advocacy in the case of mental health and mediation in the case of family breakdown have not been introduced into many prisons. This is surprising given the number of prisoners and their families affected by these two issues. In addition, large gaps or very limited provision remains—services for male foreign nationals and provision for gambling addiction are two examples. These services could probably be provided by appropriate community-based agencies without large resource implications.

(f) Ethics and whistle-blowing

For voluntary sector service providers working on a day-to-day basis within prisons, alongside and often only effectively with the active co-operation of Prison Service staff, whistle-blowing becomes more problematic. If voluntary agencies and volunteers adopt the role of 'spies' there is a danger, even a likelihood that they will be shunned and excluded. That is not to say they should ignore or condone malpractice, but that they should deal with it in a way that is appropriate, professional and effective. Gill and Mawby (1990) suggest that volunteers (as opposed to paid voluntary sector employees) who are not reliant upon income, may be more willing to whistle-blow against malpractice. They also suggest that those working within an institutional setting on a daily basis, in this case prisons, may become inculcated within the culture. Consequently they may become 'normalised' and no longer be surprised or shocked by malpractice. For the service providers (as opposed to pressure groups) open or direct criticism at an establishment level could be potentially counter productive, leading to access problems and damaging the sometimes fragile relationships between the agency and the prison. Again, it is important that this issue is discussed and addressed before the voluntary sector/volunteers starts work in a prison

(g) Cultural differences

There is no doubt that there are differences in working styles and practices between the two sectors. The differences are often expressed in crude and simplistic language and fall too readily into stereotypical and inaccurate typecasting. There are, however, as many similarities as differences between the sectors. Closer working together, joint training initiatives, job shadowing and secondments would greatly help in the understanding of each other's cultures.

When it comes to organizational planning, voluntary sector agencies can sometimes appear to be *ad hoc*, eccentric or unrealistically aspirational or idealistic. They also sometimes fail to engage extensively in strategic planning (Wilson, 1996, p.82). Herein lies a dichotomy as voluntary agencies 'are viewed in contradictory ways. They are expected to be amateur in style and motive, yet professional in their efficiency and effectiveness' (*Home Office Research Bulletin*, No 37, 1995, p.40). In contrast the Prison Service may appear to be lumbering, unresponsive and at times inflexible, an inevitable consequence perhaps of its size and status. However, an alternative perspective is that the voluntary sector, in turn, is slow to respond to Prison Service initiatives and agendas. For example, few voluntary sector agencies have fully embraced the Prison Service focus on the Basic Skills deficit amongst prisoners. Indeed, how far *should* the voluntary sector respond to Prison Service trends and agendas? What is not disputed is the contrasting styles of voluntary and statutory agencies. Each has its strengths and weaknesses.

(h) The inequality of 'partnership'
There is a perception that risk is loaded inequitably upon the voluntary sector agencies. Steve Hammer, chief executive of Compass states that 'sadly recent experience with the Prison Service is of contracts that seek to load demand on providers and limit the responsibility of the purchaser, they seem to have been less about partnership and closer to marriage Hollywood style, with contract terms that anticipate divorce and ensure that the division of the spoils is one sided' (*Criminal Justice Matters*, 40, Summer 2000, p.9). Clearly for partnership and relationships to develop further such areas of inequality and potential conflict need to be resolved.

THE IMPACT OF MANAGERIALISM

The Prison Service has, for a number of years, been undergoing a process of what has become known as 'managerialism'. This has led to the use of a new set of tools, ideas, beliefs and behaviours. The importation of private sector techniques has transformed the approach and orientation of the Prison Service and its governors (Bryans and Wilson, 2000). Governors are today focused on delivering their key performance indicators, achieving value for money and delivering quantifiable results.

This managerialist approach has brought with it some potential issues for the voluntary sector. No longer are governors willing to fund and support 'well intentioned' schemes and initiatives, unless they impact on delivering key performance indicators. Financial constraints, efficiency savings and budget reductions have led governors to assess, in a critical way, what services are being delivered by the voluntary sector.

The Prison Service is now driven by quantitative monitoring in the form of key performance indicators. Whilst some service provision can be measured in terms of outcome, such as drug rehabilitation programmes, many other services find it more difficult to be subjected to such quantitative outcome monitoring. Managerialist approaches may not be appropriate when assessing more intangible qualities, which may be an intrinsic part of a voluntary agencies' service provision. For example, how can a meaningful measurement be applied to the support given to a prisoner's family? For many voluntary sector organizations the need to demonstrate quantifiable outcomes for their work has been a new discipline which they have had to learn and adopt.

In addition, the relationship between the Prison Service and voluntary sector has become increasingly contract-based. Many voluntary sector agencies fear that 'contract culture' will distort the values and goals of voluntary agencies and change the nature of their contribution to welfare (Taylor, 1996, p.14). However, alien as it may be, voluntary sector agencies must learn to adapt to contract culture if they are to continue having a relationship with the Prison Service.

The view of the voluntary sector on these new approaches is mixed. Some claim that 'increased professionalism, greater formalisation of procedures and more complex lines of accountability have followed the introduction of contracts' (Billis and Harris, 1996, p.10). Others have concluded that 'the new management culture imported from the paid workplace is inappropriate and at odds with the culture and values of volunteering' (Dorris Smith, 1996, p.187). What is clear is that the Prison Service and the voluntary sector are entering into a new phase in their relationship, and one in which managerialism plays a major part.

MOVING FROM 'CO-OPERATION' TO 'PARTNERSHIP'

Various terms have been used in this book to describe the relationship between the Prison Service and voluntary sector including: toleration; co-operation; joint-working and partnership. These terms are used elsewhere to mean various things, in varying contexts. There has been little exploration of what these terms mean in relation to prisons and the organizations which work in them.

In order to consider various working relationships a framework has been developed. This framework, set out below, identifies the various types of relationship in the context of the level of information exchanged, objectives, activities and goal achievement. It identifies various levels of engagement on a continuum from level one (cooperation) to level three (partnership).

Levels of relationship between the Prison Service and voluntary sector

Level 1 : Cooperation	Level 2 : Joint working	Level 3: Partnership
Basic information is exchanged. Contact details, security clearance etc	Basic information is exchanged. Contact details, security clearance etc.	Basic information is exchanged. Contact details, security clearance etc.
Objectives of each agency are carried out but largely in isolation. Co-operation exists but only to the extent that it enables the work to take place.	Common objectives are shared but are pursued independently of each other with little thought of how agencies may 'add value' to each others work.	Common objectives are identified and common outcomes are agreed. Partnership is recognised as potentially adding value to each partner's activity.
Activity is seen as legitimate but peripheral to the 'real' business.	Activity is seen as legitimate and is incorporated into the prison but does not alter the practice of the prison.	The steps required to achieve the common outcomes are negotiated, defined and prioritised.
There is no common identification of users or incorporation of services into the structure of the prisons. Much is left to chance.	There is some exchange of insights and normally a sharing of outcomes but these are often achieved working in parallel rather than jointly. Lessons are learnt but on the whole do not inform future policy development because there is no comprehensive and inclusive policy review.	The tasks necessary to achieve the desired outcomes are shared. Resources are allocated according to the agreed tasks to be undertaken. Work is reviewed and new action is agreed. Results are shared nationally and locally and inform policy development. Evaluation and development ongoing.
Examples may be: A visitors' centre operating in isolation. It carries on its work of facilitating good visits but there is no discussion on how services can be jointly operated and developed and new objectives decided. An alcohol counselling service that does not share its knowledge of alcohol use within a prison, its causes and effects. Security departments that do not train and encourage service providers to consider the security aspects of their work.	Examples may be community-based education and training/pre-release courses. Shared objective in raising literacy and numeracy levels but the activities of the two agencies work around each other. Activities are not jointly managed and do not share common administrative procedures such as Sentence Planning.	Examples are hard to find—beginning to emerge in some multi-faith chaplaincy teams and young offender initiatives. The objectives are defined, appropriate partnerships developed and resourced. The partnership is evident at all stages of planning, delivery and review and evaluation.

The framework does not intend to suggest that all relationships should be at level three. It may be appropriate for some relationships only to develop to level one or two. This will depend on the organization, the services it provides and whether the Prison Service and voluntary sector want to enter into a partnership. That said, there is now wider acceptance, by politicians and professionals that the partnerships between the two sectors have an important role to play in the building of effective prison and resettlement strategies.

FUTURE PRIORITIES

While considerable progress has been made, partnership working is still in its infancy. The Prison Service Board recently adopted a Prison Service Voluntary and Community Sector Strategy and this is very welcome. This strategy seeks to establish, strengthen and develop the partnership between the Prison Service and the voluntary and community sector at national, regional and local level. However, like most strategies it will be most effective when the valuable and worthy principles it expounds are supported by adequate resources that will enable its implementation. Until then it remains a warm embrace but without any food on the table.

An insight into how partnerships between statutory and voluntary agencies could be developed is contained in *Active Partners* (Yorkshire and Humber RDA March, 2000). It lays out four dimensions, and benchmarks within each dimension. The four key dimensions that should be present in all partnerships are:

- the ability of partners to have influence over the area of engagement;
- the diverse and inclusive nature of the partnership where difference, in its many forms, is welcomed rather than seen as a threat;
- the ability of the partnership to enhance the capacity of partners to better fulfil their role within the future; and
- a clear and effective communication system that is jargon clear and responsive to different communication needs.

The map showing the road ahead is clear. An agreed strategy for joint-working between the Prison Service and voluntary sector, together with the resources necessary to implement it, are vital. What this book has demonstrated is that the relationship between the two sectors is part of a developing national mosaic, supported and promoted by government, involving hundreds of organizations and thousands of individuals working in a variety of fields. The voluntary sector is now less timid and self-effacing. It has increasing self-confidence in the expertise that it can bring for the benefit of prisoners, their families and the wider community. Joint and cooperative working with a Prison Service that does not just tolerate or humour the voluntary sector is to be welcomed. The current approach which actively encourages joint involvement in the achievement of the mutual aims of successful reintegration of prisoners into the community, and a reduction of re-offending, is now more of a reality than before. Both sectors have a responsibility to capitalise on this developing relationship, and must continue to respect differences in culture and operational aims and methods. It is appropriate to end this book with a quote from the Prison Service Corporate Plan for 2001-02 to 2003-04, which captures the thinking behind our desire to produce this book:

> The diversity and local focus of the voluntary and community based sector gives a dimension that the Prison Service itself finds hard to provide. It can be flexible in meeting particular local requirements. The Prison Service is keen to use the strengths which the sector can offer...
>
> Prison Service 2001, p14.

Appendix I: Directory of Voluntary Sector Organizations Working in the Penal Field

This is a list of some of the agencies that work with prisoners and their families. The headings indicate their main field of work. However many agencies work in different fields at any one time, and the sector is prone to rapid change. Contact the agency for more details.

General Support

1ST NIGHT IN CUSTODY PROJECT
HMP Holloway, Parkhurst Road, London N7 0NU
Tel: 020 607 6747 ex 2656

AGE CONCERN ENGLAND
Astral House, 1268 London Rd, London SW16 4ER Tel: 020 8765 7200

BLACK AND ASIAN COMMUNITY PROJECT
Centre 88, Saner Street, Anlaby Road, Hull HU3 2TR Tel: 01482 211252 Fax: 01482 211252
Email:lauriemhawkins@hotmail.com

BLACK PRISONER SUPPORT PROJECT
c/o POPS, Suite 4B, Bldg 1, Wilson Park, Monsall Road, Manchester M40 4WN
Tel: 0161 277 9066
Email: families@surfaid.org
Website: www.partnersofprisoners.co.uk

BLACK PRISONER SUPPORT PROJECT
3rd Floor, Epic House, Leicester LE1 3SH
Tel: 0116 2999 802 Fax: 0116 2999 801

COMEBACK
Ground floor, 84 Tooley Street, London Bridge, London SE1 2TF
Tel: 020 7234 1293 Fax: 020 7234 1279
Email:Comeback@netcom.co.uk

CONFEDERATION OF INDIAN ORGANIZATIONS
5 Westminster Bridge Road, London SE1 7XW
Tel: 020 7928 9889 Fax: 020 7620 4025
Email:cio@gn.apc.org

DEAF PRISON PROJECT
Birmingham Inst. For Deaf People, Ladywood Road, Birmingham B16 8SZ
Tel: 0121 246 6100 Fax: 0121 246 6125
Email: Heather@ctr.bid.org.uk

DONCASTER ASS CARE & RESETTLEMENT OF OFFENDERS
40 Netherhall Road, Doncaster DN1 2PZ
Tel: 01302 810666

HELP ASIAN PRISONERS GROUP
57 Trinity Road, London SW17

HIBISCUS
15 Great St Thomas Apostle, Mansion House, London EC4V 2BB
Tel: 020 7329 2384 Fax: 020 7329 2385

INDIA WELFARE SOCIETY
11 Middle Row, London W10 5AT

IQRA TRUST
24 Culcross Street, London W1Y 3HE
Tel: 020 7491 1572 Fax: 020 7493 7899

OUT-SIDE-IN
PO Box 119, Orpington, Kent BR6 9ZZ
Tel: 01689 835566 Fax: 01689 835566

PACER 50+
16 Gardner Court, 119 London Road, Luton LU1 3SJ Tel: 01582 451914

PAKISTANI RESOURCE CENTRE
1 Great Marlborough St, Manchester MI 5NJ
Tel: 0161 237 1125 Fax: 0161 237 9556

PRISONERS ABROAD
89-93 Fonthill Road, London N4 3JH
Tel: 020 7561 6820 Fax: 020 7561 6821
Email:info@prisonersabroad.org.uk

PROGRESS TRUST
3rd Floor, Barclay House, 35 Whitworth Street West, Manchester M1 5NG
Tel: 0161 906 0020 Fax: 0161 906 0021
Email: ruhena.begum@progresstrust.com

PROSTITUTE OUTREACH WORKERS
1st Floor, Forest Mills, Highhurst Street, Nottingham NG7 3JQ
Tel: 0115 924 9992 Fax: 0115 924 9993

ROYAL NATIONAL INSTITUTE FOR DEAF PEOPLE
19-23 Featherstone Street, London EC1Y 8SL
Tel: 0808 808 0123 Fax: 020 7296 8199
Email: helpline@rnid.org.uk
Website: www.rnid.org.uk

ROYAL NATIONAL INSTITUTE FOR THE BLIND (RNIB)
224 Great Portland Street, London W1N 6AA

SHANNON TRUST
Pinehurst Farm, Steep Road, Crowborough TN6 3RX

ST VINCENT DE PAUL SOCIETY
Westminster Central Council, 24 George Street, London W1H 5RB Tel: 0171 935 7625

TERRENCE HIGGINS TRUST
52-54 Gray's Inn Road, London WC1X 8JU
Tel: 020 7831 0330 Fax: 020 7242 0121

Directory of Voluntary Sector Organizations 175

TURNING POINT
Suite 305, New Loom House, 101 Backchurch Lane, London E1 1LU
Tel: 020 7702 2300 Fax: 020 7702 1456
Email: tpmail@turning-point.co.uk
Website: www.turning-point.co.uk

WOMEN IN PRISON
Unit 3B, Aberdeen Studios, 22 Highbury Grove, London N5 2EA
Tel: 020 7226 5879 Fax: 020 7354 8005
Email: admin@womeninprison.uk2.net Website: www.womeninprison.org.uk

Advice: Benefits, Financial, Legal, Rights

1990 TRUST
Suite 12, Winchester House, 9 Cranmer Rd, London SW9 6EJ
Tel: 020 7582 1990 Fax: 020 7735 9011

CHILDRENS SOCIETY NATIONAL REMAND REVIEW INITIATIVE
Suite 2A , The Whitehouse, 3A Chapel St, Stafford ST15 8DQ
Tel: 01785 250200 Fax: 01785 250300

FRIENDS OF FELTHAM
HMYOI Feltham, Belfont Rd, Feltham TW13 4ND
Tel: 020 8890 0061 ex 584 Fax: 020 8891 49656
Email: roma@hoop28.freeserve.co.uk

INQUEST
Alexandra National House, 330 Seven Sisters Road, London N4 2PJ
Tel: 020 8802 7430 Fax: 020 8802 7450
Email: inquest@inquest.freeserve.co.uk

LIBERTY
21 Tabard Street, London SEI 4LA
Tel: 020 7403 3888 Fax: 020 7407 5354

NATIONAL ASSOC. OF CITIZENS ADVICE BUREAUX
136-144 City Rd, London EC1V 2RL
Tel: 020 7549 0816
Email: Maroln.burgess@nacab.org.uk

PRISONERS ADVICE SERVICE
Unit 305, Hatton Square, 16 Baldwins Gardens, London EC1N 7RJ
Tel: 020 7405 8090 Fax: 020 7405 8045
Email: pas@tinyworld.co.uk

TOMORROW'S PEOPLE
70 Prince Street, Bristol BS1 4QD
Tel: 0117 925 8805 Fax: 0117 925 7699

VOICE FOR THE CHILD IN CARE
Unit 4, Pride Court, 80-82 White Lion Street, London N1 9PF
Tel: 020 7833 5792 Fax: 020 7833 8637

Education, Training, Arts

ANGLIA CARE TRUST
65 St Matthew's Street, Ipswich IP1 3EW
Tel: 01473 213140 Fax: 01473 219648
Email: admin@angliacaretrust.org.uk

BLACK ARTS ALLIANCE
PO Box 86, SDO, Manchester M21 7BA
Tel: 0161 832 7622 Fax: 0161 832 2276
Email: www.baas.demon.co.uk

BLAK (UK)
64 Douglas Road, Handsworth, Birmingham B12 9HH Tel: 0121 551 7577 Fax: 0121 551 7577
Email: blakuk@aol.com

BUSINESS IN PRISONS
HMP Sudbury, Ashbourne DE6 5HW
Tel: 01283 585511 ex 482

BWB TRAINING LTD
50 Ryde Avenue, Hull HU5 1QA
Tel: 01482 473377 Fax: 01482 470377

CENTRE FOR ADOLESCENT REHABILITATION (C-FAR)
Okehampton Camp, Okehampton, Devon EX20 1QP Tel: 01837 659556 Fax: 01837 659543
Email: info@c-far.org.uk Website: www.c-far.org.uk

CHANGING TUNES
Access House , The Promenade, Clifton Down, Bristol B58 3AQ Tel: 0117 933 1118 Fax: richard@pendleburyr.freeserve.co.uk

CLEAN BREAK THEATRE COMPANY
2 Patshull Road, London NW5 2LB
Tel: 020 7482 8600

CREATIVE AND SUPPORTIVE TRUST (CAST)
37 Kings Terrace, London NW1 0JR
Tel: 020 7383 5228 Fax: 020 7388 7252

CWM HARRY LAND TRUST
Lower Cwm Harry, Tregynon, Newtown, Powys SY16 3ES Tel:01686 650231 Fax:01686 650231
Email:cwmharrylandtrust@hotmail.com

EAST MIDLANDS OFFENDERS EMPLOYMENT CONSORTIUM
7 West End, Farndon, Newark NG24 3SG
Tel: 01636 679991 Fax: 01636 679991

ENGLISH SPEAKING BOARD
26a Princes St, Southport PR8 1EQ
Tel: 01483 562206 Fax: 01483 562206
Email: bb_singleton@hotmail.com Website: www.esbuk.demon.co.uk

ESCAPE ARTISTS THEATRE COMPANY
42 Woodlark Road, Cambridge CB3 OHS
Tel: 01223 301 439
Email: esc-arts@dircon.co.uk

176 Prisons and the Voluntary Sector

FINE CELL WORK
PO Box 30738, London WC1H ORL
Tel: 020 7278 3195
Email: enquiries@finecellwork.co.uk Website: www.finecellwork.co.uk

FOUNDATION TRAINING COMPANY
HMYOI Feltham, Bedfont Rd, Feltham TW13 4ND Tel: 020 8890 0061
Email: haqftc@yahoo.com Website: www.foundationtraining.co.uk

GEESE THEATRE COMPANY
Midlands Arts Centre, Cannon Hill Park, Birmingham B12 9QH
Tel: 0121 446 4370 Fax: 0121 446 5806
Email: mailbox@geese.co.uk Website: www.geese.co.uk

INSIDE ARTS TRUST
7-15 Greatorex Street, London E1 5NF
Tel: 020 7247 0778 Fax: 020 7247 8077

INSIDE OUT TRUST
55 High Street, Hurstpierpoint, West Sussex BN6 9PX Tel: 01273 833050 Fax: 01273 833744
Email: iotrust@pavilion.co.uk Website: www.inside-out.org.uk

IRENE TAYLOR TRUST
Unit 114 Bonmarche Centre, 241 - 251 Ferndale Rd, London SW9 8BJ
Tel: 020 7733 3222 Fax: 020 7733 3310
Email: musicinprisons@excite.co.uk

KOESTLER AWARD TRUST
9 Birchmead Ave, Pinner, Middx HA5 2BG
Tel: 020 8868 4044 Fax: 020 8422 5655

LABRISH
Three Mills Island Studios, Three Mills Lane, London E3 3DU
Tel: 020 8215 0144 Fax: 020 7363 0034

LIVIN THEATRE COMPANY
375B Ivydale Road, Nunhead, London SE15 3ED Tel: 020 7450 3315

LSW PRISON PROJECT
181a Faunce House, Doddington Grove, Kennington, London SE17 3TB
Tel: 0207 793 9755 Fax: 0207 735 5911
Email: londonswo@hotmail.com

PALS
5 Eldon Chambers, Wheeler Gate, Nottingham NG1 2NS Tel: 0115 947 0965 Fax: 0115 941 8265 Email: japiafi@nottm-di.freeserve.co.uk

POW TRUST
295A Queenstown Rd, London
Tel: 020 7720 9767 Fax: 020 7498 0477

POWER SCHEME
C/o Education Dept, HMP Leyhill, Wootton under Edge, Gloucs GL12 8BT
Tel: 01454 260681ext 414 Fax: 01454 261398

PRISM PROJECT
PO Box 6031, Bishop's Stortford, Herts CM23 1PP Tel: 01279 777007
Email: info@prismproject.org

PRISON ARTS FOUNDATION
51 Camden Street, Belfast BT9 6AT
Tel: 028 9024 7872
Email: paf@downunder.ticnet.net

PRISON WRITING
PO Box 478, Sheffield S3 8YX
Tel: 0114 272 6477 Fax: 0114 278 1892
Email: prisonwriting@aol.com

PRISONERS EDUCATION TRUST
Suite 39, Argyll House, 1A All Saints Passage, London SW18 1EP
Tel: 020 8870 3820 Fax: 020 8875 1076
Email: info@prisonerseducation.org.uk

PRISONS VIDEO MAGAZINE
P.V.M. Studios, 7 Anglers Lane, London NW5 3DG Tel: 020 7916 7707 Fax: 020 7916 7488

RUSSELL STREET PROJECT
Russell Street, Keighley, West Yorkshire BD21 2JP Tel: 01535 692050 Fax: 01535 692051

SAFEGROUND
PO Box 11525, London SW11 5ZV
Email: safe_ground_productions@compuserve.com

SOFT TOUCH COMMUNITY ARTS
120a Hartopp Road, Leicester LE2 1WF
Tel: 0116 270 2706 Fax: 0116 270 2706
Email: info@soft-touch.org.uk Website: www.soft-touch.org.uk

SOVA
Chichester House, 37 Brixton Road, London SW9 6D2
Tel: 020 7735 0404 Fax: 020 7735 4410

T.O.P.S (THE OLD POTTING SHED)
132A Station Road, Wigston, Leicester LE18 2DL

THE COMEDY SCHOOL
Three Mills Island Studio, Three Mills Lane, London E3 3DU
Tel: 020 8215 0144 Fax: 020 7363 0034

THE PRINCE'S TRUST
18 Park Square East, London NN1 4LH
Tel: 020 7543 7314 Fax: 020 7543 7421
Email: stefanna@princes-trust.org.uk Website: www.princes-trust.org.uk

THE SOBRIETY PROJECT
The Waterways Museum, Dutch River Side, Goole, E Yorks DN14 5TB
Tel: 01405 768730 Fax: 01405 769868
Email: waterwaysmuseum@btinternet.com

Directory of Voluntary Sector Organizations 177

THEATRE IN PRISON & PROBATION CENTRE (TIPP)
c/o Drama Department, Manchester University, Oxford Road, Manchester M13 9PL
Tel: 0161 275 3047 Fax: 0161 275 3877
Email: tipp@man.ac.uk

UNIT FOR ARTS & OFFENDERS
Neville House, 90/91 Northgate, Canterbury CT1 1BA
Tel: 01227 470629 Fax: 01227 453022
Email: info@a4offenders.org.uk
Website: www.a4offenders.org.uk

VOLUNTARY ARTS NETWORK
PO Box 200, Cardiff CF5 1YH
Tel: 029 2039 5395
Email:info@voluntaryarts.org.

WRITERS IN PRISONS NETWORK
17 Upper Lloyd Street, Manchester M14 4HY
Tel: 0161 226 3419 Fax: 0161 226 3419
Email: chopwood98@aol.com

YMCA: PARTNERSHIP IN PRISONS
YMCA Training, 55 High Street, Banbury OX16 5JJ Tel: 01295 252082 Fax: 01295 250013

Substance Misuse, Addiction

ACORN DRUG & ALCOHOL SERVICES
Frith Cottage, Church Road, Frimley GU16 5AD

ADDACTION
67-69 Cowcross Street, London EC1M 6BP

ALCOHOL ADVICE CENTRE
76 High Street, Watford WD1 2BP
Tel: 01923 221037 Fax: 01923 224747

ALCOHOL CONCERN
Waterbridge House, 32-36 Loman Street, London SE1 0EE

ALCOHOLICS ANONYMOUS
PO Box 1 Stonebow House, Stonebow, York YO1 2NJ Helpline: 0845 7697 555 Tel: 01904 644026 Fax: 01904 629091
Website: www.alcoholic-anonymous.org

BARNABUS DRUGS CENTRE
118A Mill St, Macclesfield, Cheshire SK11 6NR
Tel: 01625 422100 Fax: 01625 422100

BOLTON ETHNIC MINORITY SUBSTANCE MISUSE INITIATIVE
8 White Lion Brow, Bolton BL1 4AD
Tel: 01204 366388 Fax: 01204 382448

CRANSTOUN DRUG SERVICES
4th Floor, Broadway House, Broadway, London SW19 1RL
Tel: 020 8543 8333 Fax: 020 8543 4348

DRUGSCOPE
Waterbridge House, 32-36 Loman Street, London SE1 OEE
Tel: 020 7928 1211 Fax: 020 7928 1771

EXETER DRUGS PROJECT
Dean Clarke House, Southerhay East, Exeter EX1 1PQ
Tel: 01392 666710 Fax: 01392 499248
Website: www.eastDevon.net/edp

FAMILIES ANONYMOUS
DRCA Business Centre, Charlotte Despard Ave, London SW11 5JE
Tel: 020 7498 4680 Fax: 0207 498 1990
Email: office@famanon.org.uk Website: www.famanon.org.uk

GAMBLERS ANONYMOUS
19 Philippa Gardens, London SE9 6AP
Tel: 020 8265 3622

GAMCARE
Suite 1, Catherine House, 25-27 Catherine Place, London SW1E 6DU
Tel: 020 7233 8988 Fax: 020 7233 8977
Email: michael@gamcare.org.uk

MAINLINERS
38-40 Kennington Park Road, London SE1 4RS
Tel: 020 7582 5434

NARCOTICS ANONYMOUS
25 Somers Road, London SW2 2AF
Tel: 020 8355 0221

PHOENIX HOUSE
Asra house, 1 Long Lane, London
Tel: 020 7407 2789
Email:Info@phoenixhouse.org.uk

RAPt
Riverside House, 27-29 Vauxhall Grove, London SW8 1SY
Tel: 020 7582 4677 Fax: 020 7820 3716
Email: info@rapt.org.uk

SAFE COMMUNITY DRUGS AGENCY
132 Wandsworth High St, London SW18 4JP

SCOTTSWOOD WOMENS DRUG SOCIETY SUPPORT GROUP
221 Wood Stock Road, Scotswood, Newcastle upon Tyne NE15 6HE Tel: 0191 228 0642
Email: scotswood.drugs.group@talk21.com

SUBSTANCE ADVICE AND REFERRAL UNIT
Compass, 12 King Street, York YO1 9WP
Tel: 01904 632495 Fax: 01904 632490

YELDELL BRIDGES
20A Bridge Road, Towb Mills House, Andover, Hants SP10 1BL
Tel: 01264 338999 Fax: 01264 335105

Befriending, Counselling, Mediation

BEFRIENDERS INTERNATIONAL
26-27 Market Place, Kingston upon Thames KT1 1JH Tel: 020 8541 4949

CHILDLINE
Royal Mail Building, 50 Studd St, London N1 0QP
Helpline: 0800 1111 (for children living away from home) Tel: 020 7239 1000 Fax: 020 7239 1001 Website: www.childline.org.uk

COMMUNITY SERVICE VOLUNTEERS (CSV)
237 Pentonville Road, London N1 9NJ
Tel: 020 7278 6601 ex 1399 Fax: 020 7837 9318

CRUSE BEREAVEMENT CARE
126 Sheen Road, Richmond TW9 1UR
Tel: 020 8940 4818 Fax: 020 8940 7638

DEPAUL TRUST
1 St. Vincent Street, London W1M 3HD
Tel: 020 7935 0111 Fax: 020 7935 6561

DORCAS PROJECT
Furnace Bank, Great Gate, Stoke-on-Trent ST10 4HE Tel: 01889 507552 Fax: 01889 507394

IRISH COMMISSION FOR PRISONERS OVERSEAS
50-52 Camden Square, London NW1 9XB
Tel: 020 7482 4148 Fax: 020 7872 3343

LONDON MARRIAGE GUIDANCE
76a New Cavendish Street, London W1M 7LB
Tel: 020 7580 1087 Fax: 020 7637 4546

MEDIATION UK
Alexander House, Telephone Avenue, Bristol BS1 4BS
Tel: 0117 904 6661 Fax: 0117 904 3331
Email: mediationuk@cix.co.uk Website: www.cix.co.uk/-mediationuk

NATIONAL ASSOCIATION OF PRISON VISITORS
29 Kimbolton Road, Bedford MK40 2PB
Tel:01234 359763 Fax: 01234 359763

NEW BRIDGE
27A Medway Street, London SW1P 2BD
Tel: 020 7976 0779 Fax: 020 7976 0767
Email:pa.new.bridge@ukgateway.net

OPEN DOOR
24-28 Orsett Road, Grays, Essex RM17 5EB
Tel:01375 396038

OUTSIDE HELP
43 The Avenue, Lewes BN7 1QT
Tel 01273 473796

PRISON DIALOGUE
PO Box 44, Chipping Campden, Glos GL55 6YN

Tel: 01386 849186 Fax: 01386 840449
Email: PD@prisondialogue.org.uk Website: www.prisodialogue.org

PRISON LINK
29 Trinity Road, Birmingham B6 6AJ
Tel: 0121 551 1207 Fax: 0121 554 4894

PRISONERS' PENFRIENDS
Max Findlay Associates, The Business Village, Broomhill Road, London SW18 4JQ
Tel: 020 8871 5192 Fax: 020 8877 1940
Email: Gwynmorgan@maxfindlay.com

RELATE
Central Office, Hurbert Gray College, Little Church St, Rugby CV21 3AP
Tel: 01788 573 241

REMEDI
PO Box 1420, Thorne, Doncaster DN5 8XU
Tel: 01405 818866 Fax: 01405 818866
Email: doncaster@remedi.freeserve.co.uk
Website: www.remedi.cjb.net

SALVATION ARMY
101 Newington Causeway, London SE1 6BN
Tel: 020 7367 4849 Fax: 020 7367 4712
Email: thq@salvationarmy.org.uk Website: www.salvationarmy.org.uk

SAMARITANS
10 The Grove, Slough SL1 1QP
Helpline: 08457 909090 Tel: 020 8394 8300
Email: admin@samaritans.org.uk Website: www.samaritans.org

SOUTH YORKS VICTIM OFFENDER MEDIATION SERVICE
PO Box 441, Doncaster DN2 6RE
Tel: 01302 366693

THE DOOR U. K
PO Box 707, Southampton S018 2LY
Tel: 023 8063 3500 Fax: 023 8063 3500

TRAILBLAZERS MENTORING PROGRAMME
HMYOI Feltham, Bedfont Road, Feltham TW13 4ND Tel: 020 8890 0061 ex206
Email: mentoring@felthamtrailblazers.org.uk
Website: www.trail-blazers.org.uk

XMAS LETTERS TO PRISONERS
52a Whitehorse Lane, London SE25 6RE

YOUTH MENTORING SERVICE
27 Weston Road, Handsworth, Birmingham B19 1EH Tel: 0121 250 5141 Fax: 0121 250 5191

Resettlement

ADULLAM HOMES HOUSING ASSC
Pool House, Aaran Close, Great Barr
Birmingham, B43 7AD
Tel: 0121 358 3818 Fax: 0121 358 6188
info@adullam.org.uk Website: www.adullam.org.uk

Directory of Voluntary Sector Organizations 179

APEX CHARITABLE TRUST
St Alphage House, Wingate Annex, 2 Fore St,
London EC2Y 5DA
Tel: 020 7638 5931 Fax: 020 7638 5977
apextrust@charity.vfree.com Website:
www.apextrust.com

CLACC
PO Box 1269, Bristol BS99 2YD
Tel: 0117 946 6988 Fax: 0117 946 6754
Email: enquire@clacc.demon.co.uk

COMMUNITY LINKS FOR EX-OFFENDERS (CLEO)
The Gatehouse Centre, Harecliffe Road, Bristol,
Avon BS13 9JN
Tel: 0117 9020340 Fax: 0117 9020340
Email: cleo.project@virgin.net

EXTERN NORTHERN IRELAND
Graham House, 1 - 5 Albert Square, Belfast BT1 3EQ Tel: 028 9024 0900 Fax: 028 9033 1498

FOUNDATION HOUSING ASSOCIATION
8 Faraday Court, 40 Condort St, Leicester,
Leicestershire LE2 0JN Tel: 0116 254 4230

HUMBERCARE
81 Beverley Road, Hull HU3 1XR
Tel: 01482 586633 Fax: 01482 586825
janeanne.tribe@totalise.co.uk

LANGLEY HOUSE TRUST
PO Box 181, Witney, Oxon OX28 6WD
Tel: 01993 774075 Fax: 01993 772425
info@langleyhousetrust.co.uk Website:
www.langleyhousetrust.co.uk

LOOK AHEAD HOUSING & CARE LTD
1 Derry St, London W8 5HY
Tel: 020 8689 9559 Fax: 020 8665 9958

MATTHEW PROJECT
24 Potter Gate, Norwich NR2 1DX
Tel: 01603 626123

NACRO
169 Clapham Road, London SW9 0PU
Helpline: 0800 0181 259 Tel: 020 7582 6500
Fax: 020 7735 4666
Email: helpline@nacro.org.uk Website:
www.nacro.org.uk

NACRO WOMEN PRISONERS' RESOURCE CENTRE
169 Clapham Road, London SW9 0PU
Tel: 020 7840 6464 Fax: 020 7735 4366

NIACRO
169 Ormeau Road, Belfast BT7 1SQ
Tel: 01232 320157 Fax: 01232 234084

NORMAN HOUSE TRUST
134 Upperthorpe, Sheffield S6 3NF
Tel: 0114 2344038 Fax: 0114 2344038

PENROSE HOUSING ASSOCIATION
356 Holloway Road, London N7 6PA
Tel: 020 7700 0100 Fax: 020 7700 8133

RICHMOND FELLOWSHIP
80 Holloway Road, London N7 8JG
Tel: 020 7697 3300 Fax: 020 7697 3301
Email: clair.cameron@richmondfellowship.org.uk
Website: www.richmondfellowship.org.uk

RPS RAINER
Rectory Lodge, High St, Brasted, Westerham
TN16 1JE

SACRO
1 Broughton Market, Edinburgh EH3 6NU
Tel: 0131 624 7270

Shelter
3rd Floor, Ludgate Chambers, Ludgate Hill,
Leeds LS2 7HZ

ST GILES TRUST
64-68 Camberwell Church Street, London SE5
8JB Tel: 020 8874 7292 Fax: 020 8875 1648

STONEHAM HOUSING ASSOCIATION
235-241 Union Street, London SE1 0LR

THE STEPPING STONES TRUST
PO Box 344, Richmond, Surrey TW9 1GQ
Tel: 020 8287 5524 Fax: 020 8287 5524
Email: stepsto@aol.com

TRAILBLAZERS MENTORING PROGRAMME
HMYOI Feltham, Bedfont Road, Feltham TW13
4ND Tel: 020 8890 0061 ex206
Email: mentoring@felthamtrailblazers.org.uk
Website: www.trail-blazers.org.uk

WOMEN IN PRISON
Unit 3B, Aberdeen Studios, 22 Highbury Grove,
London N5 2EA
Tel: 020 7226 5879 Fax: 020 7354 8005
Email: admin@womeninprison.uk2.net Website:
www.womeninprison.org.uk

YORKSHIRE ASSOCIATION FOR THE CARE AND RESETTLEMENT OF OFFENDERS
101 Robinson Court, Walmgate, York YO1 9TR
Tel: 01904 642307 Fax: 01904 672947

Health

MIND
Grant House, 15-19 Broadway, Stratford, London
E15 4BQ

POSITIVELY IN PRISON
PO Box 6094, London SW1W 8SN
Tel: 020 7823 5472

POSITIVELY WOMEN
347 -349 City Road, London EC1 1LR

REVOLVING DOORS AGENCY
45-49 Leather Lane, London ECIN 7TJ
Tel: 020 7242 9222 Fax: 020 7831 5140
Email: admin@revolving-doors.co.uk Website:
www.revolving-doors.co.uk

SANELINE
1st Floor, Cityside House, 40 Adler Street,
London E1 1EE
Helpline: 0845 678000 Tel: 020 7375 1002 Fax:
020 7375 2612
Email: sane@saneline.org.uk Website:
www.mkn.co.uk/help/charity/sane

SCHIZOPHRENIA ASSOCIATION OF GREAT BRITAIN
Bryn Hyfryd, The Crescent, Bangor LL57 2AG
Tel: 01248 354048 Fax: 01248 354048
Email: sagb@btinternet.com Website:
www.btinternet.com/-sagb

SIRI BEHAVIOURAL HEALTH
13 Wembley Hill Road, Wembley HA9 8AF
Tel: 020 8795 3770 Fax: 020 8795 3775
Email: tony_siri@compuserve.com

THRESHOLD NATIONAL WOMEN AND MENTAL HEALTH INFOLINE
14 St George's Place, Brighton BN1 4GB
Helpline: 0845 3000911 Fax: 01273 626 444
Email: thrwomen@globalnet.co.uk Website:
www.thresholdwomen.org.uk

WISH: WOMEN IN SECURE HOSPITALS
15 Great St Thomas Apostle, London EC4V 2BB
Tel: 020 7329 2415 Fax: 020 7329 2416
Email: wish@wishlondon.freeserve.co.uk

Personal Development

ALTERNATIVES TO VIOLENCE PROJECT
Old Painswick Inn, Gloucester Street, Stroud
GL5 1QG
Tel: 01453 756751 Fax: 01453 767823
Email: avpbritain@waitrose.com

BRAHMA KUMARIS
Global Co-operation House, 65 Pound Lane,
London NW10
Tel: 020 7727 3350 Fax: 020 7727 6480
Email: bk@bkwsugrc.demon.co.uk Website:
www.bkwsu.com

CRIMINON UK
PO Box 200, East Grinstead RH19 4AR
Tel: 01342 324181 Fax: 01342 326948
Email: suechalm@hotmail.com Website: www.criminon.org

PRISON PHOENIX TRUST
PO Box 328, Oxford OX1 1PJ
Tel: 01865 798647 Fax: 01865 248098

Spiritual Guidance

12 TRIBES OF ISRAEL
107 Norton St, Old Trafford, Manchester M16
Tel: 0976 794321

ALPHA IN PRISONS
Holy Trinity Brompton, Brompton Road, London
SW7 1JA
Tel: 020 7590 8258 Fax: 020 7584 8536
Email: prisons@htb.org.uk Website:
www.alphacourse.org

BUDDHIST PRISON CHAPLAINCY ORGANIZATION
The Forest Hermitage, Lower Fulbrook CV35 8AS

CHAPLAIN FOR THE DEAF
3 Hawthorn Rd, Cherry Willingham, Lincoln LN3 4JU

DAVID STILLMAN EVANGELIST ASSOCIATION
PO Box 102, Reading RG30 3NP
Tel: 0118 983 2221
Email: davidstillman@breathemail.net

HAILE SELASSIE I PEACE FOUNDATION
10 Holyhead Rd, Birmingham B21 0LT
Tel: 0121 551 6709

ISKCON PRISON MINISTRY
Bhaktivedanta Manor, Letchmore Heath,
Watford, Herts WD2 8EP

ISLAMIC CULTURAL CENTRE
146 Park Road, London NW8 7RG
Tel: 020 7724 3363 Fax: 020 7724 0493

JEWISH VISITATION COMMITTEE
735 High Road, London N12 0US

METHODIST CHURCH PRISON MINISTRY
Methodist Chaplain, Methodist Church House, 25
Marylebone Road, London NW1 5JR
Tel: 0207 467 5248 Fax: 0207 467 5282

NEW TESTAMENT CHURCH OF GOD
Main House, Overston Park, London N6 6A
Tel: 07930 142470

PRISON FELLOWSHIP ENGLAND AND WALES
PO Box 945, Maldon, Essex
Tel: 01621 843232 Fax: 01621 843303
Email: fi34@dial.pipex.com

QUAKER PRISON MINISTERS
Friends House, 173 Euston Road, London NW1
2BJ Tel: 020 7663 1000 Fax: 020 7663 1001

RASTAFARIAN ADVISORY CENTRE
17A Netherwood Road, London W14

SIKH PRISON CHAPLAINCY SOCIETY
PO Box 239, Southall, Middlesex UB2 2DR

Directory of Voluntary Sector Organizations **181**

YOUTH AT RISK
The Impact Centre, 12-18 Hoxton Street, London N1 6NG Tel: 020 7920 7600 Fax: 020 7920 7649
Email:info@youthatrisk.org.uk

YOUTH WITH A MISSION
Highfield Oval, Harpenden, Herts AL5 4BX
Tel: 020 7720 3489
Email:bshermo@compuserve.com

Immigration

ASSC OF VISITORS TO IMMIGRATION DETAINEES
PO Box 7, Oxted RH8 0YT
Tel: 01883 712713 Fax: 01883 712713
Email: ireland@hj44.freeserve.co.uk Website: www.aviddetention.org.uk

DETENTION ADVICE SERVICE
308 Seven Sisters Road, London N4 2AG
Tel: 020 8802 0684 Fax: 020 8802 0684

JOINT COUNCIL FOR THE WELFARE OF IMMIGRANTS
115 Old Street, London EC1V 9JT

REFUGEES ARRIVAL PROJECT
Room 2005, 2nd floor, Queens Buildings, Heathrow Airport, Hounslow TW6 1DL

U K IMMIGRANTS ADVISORY SERVICE
67-71 Grove Road, Hounslow, Middx TW3 3PR

Specialist Support

AFTER ADOPTION
12 – 14 Chapel Street, Manchester M7 3NN
Tel: 0161 827 7804 or 0161 839 4930 Fax: 0161 832 2242 Email: aadoption@aol.com

DYSLEXIA INSTITUTE
133 Gresham Road, Staines TW18 2AJ

Family Support

ADFAM NATIONAL
Waterbridge House, 32-36 Loman St, London SE1 0EE Helpline: 020 7928 8900 Tel: 020 7928 8898 Fax: 020 7928 8923

AFTERMATH
PO Box 414, Sheffield S4 7RT
Tel: 0114 275 8520 Fax: 0114 275 8520
Website: www.soft.net.uk/turner/aftermath

CALDERDALE & KIRKLEES PARENTS & RELATIVES SUPPORT GROUP
10 Thornhill Bridge Lane, Brighouse HD6 4AW
Tel: 01484 722223

CHILDLINE
Royal Mail Building, 50 Studd St, London N1 0QP Helpline: 0800 1111 (for children living away from home)
Tel: 020 7239 1000 Fax: 020 7239 1001
Website: www.childline.org.uk

CONTACT
The Council House, Northwich, Cheshire CW9 5PD Tel: 01606 47107 Fax: 01606 350616

FAMILY SERVICE UNITS
207 Old Marylebone Road, London NW1 5QP
Tel: 020 7402 5175 Fax: 020 7724 1829

FAMILY SUPPORT NETWORK
8 Johnson Terrace, Edinburgh EH1 2PW
Tel: 0131 225 8500

FAMILYTIME: MILTON KEYNES PRISONER FAMILIES SUPPORT GROUP
City Counselling Centre, 320 Saxon Gate West, Milton Keynes
Helpline: 01908 309632

FEDERATION OF PRISONER'S FAMILY SUPPORT GROUPS
Cambridge House, Cambridge Grove, London W6 0LE
Tel: 020 8741 4578 Fax: 020 8748 5867
Email: info@fpfsg.demon.co.uk Website: www.fpfsg.org.uk

GASPED
5a Cheapside, Wakefield WFI 2SD
Tel: 01924 787501 Fax: 01924 787502
Email: Gasped@wkfdresourcecentre.fsnet.co.uk

HARP
51 Cambridge Road, Milton, Cambridge CB4 6AW
Helpline: 01223 425604 Tel: 01223 426148 Fax: 01223 425604
Website: www.harpinfo.org.uk

HOME-START
2 Salisbury Road, Leicester LE1 7QR
Tel: 0116 233 9955 Fax: 0116 233 0232
Email: Info@home-start.org.uk

HOPE PRISONERS FAMILY SUPPORT GROUP
The Hope Visitors' Centre, HMP Perth, 3 Edinburgh Road, Perth PH2 8AS

KIDS V.I.P
Old Dairy Cottage, Andover Road, Winchester S022 6AZ
Tel: 01962 889370 Fax: 01962 889370
Email: kidsvip@mcmail.com

MOTHERS' UNION
Mary Sumner House, 24 Tufton Street, London SWIP 3RB
Tel: 020 7222 5533 Fax: 020 7222 1591
Email: mu@themothersunion.org

NEPACS
22 Old Elvet, Durham DH1 3HW
Tel: 0191 382 2110

NSPCC
Western House, 42 Curtain Rd, London EC2A 3NH Tel: 020 7825 2500 Fax: 020 7825 2525
Email: infounit@nspcc.org.uk Website: www.nspcc.org.uk

ORMISTON CHILDREN & FAMILIES TRUST
333 Felixstowe Rd, Ipswich IP3 9BU
Tel: 01473 724517 Fax: 01473 724517

PARTNERS OF PRISONERS AND FAMILIES SUPPORT GROUP
Suite 4B, Bldg 1, Wilson Park, Monsall Road, Manchester M40 4WN
Tel: 0161 277 9066 Fax: 0161 277 9066
Email: families@surfaid.org Website: www.partnersofprisoners.co.uk

PRISON ADVICE AND CARE TRUST (PACT)
Lincoln House, I-3 Brixton Road, London SW9 6DE Helpline: 0800 085 3021 Tel: 020 7582 1313 Fax: 020 7735 6077
Email: info@pact.org.uk Website: www.imprisonment.org.uk

PRISONERS' FAMILIES AND FRIENDS SERVICE
20 Trinity Street, London SE1 1DB
Helpline: 0800 808 3444 Tel: 020 7403 4091
Fax: 020 7357 9722
Email: pffs@btclick.com
Website: www.home.btclick.com

SCOTTISH FORUM ON PRISONS AND FAMILIES
1st Floor, 17 Waterloo Place, Edinburgh EH1 3BJ Helpline: 0500 839383 Tel: 0131 557 9800 Fax: 0131 557 9812

SINGLE PARENT ACTION NETWORK UK
Millpond, Baptist St, Bristol BS5 0YW
Tel: 0117 951 4231

SOFA (SERIOUS OFFENDERS FAMILIES ASSOC)
2 The Chestnuts, Ella Street, Hull HU5 3AR

THE HUMBER PRE-SCHOOL LEARNING ALLIANCE
C/o Centre 88, Saner Street, Hull HU3 2TR
Tel: 01482 229859 Fax: 01482 329472
Email: tobystewart@thehumberpla.freeserve.co.uk

ULSTER QUAKER SERVICE COMMITTEE
541 Lisburn Road, Belfast BT9 7GQ
Tel: 028 9020 1444 Fax: 028 9020 1881
Email: uqsc@btinternet.com

WOMEN'S ROYAL VOLUNTARY SERVICE
44 Albany St, Edinburgh EH1 3QR
Tel: 0131 558 8028 Fax: 0131 558 8014

WOMEN'S ROYAL VOLUNTARY SERVICE
Milton Hill House, Milton Hill, Abingdon, Oxford OX13 6AF
Tel: 01235 442914 Fax: 01235 861166
Email: info@wrvs.org.uk

Campaigning

ACTION AGAINST INJUSTICE
PO Box 858, London E9 5HU

HOWARD LEAGUE FOR PENAL REFORM
1 Ardleigh Road, London NI 4HS
Tel: 020 7249 7373 Fax: 020 7249 7788
Email: howard.league@ukonline.co.uk Website: www.web.ukonline.co.uk/howard.league

INNOCENT
1 Kingsway, Middleton, Manchester M24 1LR
Tel: 0161 643 4194
Email: Innocent@mail.uk2.net

JUSTICE
59 Carter Lane, London EC4V 5AQ

JUSTICE FOR WOMEN
55 Rothcoole Gardens, London N8 9NE
Tel: 020 8374 2948 Fax: 020 8374 2948
Email: jfw@sprynet.co.uk

PENAL AFFAIRS CONSORTIUM
C/o Law Dept, Room 1024a University of East London, Longbridge Rd, Dagenham SW9 OPU
Tel: 020 8223 2902 Fax: 01621 969219
Email: plkiff@aol.com

PRISON REFORM TRUST
15 Northburgh Street, London EC1V OJR
Tel: 020 7251 5070 Fax: 020 7251 5076
Email: Prt@prisonreform.demon.co.uk

SUZY LAMPLUGH TRUST
14 East Sheen Avenue, London SW14 8AS

UNLOCK (NATIONAL ASSOCIATION OF EX-OFFENDERS)
Tel: 01925 721021 Fax: 01925 721021
35A High Street, Snodlands, Kent ME6 5AG
Tel: 01634 247350
Email: unlock@tphbook.dircon.co.uk

Relevant National Organizations

ACTIVE COMMUNITY UNIT
Room 259, 50 Queen Annes Gate, London SW1H 9AT
Tel: 020 7217 8632 Fax: 020 7217 8500

BOARD OF SOCIAL RESPONSIBILITY (C of E)
Church House, Great Smith St, London SW1P 3NZ Tel: 020 7898 1531/1537 Fax: 020 7898 1536 Email: Peter.sedgwick@c-of-e.org.uk

Directory of Voluntary Sector Organizations 183

BOARD OF VISITORS SECRETARIATS
HM Prison Service, 3rd Floor Horseferry House, Dean Ryle Street, London SW1P 2AN
Tel: 020 7217 8407 Fax: 020 7217 8596

CATHOLIC ASSC FOR RACIAL JUSTICE
9 Henry Road, London N4 2LH
Tel: 020 8802 8080 Fax: 020 8211 0808
Email: info@carj.freeserve.co.uk

CHURCH OF ENGLAND BOARD OF SOCIAL RESPONSIBILITY
Church House, Great Smith St, London SW1P 3NZ Tel: 020 7898 1531 Fax: 020 7898 1536

CLINKS
15 Priory Street, York YO1 6ET
Tel: 01904 673970 Fax: 01904 613756
Email: CLINKS@yorks.globalnet.co.uk

COMMISSION FOR RACIAL EQUALITY
Elliot House, 10/12 Allington Street, London SW1E 5EH

ISLAMOPHOBIA COMMISSION
CRE, 10-12 Allington St, London SW1
Tel: 0207 794 7301

NATIONAL ASSOCIATION OF VOLUNTEER BUREAUX
New Oxford House, 16 Waterloo Street, Birmingham B2 5UG

NATIONAL BOARD OF CATHOLIC WOMEN
38 Winton Ave, London N11 2AT

NATIONAL BODY OF BLACK PRISONERS SUPPORT GROUPS
c/o POPS, Suite 4B, Bldg 1, Wilson Park, Monsall Road, Manchester M40 4WN
Tel: 0161 277 9066
Email: families@surfaid.org

NATIONAL CENTRE FOR VOLUNTEERING
Regent's Wharf, 8 All Saint's Street, London N1 9RL.
Tel: 020 7520 8900 Fax:
Email: www.volunteering.org.uk

NATIONAL CHILDREN'S CENTRE
Brian Jackson House, New North Parade, Huddersfield HD1 5JP
Tel: 01481 519988 Fax: 01484 435150

NCVO
Regent's Wharf, 8 All Saints St, London N1 9RL
Tel: 020 7713 6161020 7520 2540 Fax: 020 7520 2587 Email: Jane.Hatfield@ncvo-vol.org.uk

PRISON GOVERNOR'S ASSOCIATION
409 Horseferry Hse, Dean Ryle Street, London SW1P 2AW

PRISON OFFICERS' ASSOCIATION
245 Church St, London N9 9HW

RESTORATIVE PRISON PROJECT
Dunelm, 3 Church Lane, Shepley, Huddersfield HD8 8AF

THE BUTLER TRUST
Howard House, 32-34 High St, Croydon CR0 1YB Tel: 020 8688 6062 Fax: 020 8688 6056
Email: bt@thebutlertrust.demon.co.uk

THRIVE
The Geoffrey Udall Centre, Beech Hill, Reading, Berks RG12 7NF
Tel: 0118 988 5688
Email: neilk@thrive.org.uk

UNITARIAN PENAL AFFAIRS PANEL
6 Saxon Ave, Crumpsall, Manchester M8 4QH
Tel: 0161 740 0778

Compiled by CLINKS (2002). **Disclaimer:** Considerable effort has been made to make the list accurate and neither CLINKS nor the publishers of *Prisons and the Voluntary Sector* can accept responsibility for the consequences of any inaccuracies. Inclusion in this list does not represent a statement of quality or other guarantee with respect to organizations listed. Readers should always make their own inquiries concerning up-to-date information and exercise their own judgement in relation to organizations.

Appendix II: Charitable Trusts Working in the Penal Affairs Field and Crime Prevention

Allen Lane Foundation
AW.60 Charitable Trust
Beatrice Laing Trust
The Bromley Trust
Noel Buxton Trust
W.A.Cadbury Charitable Trust
Sir John Cass's Foundation
The Church Urban Fund
Esmee Fairbairn Charitable Trust
Paul Hamlyn Foundation
The Hayward Foundation
Hilden Charitable Fund
J Paul Getty Jr Charitable
Irish Youth Foundation Ltd
The Lankelly Foundation
The Leigh Trust
Lloyds TSB Foundation
Lyndhurst Settlement
The Mental Health Foundation
The Monument Trust
The Northmoor Trust
The Oakdale Trust
The Pilgrim Trust
St James' Trust Settlement
Sir Halley Stewart Trust
Swan Mountain Trust
Sir Jules Thorn Charitable Trust
The Tudor Trust
The Garfield Weston Foundation
Weavers Company Benevolent Fund
The Wates Foundation
Zochonis Charitable Trust

This list is not exhaustive. Further details can be found in *A Guide to the Major Trusts, Volume 1* (largest 300 trusts, ISBN 1 900360 38 1) and *Volume 2* (a further 700 trusts, ISBN 1 900360 13 6), published by the Directory of Social Change, 24 Stephenson Way, London NW 1 2DP. Tel: 0171 209 5151. Fax: 0171 209 5049.

Appendix III: The Laming Report

SECTION FIVE - THE ROLE OF THE COMMUNITY

1. Organizations based outside prisons, in the community, have long had a role in providing services to prisoners. Over the past twenty years prisons have become increasingly receptive to community-based agencies and the range and scope of organizations involved and services provided is very impressive. They are important because they provide prisoners with access to services they may be able to continue to use after their release, and because they offer contact with the outside world.

2. Community based organizations working in prisons vary from large-scale bodies employing only paid staff and working under contract in a number of prisons, to smaller agencies using a combination of paid staff and volunteers or, in some cases, volunteers alone. Some are funded entirely by the prison (such as many drug service providers and education contractors), other rely on a mix of funding or have the support of a funder outside the prison. Some are charities or not-for-profit organizations; others operate within the private structure.

3. Community based organizations offer an important resource to prisons, but one that is not efficiently used at present. Many prisons have no centralised information about which agencies are active in the prison, let alone what they do and how. Every prison should be able to provide detailed information about which agencies are actively involved with prisoners, what sort of work they undertake and how it sits with work undertaken by the prison itself and with other community agencies. We recommend that a named member of staff - either employed specifically for the purpose from a community agency background or a member of prison staff with facility time to undertake the task – is given the job of acting as the main point of contact for community agencies. This task would involve finding suitable agencies to work in the prison and providing for the identified needs of prisoners. This individual would also have responsibility for the reporting and review of agencies' work and would be directly accountable to a governor – possibly the Head of Prisoner Activities in a large prison or the Governor in a small one.

4. Unless community based organizations are involved in contracts with prisons they often have no formal agreements about the work they do and how it is to be undertaken. This haphazard approach does nothing to ensure best use is made of them. Relations between prisons and community based organization can be clarified and made more purposeful by the introduction of formal agreements which should define the purpose of the agency's work in the prison, how the work will be carried out, what the agency will provide and what the prison will provide, how the work will be reviewed and mechanisms for resolving difficulties and for terminating the agreement.

5. Where formal partnerships are created with community based service providers, prisons must be sure that their expectations are fair and realistic. They are in a very powerful position as large-scale purchasers of services. One service provider told us "... contracts rarely reflect partnership and are inequitable, loading unrealistic demands on providers and limiting the responsibilities of the purchaser".

6. Unrealistic expectations sometimes extend to the cost of services provided by community based agencies. Unless funding is provided from another source prisons must recognise that the use of community based agencies has a cost, which is likely to include overheads and possibly capital expenditure. Even providing adequate support to volunteers has resource implications – volunteers must be adequately trained and supported and should be offered expenses.

7. The lack of integration of the work of many community based agencies into the mainstream work of the prison has meant that it has been vulnerable to changing priorities, changes of Governor and pressures affecting the system.

Governors may find that the work of community agencies is helpful in achieving some of the desired outcomes in terms of performance measures. A more strategic approach is required at all levels and the work of community based agencies should feature in prisons' business plans agreed between Governors and Area Managers.

8. Prisoners at similar prisons are likely to require the services of broadly similar community based agencies. A 'menu' of suggested types of service for each section of the prison population should be drawn up. Area Managers should monitor the involvement of community based agencies in the provision of services.

9. Many community based agencies offer opportunities to prisoners in areas not (and unlikely to be) covered by accredited programmes designed to have a clear impact on reconviction rates. There is a danger that the value of other interventions will be dismissed when set alongside the large-scale highly developed programmes which are now available, and that they will be deprived of resources. Many of the small scale interventions are designed to offer prisoners information and resources relating to other aspects of their lifestyles – such as health information, the constructive use of leisure time, help with budgeting or support in coping with their family relationships. Many of these interventions aim for primary outcomes other than the reduction of re-offending. They tend to be less resource intensive and of much shorter duration that accredited programmes, and are therefore potentially available to many more prisoners. This Group recommends that the Prison Service investigate the adoption of a system of Approved Activities, similar to that used in the Scottish Prison Service, which would provide prisoners with a range of high-quality evaluated options. They would be available to short-term prisoners (who are often unable to complete longer accredited programmes) and as a constructive supplement to accredited programmes for longer-term prisoners.

10. Relationships between prison staff and community based agency staff are very variable. At best there is a high degree of co-operation, at worst hostility, stereotyping and a lack of trust. Governors should have access to training on multi-disciplinary working and the role of community agencies. Community agency liaison officers should ensure that information about the work of community agencies in the prison is made widely available to staff. Staff – whether paid or voluntary – from community agencies need to understand the prison environment in order to be able to provide appropriate services. Induction programmes should be developed to provide an insight which goes beyond routinely provided security information.

11. The recent activity highlighting the existence of the Compact between Government and the Community and Voluntary Sector in the form of Prison Service roadshows attended by the Minister has been very welcome, as has the commissioning of Good Practice Guidelines for Governors in this area. Sensitivity to the issues such as the difficulty caused to small community based agencies by paying them in arrears, and a willingness to review arrangements has been evident and is commendable.

12. Community-based agencies can have a role in both the identification of failing prisons and their recovery. An education provider described how the Quality Indicators it was set were sometimes not achieved due to other weaknesses in the prison. One example given was:

A significant number of prisoners on the list do not arrive. Continuity for students in classes varies significantly damaging consistency' as a result of 'Poor co-ordination between the [education] department and the wings. Regime activities are not valued.

The [education] programme is a mystery to all officer staff. They do not think it is their job to direct inmates to Education.' *The issues being* 'A minority of staff resent the education on offer and feel the money would be better spent on their children etc. there are incidents racism and harassment. Prisoners are not unlocked on time. Prisoner morale is low.

13. When a community based agency or provider has clearly defined quality standard to meet failures like this and the reasons for them, become very clear. Where no such formal agreements exist the same impressions may be formed, but the evidence may be weaker. In such situations these agencies need to have clear agreed procedures in place to enable them to raise their concerns with the Governor, and, if necessary, the Area Manager.

RECOMMENDATIONS Links between prisons and community-based agencies should be strengthened and co-ordinated more effectively. Prison and community based agency staff should be provided with training to enable them to work together more effectively. Community based agency staff should be able to convey any concerns they have about the prison to the Governor or Area Manager.

Boards of Visitors

14. Boards of Visitors have a key role to play in highlighting difficulties in prisons. They currently operate on an entirely voluntary basis and their task is to represent the public 'stake' in imprisonment by monitoring the

fair treatment of prisoners. They have a right of access at any time to all parts of the prison and to all prisoners. They are expected to raise their concerns with the Governor, or more senior personnel in the Prison Service, and where necessary take matters directly to the Secretary of State to whom their annual reports are addressed. Sadly the repeated concerns expressed by Boards of Visitors were not heeded in relation to some of the prisons which have recently attracted attention for their poor performance.

15. The last review of the role of Boards of Visitors, chaired by the Rt. Hon Michael Forsyth MP, was conducted in 1995. Its recommendations resulted in the establishment of the National Advisory Committee and the Secretariat of Boards of Visitors and these two bodies have subsequently worked together to highlight improvements which could be made to the effectiveness of Boards. Five years after the Forsyth review this Group feels that the time is right for a further review concentrating on the work of Boards of Visitors, how they can become more effective, and how the Prison Service can become more responsive when they raise concerns.

16. We would like this review to consider the following questions:

- How links to the Prison Service above the level of Governor might be improved – in particular the question of the relationship between the Board of Visitors and the Area Manager and his/her team;
- Whether it would be helpful to create an obligation and a procedure for raising certain concerns with the Area Manager at the same time as with the Governor – examples might be allegations of brutality made against staff by prisoners, allegations of racism, an impoverished regime sustained over a certain period of time – even if the solution is provided without the Area Manager's direct intervention;
- Whether Boards of Visitors should retain the task of sanctioning prisoners' segregation, a management role, or whether this role should be taken by the Governor leaving Boards with an obligation to see all segregated prisoners on a regular basis to check on their welfare;
- How better support to Boards might be provided on specific areas such as race, education and human rights;
- How training and information for members of Boards of Visitors might be improved and the possible role of IT in this;
- Whether it is reasonable to expect Board Chairmen to fulfil such a demanding role without pay; and
- How to offer examples of best practice and avoid isolation.

RECOMMENDATION There should be a review of the role, resources and responsibilities of Boards of Visitors

APPENDIX IV: Chronology of Relevant Development

1756	The Marine Society started a school for convicts.
1773	The Society for the Relief and Discharge of Debtors was formed
1777	Publication of John Howard's 'The State of the Prisons'.
1788	Founding of New Asylum for the Prevention of Vice and Misery among the Poor. This became the Philanthropic Society in 1790.
1790	The Philanthropic Society founded
1808	Founding of the Society for the Improvement of Prison Discipline, which carried out frequent jail inspections and published reports of their findings as well as numerous pamphlets.
1815	Founding of The Society for Investigating the Causes of the Alarming Increase in Juvenile Delinquency in the Metropolis.
1816	Founding by Elizabeth Fry of the first society of voluntary workers in an English Prison 'The Ladies Association for the Improvement of the Female Prisoners in Newgate' soon followed by the wider reaching 'British Ladies Society for the Reformation of Female Prisoners'.
1817	Founding of 'The Society for the Improvement of Penal Discipline'.
1823	Peel's Goal Act which authorised Justices to provide prisoners with food, clothes, working tools and the means of returning home, and the first of a number of Acts to impose some standards and uniformity on the running of local prisons.
1835	The Prisons Act 1835 provided for the appointment of inspectors of prisons and the first accurate prison occupation statistics were compiled.
1849	The Philanthropic Society established an agricultural colony for delinquent boys at Redhill.
1851	Mary Carpenter published her influential book 'Reformatory Schools for the Children of the Perishing and Dangerous Classes and for Juvenile Offenders'.
1854	The Youthful Offenders Act gave provision for voluntary societies to provide Reformatory Schools.
1854	Feltham School inaugurated.
1857	The Certified Industrial Schools Act allowed voluntary organizations to care for potentially delinquent children in Industrial Schools.
1862	The Discharged Prisoners' Aid Act officially recognised aid societies and their legitimacy.
1877	The Prison Act 1877 transferred power and responsibility for prisons from local justices to the Home Secretary. The administration of the system was delegated to a new body of up to five members, the Prison Commission. Unpaid Visiting Committees were appointed to every prison with free access to every prisoner and every part of the prison. These were later called the Board of Visitors.
1886	Founding of The Howard League for Penal Reform.
1895	Publication of the Gladstone Report with its influential wide ranging review of penal policy and practice
1898	Prison Act 1898 introduced measures to improve prison conditions, defining the role of Visiting Committees and setting up Boards of Visitors at Aylesbury, Rochester, Dartmoor, Parkhurst and Portland. The Prisons Act 1898 established the Central Discharged Prisoners Aid Society to co-ordinate the work of all the local aid societies. The Act also abolished the crank and treadwheel.
1898	Founding of the Bourne Trust formally the Catholic Social Service for Prisoners.
1901	Lady Visitors' Association founded under the presidency of Adeline, Duchess of Bedford.
1907	Probation of Offenders Act 1907 established statutory provision of probation formerly provided by Church of England Temperance Society and other charities through their police court missionaries
1908	Prevention of Crime Act 1908 allowed released offenders to be paroled to the newly established Central Association for the Assistance of Discharged Convicts.
1911	Formation of the Central Association for the Aid of Discharged Convicts. It was an umbrella group with a council of representatives of the leading societies.
1922	The National Association of Prison Visitors for Men founded.
1923	The National Association of Prison Visitors founded.

Appendices 189

1937	Ten philanthropic and religious organizations set up a committee to supplement borstal aftercare.
1947	Women Voluntary Service provided a 'First Aid' scheme for meeting the immediate domestic needs of women in Holloway.
1950	High Beech Probation Home, Redhill founded by the London Police Court Mission (now the Rainer Foundation). This was one of the voluntary organizations that continued to provide a probation service until the State took over in 1940.
1952	The Prison Act 1952 created the Office of HM Chief Inspector of Prisons.
1956	New Bridge founded.
1963	The Report of the Advisory Council on the Treatment of Offenders 'The Organization of Aftercare' which recommended that the work carried out by the National Association of Discharged Prisoners' Aid Societies (NADPAS)A should be taken over by the Probation Service.
1965	The Apex Trust founded.
1966	NADPAS changes its name to NACRO.
1970	Radical Alternatives to Prison founded (RAP).
1972	PROP - The National Prisoners' Movement was founded.
1974	Prison Fellowship founded.
1975	SOVA founded.
1981	Prison Reform Trust founded.
1983	Women in Prison founded.
1987	IQRA Trust founded.
1988	POPS founded.
1989	The Penal Affairs Consortium founded
1994	Voluntary Sector Consortium initiated by Robert Hardy, Bishop of Lincoln, the Prisons' Bishops.
1996	The Voluntary Sector Consortium founded.
1998	CLINKS founded.
1998	Compact on Relations between Government and the Voluntary and Community Sector in England published.
1998	Unlock founded
1999	Restorative Justice Consortium founded
2000	The Inside Out Trust Penal Voluntary Sector Conference held at HMYOI Huntercombe
2000	Appointment of Voluntary Sector Co-ordinator at Prison Service HQ
2001	Publication of the Joint CLINKS / Prison Service *Good Practice Guide*.

Appendix V: Further Reading

The references section contains the details of all the books referred to in the chapters of this book. The following are key texts we would recommend to people as additional reading about the Prison Service and voluntary sector.

Bryans, S. and Jones, R. (2001) *Prisons and the Prisoner: An Introduction to the work of Her Majesty's Prison Service*, The Stationery Office.
Bryans, S. and Wilson, D (2000) *The Prison Governor: Theory and Practice*, (2nd edition), Prison Service Journal Publications.
Cavadino, M. and Dignan, J. (1997) *The Penal System: An Introduction*, Sage.
Coyle, A. (1994) *The Prisons We Deserve*, Harper Collins.
Devlin, A. (1998) *Invisible Women: What's Wrong With Women's Prisons*, Waterside Press.
Devlin, A. (1996) *Prison Patter: A Dictionary of Prison Slang*, Waterside Press.
Flynn, N. (1998) *Introduction to Prisons and Imprisonment*, Waterside Press.
Goodman, A and Mensah, B. (1999) *The Prison Guide*, Blackstone Press.
Gravett, S. (1999) *Coping with imprisonment: A Guide to Practitioners on the Realities of Imprisonment*, Cassell.
Ignatieff, M. (1978) *A Just Measure of Pain :The Penitentiary in the Industrial Revolution 1750-1850*, Macmillan.
Leech, M. and Cheney, D. (2001) *The Prisons Handbook*, Waterside Press.
Lewis, D. (1997) *Hidden Agendas: Politics, Law and Disorder*, Hamish Hamilton.
Mathews, R. (1999) *Doing Time: An Introduction to the Sociology of Imprisonment*, Macmillan.
May, T. (1995) *Probation :Politics, Policy and Practice*, Open University.
Pettifer, E. (1939) *Punishments of former days*, Waterside Press (reprinted 1992).
Martin, C. and Player, E. (2000) *Drug Treatment in Prison*, Waterside Press.
Prison Reform Trust (1997) *Race Equality in Prisons: the Role of RRLO*, Prison Reform Trust.
Rutherford, A. (1993) *Criminal Justice and the Pursuit of Decency*, Waterside Press.
Simon, F. (1999) *Prisoners' Work and Vocational Training*, Routledge.
Stern, V. (1998) *A Sin Against The Future: Imprisonment in the World*, Penguin.
Stern, V. (1987) *Bricks of Shame: Britain's Prisons*, Penguin.
West, T. (1997) *Prisons of Promise*, Waterside Press.
Whitfield, D. (1998) *Introduction to the Probation Service* (2nd edition), Waterside Press.
Wilson, A. and Charlton, K. (1997) *Making Partnerships Work: A practical guide for the public, private, voluntary and community sectors*, Joseph Rowntree Foundation.
Wilson, D. and Ashton, J. (1998) *Crime and Punishment: What Everyone Should Know*, Blackstone Press.
Wilson, D. and Reuss, A. (2001) *Prison(er) Education*, Waterside Press.

In addition:
'Active Partners - Benchmarking Community Participation' published by Yorkshire and Humberside Development Agency can be obtained from the agency at:

Victoria House, 2 Victoria Place, Leeds LS11 5AE or www.yorkshire-forward.com

All the Compact documents - the Compact itself, Funding document, Black and Minority Ethnic, Community Groups, Consultation and Policy Appraisal, and Volunteering are available from:

The Active Community Unit, Room 235, Horseferry House, Dean Ryle Street, London SW1P 2AW.

The CLINKS/Prison Service *Good Practice Guide* can be obtained from: Voluntary Sector Co-ordinator's Office, Room 705, Cleland House, Page Street, London SW1P 4LN, 0207 217 6842

References

Alcohol Concern (2000) *A DIY Guide to Implementing Outcome Monitoring.* London: Alcohol Concern.
Aves, G. (1969) *Voluntary Workers in the Social Services.* London: Allen and Unwin/BASW.
Banton, M. (1973) *Police Community Relations.* London: Collins.
Barr, H. (1971) *Volunteers in Prison Aftercare.* London: Allen and Unwin.
Billis, D. and Harris, M. (eds) (1996) *Voluntary Agencies: Challenges of Organization and Management.* London: Macmillan Press.
Blair, T. (1998) *The Third Way: new politics for the new century.* London: Fabian Society.
Blom-Cooper, L. (ed) (1974) *Progress in Penal Reform.* Oxford: Clarendon Press.
Boateng, P. (2000)
Brenton, M. (1985) *The Voluntary Sector in British Social Services.* London: Longman.
Brodie, A., Croom, J. and Davies, J. (1999) *Behind Bars: The Hidden Architecture of England's Prisons.* Swindon: English Heritage.
Bryans, S. and Jones, R. (2001) *Prisons and the Prisoner: an introduction to the work of HM Prison Service.* London: The Stationery Office.
Bryans, S. and Walker, R. (2000) 'Delivering Constructive Prisons in Partnership', *Prison Service Journal*, No. 131.
Bryans, S. and Walker, R. (2001) 'An introduction to the role of the voluntary and community based sector' in Leech, M. and Cheney, D. (2001) *The Prisons Handbook 2001.* Winchester: Waterside Press.
Bryans, S. and Wilson, D. (2000) *The Prison Governor: Theory and Practice*, (2nd edition). Grendon Underwood: Prison Service Journal Publications.
Cabinet Office (2000) *Top Management Programme: Prison Service Case Study.* Unpublished.
Cabinet Office (2001) *Modernising the legal and regulatory framework for charities and the voluntary sector*
(www.cabinet-office.gov.uk/innovation/2001/charity/charityscope.shtml)
Carley, M., Chapman, M., Hastings, A., Kirk, K. and Young, R. (2000) *Urban Regeneration Through Partnership: a study in nine urban regions in England, Scotland and Wales.* London: Policy Press.
Casale, S. and Haughton, P. (1997) *Penal Programme Report.* London: City Parochial Foundation.
Charities Aid Foundation (2000) Dimensions, Vol 3
CLINKS (1999) *Community-based Organizations and Four Prisons in England.* York: Prisons-Community Links.
CLINKS (2000) *Good Practice Guide - consultation document.* York: Prisons-Community Links.
Davis Smith, J. (1995) The Voluntary Tradition: philanthropy and self-help in Britain 1500-1945. In J. Davis Smith, C. Rochester & R. Hedley (eds) *An Introduction to the Voluntary Sector.* London: Routledge.
Davis Smith, J., Rochester, C. and Hedley R., (eds) (1995) *An Introduction to the Voluntary Sector.* London: Routledge.
Deakin, N. (1995) The Perils of Partnership: the voluntary sector and the state, 1945-1992. In J. Davis Smith, C. Rochester & R. Hedley (eds) *An Introduction to the Voluntary Sector.* London: Routledge.
Demos (1997) *Holistic Government.* London: Demos
Deverson, P (2000) *Society of Voluntary Associates (SOVA).* Unpublished Research Project. HMYOI Feltham.
Deloitte, Haskins and Sells (1989) *Report on the Practicality of Private Sector involvement in the Remand System.* London: Home Office.
Davis Smith, J (1996) 'Should Volunteers be Managed?' in Billis, D. and Harris, M. (1996) *Voluntary Agencies: Challenges of Organization and Management.* London: Macmillan.
Draycott, R. (1998). *A Brief History of the Boards of Visitors.* London: The Stationery Office.
Fielding, N. (1988) *Joining Forces.* London :Routledge.
Fitzherbert, Addison & Rahman 1999 *A Guide to the Major Trusts* Vol. 1&2

The Directory of Social Change
Forsythe, W. J. (1991) *Penal Discipline, Reformatory Projects and the English Prison Commission 1896-1939*. Exeter: University of Exeter Press.
Fox, L. (1952) *The English Prison and Borstal System*. London: Routledge and Kegan Paul.
Freeman, J. (ed) (1978) *Prisons past and future*. London: Heinemann.
Gill, M. and Mawby, R. (1990) *Volunteers in the Criminal Justice System: a comparative study of probation, police, and victim support*. Milton Keynes: Open University Press.
Gordon et al (1995) 'Functional Family Therapy for Delinquents on Adult Criminal Behaviour', *Criminal Justice and Behaviour*, vol. 22, no. 1.
Hammer, C. (2000) in Criminal Justice Matters, No 40. Centre for Crime and Justice Studies.
Haxby, D. (1978) *Probation: a Changing Service*. London: Constable.
Hedley, R. (2000) 'Jos Sheard – A memoir', *Voluntary Action: The Journal of the Institute for Volunteering Research*, Volume 2, Number 2.
Hems, L. and Passey, A. (1998) *The UK Voluntary Sector Almanac 1997/98*. London: NCVO Publications.
HM Inspectorate of Prisons (1999) *Annual Report of HM Chief Inspector of Prisons for England and Wales*. London: The Stationery Office.
Hobhouse, S. and Brockway, A.F. (1922) *English Prisons Today*. London: Longmans, Green and Co.
Home Office, (1995) *Home Office Research Bulletin, No 37, p.40*.
Home Office (1998) *Reducing Offending: An Assessment of Research Evidence on Ways of Dealing with Offending Behaviour*. Home Office Research Study 187. London: Home Office.
Home Office (1998) *Compact: getting it right together. Compact on Relations between Government and the Voluntary and Community Sector Sector in England*. Cm 4100. London: Home Office.
Home Office (1999) *Reconvictions of Offenders Sentenced or Discharged from Prison in 1995, England and Wales*. Home Office Statistical Bulletin. London: Government Statistical Service.
Home Office (2000a) *Funding: a code of good practice*. London: Home Office.
Home Office (2000b) *Consultation and Policy Appraisal: a code of good practice*. London: Home Office.
Home Office (2000c) *Business Plan 1999/20002/ Aim 4*. London: The Stationery Office.
Home Office (2000d) *Prison Statistics England and Wales 1999*. London: The Stationery Office.
Home Office (2001a) *A Report on the Working Group Chaired by The Rt Hon Sir Peter Lloyd MP*. London: The Stationary Office.
Home Office (2001b) *£18 million in new grants to build strong active communities*
Home Office Press Release 30 March 2001
Howard, J. (1929) *The State of the Prisons*. London: J.M. Dent and Sons Ltd. Original Publication 1777
Hyland, J. (1993) *Yesterday's Answers: Development and Decline of Schools for Young Offenders* London: Whiting and Birch.
Ignatieff, M. (1978) *A Just Measure of Pain: The Penitentiary in the Industrial Revolution 1750 - 1850*. London and Basingstoke: Macmillan.
The Joseph Rowntree Trust : Sourcebook of Juvenile Offenders
Kaplan, R. and Norton, D. (1996) *The Balanced Scorecard, translating strategy into action*. Boston: Harvard business School Press.
Kauffman, K. (1988) *Prison Officers and their World*. Harvard: Harvard University Press.
Kendall, J. (2000) *The Mainstreaming of the Third Sector into Public Policy in England in the Late 1990s: whys and wherefores*. London School of Economics, Civil Society Working Paper 2.
Kendall, J. and Almond, S. (1999) 'United Kingdom' in Salamon et al (1999) *Global Civil Society: dimensions of the nonprofit sector*. Baltimore: The Johns Hopkins University pp179-200.
Kendall, J.and Knapp, M. (1996) *The UK Voluntary Sector*. Manchester: Manchester University Press.
King, R.D. and Morgan, R. (1980) *The Future of the Prison System*. Farnborough:Gower.

Kirkby, T. (1999) *The Prison Service of England and Wales: Facts and Figures*, Unpublished paper. London: International Centre for Prison Studies.
Knight, B. (1993) *Voluntary Action*. London: Centris.
Laming, Lord (2000) *Modernising the Management of the Prison Service: An Independent Report by the Targeted performance Initiative Working Group Chaired by Lord Laming of Tewin CBE* (The Laming Report). London: Home Office
Learmont, Gen. Sir John (1995) *Review of Prison Service Security in England and Wales and the Escape from Parkhurst Prison on Tuesday 3rd January 1995* (The Learmont Report), Cm 3020, London: HMSO.
Leech, M. and Cheney, D. (2001) *The Prisons Handbook 2001*. Winchester: Waterside Press.
Lewis, P. (1988) 'When cash is a drug'. *Community Care: Inside the Voluntary Sector*, 25, February.
Lewis, J. (1999) Reviewing the Relationship Between the Voluntary Sector and the State in Britain in the 1990s. *Voluntas* 10 (3) pp.255-270.
Light, R. (1984). 'Pressure Groups, Penal Policy and the Goals', *Prison Service Journal*. Oct 1984, No. 56, p.7
Lochhead, S.R. (1993). *Outside In: A Study of Prison Visiting*. York: William Sessions.
Lombardo, L. (1981) *Guards Imprisoned: Correctional Officers at work*. New York: Elsevier.
Martin, C. (2000) 'CLINKS and the work of community based and voluntary groups within prisons'. *Prison Service Journal*, No.131.
Morris, R. (1976) *Prisons*. London: Batsford.
Morris, N. and Rothman, D. (1995) *Oxford History of the Prison: The Practice of Punishment in Western Society*. Oxford: Oxford University Press.
Mountbatten, Earl (1966) *Report of the Inquiry into Prison Escapes and Security*. (The Mountbatten Report). London: HMSO.
National Centre for Volunteering (2000) 'Volunteering', *Volunteering - The Magazine*, August 2000
National Coalition for Black Volunteers (2000) 'Charities Colour Blind Approach Discriminates Against Black Volunteers' Press release: June 2000
National Coalition for Black Volunteers (2000) 'Noticeable By Their Absence: Black Volunteers in Charities', Press Release: June 2000
National Council for Voluntary Organizations (NCVO) (1998) Blurred Vision. *Research Quarterly 1*. London: NCVO Publications.
National Council for Voluntary Organizations (NCVO) (2000a) Co-operation, Participation and Complexity: local partnerships and public policy. *Perspectives on Public Policy (3)*. London: NCVO Publications.
National Council for Voluntary Organizations (NCVO) (2000b) *Local Compact Guidelines*. London: NCVO Publications.
Newburn,T.(1995) *Crime and Criminal Justice Policy*. London: Longman.
Pahl, J. (1979) 'Refuges for Battered Women: Social Provision or Social Movement?'. *Journal of Voluntary Action Research*, 8, 25-35.
Passey, A., Hems, L. and Jas, P. (2000) *The UK Voluntary Sector Almanac 2000*. London: NCVO Publications
Passey, A. and Tonkiss, F. (2000) Trust, Voluntary Association and Civil Society. In F. Tonkiss, and A. Passey (eds) *Trust and Civil Society*. Basingstoke: Macmillan.
Prison Service (1997) *Prison Service Review*. London: HM Prison Service.
Prison Service (1999a) *Quinquennial Review of the Prison Service: prior Options Report*. London: The Stationery Office.
Prison Service (1999b) *A Framework Document*. London: The Stationery Office.
Prison Service (1999c) *Prison Service Order 1000*. London: HM Prison Service.
Prison Service (2000a) *Business Plan 2000/2001*. London: HM Prison Service.
Prison Service (2000b) *Annual reports and accounts April 1999-2000*. London: The Stationery Office.
Prison Service (2000c) *HR Planning-Diversity statistics*. London: HM Prison Service.
Prison Service (2000d) *Pre-Release Volunteering, The Facts*. London: HM Prison Service.

Prison Service (2001) *Corporate Plan 2001-02 to 2003-04 and Business Plan 2001-02.* London: HM Prison Service
Ryan, M. (1996) *Lobbying from below.* London : UCL Press.
Samaritans (2000) *Facing the Future.* Annual Review of the Samaritans 1999-2000 London: Samaritans:
Sandiford, D. (1998). *Speech to the Boards of Visitors Centenary Conference.* Unpublished.
Shaw, S. (2000) 'Pressure Groups and the Prison Service', in S. Bryans and R. Jones (2001) eds *Prisons and the Prisoner: an introduction to the work of HM Prison Service.* London: The Stationery Office.
Sheard, J. (1992). 'Volunteering and Society, 1960-1990', in R. Hedley and J. Davis Smith (eds), *Volunteering and Society.* London: Bedford Square Press.
Straw, J. (1998) *Speech to the Prison Reform Trust.* Unpublished speech, 22nd July 1998.
Taylor, M. (1996) 'What are the Key Influences on the Work of Voluntary Agencies?' in Billis, D. and Harris, M. (1996) *Voluntary Agencies: Challenges of Organization and Management.* London: Macmillan.
Thomas, J. (1977) *The Prison Officer since 1850: A Study in Conflict.* London: Routledge.
Thornton, D. (1996) *Criteria for Accrediting Programmes.* London: HM Prison Service.
Tonkiss, F. and Passey, A. (1999) Trust, Confidence and Voluntary Organizations: between values and institutions. Sociology 33 (2) pp257-274.
Vincent, J. and Pharoah, K. (2000) *Patterns of Independent Grant-Making in the UK.* Charities Aid Foundation: London.
Waghorn, J. (2000). 'Samaritans in Prison', *Prison Service Journal,* No. 131.
Walker, N. (1965) *Crime and Punishment in Britain.* Edinburgh: Edinburgh University Press.
Whitfield, R. (1980). *The Role of Volunteers in the Penal System.* London: Howard League for Penal Reform.
Wilson, D. (1996) 'How do Voluntary Agencies Manage Organizational Change?' in Billis, D and Harris, M. (1996) *Voluntary Agencies: Challenges of Organization and Management.* London: Macmillan.
Wilson, A. and Charlton, K. (1997) *Making Partnerships work.* London: Joseph Rowntree Foundation.
Wolfenden, Lord (1978) *The Future of Voluntary Organizations,* Report of the Wolfenden Committee, London: Croom Helm
Wolman, H. and Page, E. (2000) Policy Transfer Among Local Regeneration Partnerships. *Findings* (530). York: Joseph Rowntree Foundation.
Woodcock, Sir John (1994) *The Escape from Whitemoor Prison on Friday 9th September 1994* (The Woodcock Report). Cm 2741. London: HMSO.
Woolf, Lord Justice and Tumim, Judge S. (1991) *Prison Disturbances April 1990: Report of an Inquiry by the Rt Hon. Lord Justice Woolf and His Hon. Stephen Tumim* (The Woolf Report). Cm 1456. London: HMSO.
Worrall, J. (2000) *The needs of prisoners serving less than three months.* Unpublished report by NACRO to the Prison Service
Young, A.F. and Ashton, E.T. (1956). *British Social Work in the Nineteenth Century.* London: Routledge and Kegan Paul.
Zedner, L. (1995). 'Wayward Sisters', in N. Morris and D. Rothman (eds.), *The Oxford History of the Prison: The Practice of Punishment in Western Society.* Oxford: Oxford University Press.

Index

abbreviations vi
accommodation (ex-prisoners) 154
accountability 23 24
accreditation 88
  courses 89
  Accreditation Panel (Scotland) 89
acknowledgements iv
active community involvement 80 102
Active Community Unit (ACU) (Home Office) 70 73 76 91 103 148
Active Partners 172
addiction 154
adding value 153
'additionality'/extension of services 145 152 163
alcohol 135
Alcoholics Anonymous (AA) 95 132 136
Al-Koei
  Foundation 107
  Yousif 106
agency status (Prison Service) 33 65
agreement
  minimum standards 125
  national 23
  protocols 126
  written 87
Ahmed, Maqsood 107
aid societies 50 *et seq* 57 *et seq*
anonymous funding 156
appropriateness 153
audit
  existing provision, of 127
  outcomes, of 135 150 155
authors i

Barnardos 61
Basic Skills 169
befriending 99
best practice 23
best value 24
Bishop of Lincoln's Group
  See *Voluntary Sector Consortium*

black issues 72 107 110 114 158 163
Black Prisoner Support Group/Project (BPSG/P) 94 110 113
Blunkett, David MP 117 120
Board of Visitors 35 57 93 96 *et seq*
Boeteng, Paul MP 13 75 76
Borstal Association 60
Bourne Trust 106
Butler Trust 101
Bryans, Shane 149 162

campaigns/campaigning 14 17
CARATS 84 123 133 137 143
Carey, Margaret 50
Carpenter, Mary 56 61
Casale, Sylvia 66
categorisation (prisoners) 29 41
Centre for Crime and Justice Studies 75 84
Centris report 21
chaplain/chaplaincy 54 58 117
charity 18 50 *et seq* 60 62 145 156 184
  Association of Charitable Trusts Penal Affairs Interest Group 140
  Charity Commission 82
  Charity Aid Foundation 140 141
Church of England Temperance Society 54 60
church involvement 53 61 62 70 141
chronology 188
citizenship 62 66
Clarke, Kenneth MP 33
CLINKS 15 24 62 66 75 84 90 103 113 120 146 148
  pilot project 67 154
codes 23
Comeback 144
Commission on the Future of the Voluntary Sector 65
communication 98 124 128 172
  absence of jargon 172
community

Index

active 102
Community Fund (National Lottery) 139 157
commmunity service volunteers 101
  links 122 160
  and see *CLINKS*
  responsibility xi
community-based developments 63 *et seq*
  and see *active community involvement, Active Community Unit, safer community*
compact 17 21 23 65 90
  Compact on Relations between Government and the Voluntary etc sector (Voluntary Sector Compact, or COMPACT) 65 *et seq.* 90 164
Compass 84 169
confidentiality 122 126
Connexion Service 100
conservative 61
consistency 152 160
contract/contracting 133 157
  contract culture 25 150 170
  Prison Service Contracts and Procurement Group 157
contributors vii-x
control (prisoners) 61
co-ordination 160
  and see *Voluntary Sector Co-ordinator*
costings 127
  cost effectiveness 165
  and see *funding*
Councils of Voluntary Service 144
counselling 154
Cranstoun 84
creativity 22
Crime Concern 101 147
Criminal Justice Act 1991 30 47
criteria 160
criticise, ability to 164
cropwood Fellowship 122
cultural aspects 125 168
Custody, Care and Justice 30

Dalton Youth Project 94

database 84
Deakin Commission 21 65
Deakin, Nicholas 65
dedication iv
Dell, Richie 106 114
deterrence 27 31
development 22
  freedom to develop 22
  plans 22 127
difference 172
Directory of Social Change 141
Discharged Prisoners' Aid Society(ies) 57
dispersal system 29
Divert Trust 101
drugs 122 130 135 169
  rehabilitation 122
  Prison service Drugs Strategy 130
  treatment contracts 82 133
  and see *RAPt*
Dostoevsky, Fyodor 117
Du Cane, Sir Edmund 28

education 61 94
  HIV, aids 154
employment/unemployment 121 154
escape 29 31 33
Etherington, Stuart 17
ethical issues 145 168
evidence-based
  approach, generally 153
  effectiveness 131 153
  policy 23
  provision 127
evaluation 146 154 159 160
equal opportunities 156

facilities 124 154
faith issues 84 106 117
family 121 154
Family Ties Consultative Group 70
Federation of Prisoners' Families Support Groups 79 85 161
Feltham YOI 94
  Radio Feltham 102
Foreword xi

Fresh Start 30
Fry, Elizabeth 52 62 96 117
funding/spending etc. 13 55 74 82 85
  86 103 114 123 131 132 138 156 *et seq*
  167
  anonymous 156
  Department of Health 145 147
  devolution to governors 74 142
  ethical issues 145
  European Union 144 157
  evaluation 146
  health authorities 145
  in-advance 76
  in arrears 147
  independent funding 140 145
    bodies 139
  joint bids 123
  Prison Service 142
  Prison Service Finance Manual 76
  Prison Service Order 142 156
  statutory bodies 143
  and see *Community Fund/NLCB*
future, the 24 102 114 162
  priorities 172

gambling 154
Gladstone
  Herbert 28
  report 58
Glen Parva 112
glossary vi
Good Practice Guide 24 71 78 103 113 120
  146 152 153 155 158
Gordon, Jo 74 76 120
government 21 65 74 142 162
governors (prison) 42 121 *et seq* 149
Green, Robert 110

Hammer, Steve 169
Hardy, Bishop (Bishop of Lincoln) 62 67
Haughton, Paulette 66
health
  healthcare 21 35
  'healthy prison' 72 120 153 154
  'healthy voluntary agency' 155

Hibiscus 110
history 17 50 *et seq*
home, loss of following imprisonment
  121
Home Office 21 29 31 32 59 70 85 89
  98 103 112 134 151 154
  and see *Active Community Unit,*
  Pathfinders programme
Hooper, Roma 92
housing (ex-prisoners) 154
Howard, John 28 51 62 117
Howard League 55 85 93
Howard, Michael MP 31 33
humane values/considerations 28 56 95
  119
Huntercombe YOI 100

imprisonment
  history of 27
  independence 139
  industrial schools 57 61
    Industrial Schools Act 1857 61
  inequality and partnership 169
  innovation 22 54 164
  Inside Out Trust 94
  inspectorate/inspector 13 29 34 89 97
  151
IQRA Trust 107
Islamic Cultural Centre 107

key performance indicators (KPIs) 34 88
  89 150
keys 159
Kilgariff, Peter 77 138 *et seq* 157

JADE project 144
joined-up thinking/provision 146

Labour 14 17 21 65
Lankelly Foundation 77 138 143
Laming Committee/report 15 31 89 90
  91 185 *et seq*
Lawrence, Stephen/Lawrence inquiry
  103 112
leadership 22 24

Learmont report 31
legislation 56
Lewis, Derek 33
liaison 128 160
Listener Scheme 99 121 155
literacy 102 154
lobbying 56 62
local
    authorities 122
    compact guidelines 24
    Local Learning Unit (LLU) 22

magistrates 57 58 60
'mainstreaming' 159
management
    Management Board (Prison Service) 37 76 77 172
    managerialism, impact of 169
    structures 39 *et seq*
Manning, Alton 114
Martin, Clive 63 75 162
Martin, Sarah 52 62
May Committee 29 41
mental health issues 121 145 154
mentors/mentoring 94 95 100 154
minority
    ethnic issues 72 84 106 110 154 158 162
    issues 114
missionaries 53 57 60
monitoring 159 170
Moorland 112
Mountbatten report 29 41
Mubarek, Zahid 114
multi-agency work 155
Muslims 106 *et seq*
    Muslim Advisor (Prison Service) 107
    National Council for the Welfare of Muslim Prisoners 107
mutualism 20

Narey, Martin 119
Narcotics Anonymous 132 136

National Association for the Care and Resettlement of Offenders (NACRO) 59 64 85 114 121 142
National Association of Prison Visitors 74 118 155
National Body of Black Prisoners Support Groups 85 111
National Children's Homes 61
National Coalition for Black Volunteers 103
National Council for the Welfare of Muslim Prisoners (NCWMP) 107
National Drugs Strategy 143
National Probation Service/Probation Service 31 33 44 59 72 101 110 122 135 144 147
National Treatment Agency 135
networking 161
New Bridge 94
New Deal for Communities 22
NLCB 140 *et seq* 145
Noblett, The Venerable William 106 117
non-governmental organization (NGO) 74
numeracy 102 154
Nutley, Katie 121

official stance
    opposition to 55
officers (prison) 29 30
    Prison Officers Association (POA) 29 44

Obaze, David 103
Ombudsman (Prisons and Probation) 34 97
Open College Network 88
outcomes 134 135 169

Padel, Una 75 82
partnership 17 66 71 *et seq* 75 91 110 121 149 *et seq*
    benefits of 121
    COMPACT 66 164
    Labour 17

pitfalls 124
practical steps towards 149
reputable links 124
'right partner' 155
UK voluntary sector with 21
Passey, Andrew 17
Pathfinders programme (Home Office) 143
Penal Affairs Consortium 62
Penal Reform International 85
penal voluntary sector 50
performance 37
    Performance and Innovation Unit (Cabinet Office) 162
philanthropy 50 53 57 163
planning 37 86 127
police court missionaries 60
    and see *missionaries*
positive custody 29
positive partnership 73
pragmatism 130 136
preparation 124
Prince's Trust, The 64
principles 130 136
prison
    establishments 39
    director general 35
    discipline 55 56 61
    governors 42
    minister 13 75 76
    officers (including rank) 29 30
        Prison Officers Association (POA) 29 44
    Prison Commission 29 57 58
    Prison Department 29
    Prison Service (generally) 27 *et seq*
        Business Plan 151
        contracting with 133
        headquarters 35 *et seq* 77 79 91 103 124 149 153 156
        management 30 35 *et seq*
        offending behaviour courses etc 154
            accreditation 88
        Offending Behaviour Unit 72
    policy on partnerships etc 74 79

politics 133
Race Advisory Group 111
    Strategy Board 34 37
    Voluntary Sector Co-ordinator 76 *et seq* 120 153
        local co-ordinators (proposal) 87
    Voluntary and Community Sector Strategy 172
    security 27 29 31 41 61 93 122 125 150
prisoners 47 *et seq*
Prisoners' Information Pack 85
Prison Fellowship 94
Prison Reform Trust 64 85
Prisons Act 1877 28 57 96
Prisons Act 1952 41 106
Prisons Handbook, The 61
Prison Visitors' Association 96 *et seq*
    and see *Board of Visitors, women*
private sector management 30
probation 60
    probation officers 60
    Probation of First Offenders Act 1877 60
    Probation of Offenders Act 1907

Quakers 52
quality 21 24 86 162

race 72 108 110 111 112 114
Radzinowicz, Sir Leon 29
Ramsbotham, Sir David 13
RAPt 84 132 134 136 *et seq*
reality 14 149 *et seq* 161
relevance 153
reform 27 50 62
reformatory schools 56
regimes
    constructive 102 153
rehabilitation 27 31 50 73 169
    drugs 122 130 135 169
reintegration 173
relationships, developing 86 128 171
re-offending 28 88 121 134
    reducing 134 153 154 173

research 55 66 *et seq* 132
resettlement 63 72 143 144
RESPOND 113
Revolving Doors 145
rewards of volunteering 101
rhetoric 149 *et seq* 161
Rimmer, Stephen 121
risk
   risk assessment (Prison Service by) 122
   risk factors 134
   risk-taking 22
Rowntree, Joseph (Foundation) 101
RPS Rainer 101
Runnymede Trust Commission on Muslims etc. 109
Ruggles-Brise, Sir Evelyn 28 58

safer community 72
Salvation Army 61 118
Samaritans 62 64 81 84 93 95 98 99 121 155
Sampson, Adam 130
Sanderson, Nick 74
Sandiford, Delbert 97
school
   exclusion from 121
Seattle 26
secure hospitals 33
security 27 29 31 41
   categories/categorisation 41 112
   checks 86
Sentence Management Group etc. 161
service delivery/providers 14 51 54 127 134 155
   ensuring effective delivery 158
   Service Delivery Agreement 127 *et seq* 150 153
   service level agreement (SLA) 128
sexual abuse 154
skills 22
social change 61
social cohesion 165
Society of Voluntary Associates (SOVA) 94 101 102
   Literacy and Numeracy Project 102

standards
   agreed 134 135
   Prison Service 27
staff (Prison Service) 35 *et seq* 124 *et seq*
   goodwill 137 167
   minority ethnic 113
   mobility, problems presented by 87
   suspicion 150
   tensions 166
   and see *training*
Strategy Board (Prison Service) 34 37
Straw, Jack MP 31
Stow, Sir Kenneth 65
Suicide Awareness Team 99
sustainability 147

target 160
   Targeted Performance Initiative Working Group 31
   targeted intervention 134
   and see *performance, key performance indicators*
Teeside Probation Service 100
third parties 140
Thorn Cross YOI 144
Thornton, David 72
Trail-Balzers 94
training 124 128 154 156 159 168
trauma 154

umbrella organizations 86 122
Unlock 85 93
Uplift 94

value for money 88
visitors 52
   Prison Visitors' Association 96 *et seq*
   and see *Board of Visitors, women*
   Guide for Visitors to Prisons 79
voluntary sector
   benefits of 94
   democracy, a vital part of 145
   Directory of Voluntary Sector Organizations 174 *et seq*
   generally 17

government and 21 143
growth of 13
'healthy voluntary agency' 155
managing the voluntary sector
contribution 127
meaning of 18 82 92
responsiveness 123
staff 122 124 *et seq* 156
   regulation of 135
   and see *training*
tensions 56 *et seq* 166 *et seq*
UK: scale and scope etc. 18 162
Voluntary Sector Consortium (Bishop of Lincoln's Group) 62
Voluntary Sector Forums 71
volunteer 83 92
   database 161
volunteering 92
   rewards of 101
'watchdog function' 165

Waite, Terry CBE xi
Walker, Roma 50 162 164
Welcome Trust 140
welfare state 61
'what works' 154
Wolfenden Committee 61

women 41 96 110 115
   foreign nationals 110 154
   Ladies' Association etc. 96
   visitors 54 58
Women in Prison 85 93
Women's Policy Group Liaison Forum 79
Women's [Royal] Voluntary service (W[R]VS) 55 74
Woodcock report 31
Woolf report 30 90 122
Working Group on Government Relations 23
Working Group on the Active Community 102
'Working with Prisoners Directory' 71 148
Working with the Voluntary and Community Sector (Prison Service) 24

young criminals/offenders 28
Young Offender Institution Rules 1988 39
Youth at Risk 94
Youthful Offenders Act 1854 61
Youth Justice Board 33 100
youth offending team (YOT) 33

Also at www.watersidepress.co.uk

For a wide range of books on criminal justice and penal affairs see the

Waterside Press Catalogue

Opening Up a Closed World

Crime, Punishment, Policing, Criminology

Courts, Sentencing, Criminal Policy

Citizenship, Human Rights

Youth Justice

Restorative Justice, Mediation, Conflict Resolution

The Prisons Handbook and Prison Writing

The Waterside Press Prison List

Child Law, Family Law, Domestic Violence

Capital Punishment: Britain and Around the World

Drugs

Electronic Monitoring

Guides for Newcomers

The Waterside Press Criminal Policy Series

Telephone 01962 855567

Full details of all these publications also appear at our web-site

WATERSIDE PRESS IS AN INDEPENDENT IMPRINT

Excellent value: Beginners Guides
A 'mini-library' for newcomers, practitioners, colleges - and general interest

Introduction to the Criminal Justice Process Bryan Gibson and Paul Cavadino. An outline of the system from investigation and arrest to prosecution, conviction, sentence and beyond. An excellent description of roles, powers and responsibilities. Accessible and highly readable - including for people with little or no experience: 'Rarely, if ever, has this complex process been described with such comprehensiveness and clarity' *Justice of the Peace* (First edition) NEW **SECOND EDITION** AVAILABLE MID-2002 172 pages. ISBN 1 872 870 27 9. £15

Introduction to the Magistrates' Court Bryan Gibson with Winston Gordon and Andy Wesson. The **FOURTH EDITION** of this popular work contains a basic explanation of the work of the magistrates' court and an outline of jurisdiction, procedures, sentencing and other powers – plus proposals for reform. Contains a **Glossary of Words, Phrases and Abbreviations** – 'The Language of the System'. 'An ideal introduction' *Law Society Gazette* (First edition). Other editions received excellent reviews, including from *The Magistrate* and *Victim Support* etc. 2001 192 pages. ISBN 1 872 870 99 6. £15

Introduction to the Probation Service Dick Whitfield SECOND EDITION A straightforward account of the Probation Service, its history and modern-day role including its primary functions in relation to the courts, pre-sentence reports (PSRs) and community sentences. An ideal companion to other books in this range. **Reprinted 2001 with extra material by Mike Nellis dealing with the coming of the National Probation Service.** 192 pages. 1998 ISBN 1 872 870 81 3. £15

Introduction to Prisons and Imprisonment Nick Flynn. With a Foreword by **Lord Hurd of Westwell.** Basic information about imprisonment in England and Wales, HM Prison Service and prison regimes. Ideal for people who want a clear guide about how English prisons operate. 160 pages. *Under the auspices of the Prison Reform Trust.* 1998 (Reprinted 2002) ISBN 1 872 870 37 6. £15

Introduction to Youth Justice Winston Gordon, Philip Cuddy and Jonathan Black Edited by Bryan Gibson. 1999 ISBN 1 872 870 75 9. £13.50

Introduction to Road Traffic Offences Winston Gordon, Philip Cuddy and Andy Wesson. Everything for the general reader: commonplace road traffic offences, licence endorsement and disqualification from driving. Highly accessible – and an ideal aide memoire. 176 pages. 1998 ISBN 1 872 870 51 1. £13.50

Introduction to the Scottish Children's Panel Alistair Kelly. An outline of the Scottish system of justice for children. 'Very interesting reading' *The Law.* 1996 ISBN 1 872 870 38 4. £13.50

Introduction to the Family Proceedings Court Elaine Laken, Chris Bazell and Winston Gordon Foreword: Sir Stephen Brown. Excellent reviews. 1997 ISBN 1 872 870 46 5. £13.50

Introduction to Criminology Russell Pond. 'Most helpful and readable' . . . 'fascinating and thought provoking': *The Magistrate.* For anyone wanting to get speedily to grips with the central ideas, beliefs, sources and terminology of an otherwise complex – sometimes mystifying - topic. **Sound pre-course reading at various levels.** 160 pages 1999. ISBN 1 872 870 42 2. £13.50

WATERSIDE PRESS • DOMUM ROAD • WINCHESTER • SO23 9NN
Tel/Fax 01962 855567

Direct mail prices quoted Please add £2.50 per book p&p (UK). Cheques **'Waterside Press'** Firms, organizations and public utilities can be invoiced for orders of over £25 in value.

VISA • MASTERCARD • SWITCH Etc

Orders can be placed by E-mail: **watersidepress@cs.com** Online bookstore **www.watersidepress.co.uk**

Please give a day-time telephone number – and/or e-mail address

Attention is drawn to the Consumer Protection (Distance Selling) Regulations 2000 (SI 2334) for customers' rights.

Extracts from the Waterside Press Prison List

There could not be a better reference book
Martin Narey, Director General HM Prison Service (January 2002)
Highly recommended *Criminal Practitioners Newsletter* (Review of 2001 Edn.)

The Prisons Handbook 2002
Edited by MARK LEECH and DEBORAH CHENEY

This definitive annual work always attracts outstanding reviews for its scale, comprehensiveness, accuracy, clarity and reliability. It has the support of the director general of HM Prison Service and many serving governors, officers and prisoners contribute to it with current information. The handbook is quite simply the best day-to-day work that there is on prisons in England and Wales. Contains in Section 1 a detailed A to Z of the Prisons of England and Wales (one to two pages per entry and including this year, for the first time, 'governor profiles' where supplied) and nine further substantial sections dealing with virtually every aspect of imprisonment: law; human rights; prison regimes; minority rights and a host of other topics – including, new this year, a section on Prison Officers and Prison Governors.

NEW SIXTH EDITION: BIGGER AND BETTER THAN EVER AT WELL OVER 700 PAGES

ISBN 1 872 870 16 3 Price £57.50 (NB to add £5 p&p)
Prisoners, Families, Friends and HM Prison Service £44.50 (plus £5 p&p)

Going Straight Angela Devlin and Bob Turney
Foreword Jack Straw, Former Home Secretary

Based on first-hand accounts, *Going Straight* seeks to identify turning points and key influences in the lives of criminals (some well-known) who - often against all odds - turned their lives around. Includes contributions by **His Honour Sir Stephen Tumim** and broadcaster **Roger Graef**
1998 Reprinted 2001 ISBN 1 872 870 66 X £18

Prison(er) Education: Stories of Change and Transformation
David Wilson and Anne Reuss

An unswerving challenge to penal policy-makers to accept the value of education – beyond 'basic skills'. With contributions Dr Ray Pawson, Stephen Duguid and Emma Hughes. **The first major collection of writings about the transforming power of education in British prisons.**
As featured by Jeremy Paxman on BBC 'Start the Week'. 2000 ISBN 1 872 870 90 2. £18

Murderers and Life Imprisonment
Eric Cullen and Tim Newell.

The range of this major work is wide: from an examination of 'Who Are the Lifers?' (including a UK/USA comparison), lifer profiles, 'The Structure of a Life Sentence' and 'The Psychology of the Murderer', 'Containment and Treatment', 'Discretionary Lifer Panels' and a range of ethical, Human Rights and associated issues. With contributions by **Professor David Wilson** ('Delusions of Innocence') and **Roland Woodward** now director of HMP Dovegate ('Lifer Risk Assessment'). The work is further enhanced by anonymised case studies. An expert analysis by two people who have spent their careers with lifers. **'An extremely timely addition to Waterside's remarkable series of criminal justice texts': Stephen Shaw** (Foreword). ISBN 1 872 870 56 2. 1999. £18

Prisons of Promise
Tessa West **Foreword** Sir David Ramsbotham
This forward-looking book counteracts images of prisons as negative places and challenges people to identify 'goodwill', energies and skills which might be maximised to make prisons safe and purposeful communities. 'A positive and purposeful book . . . which I commend, unreservedly, to anyone who has an interest or involvement in prisons' *Sir David Ramsbotham.* 'Extremely well-researched . . . Should be seriously considered by the Home Secretary' *Justice of the Peace.* 1997 ISBN 1 872 870 50 3. £16

Prison Patter Angela Devlin
A dictionary of prison slang culled from prisoners, prison officers and other people working inside prisons. 'Useful for the custody suite' *Police Journal.*
1996 ISBN 1 872 870 41 4. £13.50

Punishments of Former Days Ernest Pettifer
One of Waterside's earliest publications, this survey of old-time punishments serves to inform the present day. Historical and absorbing. 'A good read' *The Magistrate.*
1992 ISBN 1 872 870 05 8. £12

Deaths of Offenders The Hidden Side of Justice Alison Liebling (Ed.)
Examines deaths in police, prison and special hospital custody - including on remand and in court/police cells. Contains a range of expert contributions. Published on behalf of ISTD (Now the Centre for Crime and Justice Studies). 1998 ISBN 1 872 870 61 9. £18

IN 2002 WATCH ALSO FOR **No Truth, No Justice** Audrey and Paul Edwards – The personal account of parents whose son was killed whilst on remand, their struggle to find out what happened and the barriers which – with endless determination and tenacity – they finally overcame until the tragic events were referred to Europe. Further details to be announced

The Pain and the Pride: Life Inside the Colorado Boot Camp
Brian P Block
A fly-on-the wall account of life inside an American Boot Camp.
2000 ISBN 1 872 870 84 3 £10

Invisible Women What's Wrong With Women's Prisons Angela Devlin
Highly acclaimed – Angela Devlin's classic account of women's prisons: 'What an excellent book' *Justice of the Peace.* 1998. Second reprint 2002 ISBN 1 872 870 59 7 £18.

Anybody's Nightmare The Sheila Bowler Story
Angela and Tim Devlin
As dramatised by ITV and starring Patricia Routledge. One woman's fight to clear her name of murder – in the end successfully. ISBN 1 901470 04 0 £12.50

I'm Still Standing Bob Turney
The widely acclaimed autobiography of a dyslexic ex-prisoner (who later became a probation officer). 'A truly remarkable book' *Prison Writing.* (1997, reprinted 2001)
ISBN 1 872 870 43 0 £13.50

Drug Treatment in Prison An Evaluation of the RAPt Treatment Programme
Carol Martin and Elaine Player (Eds.)
The findings of a two-year study into the effectiveness of the RAPt programme which enables male prisoners with self-confessed problems of substance misuse to lead a drug and alcohol-free life in prison and in the community after release. The report also assesses whether completion of the programme is associated with a reduction in the likelihood of reconviction post-release. A unique and highly significant collection of data and information. 2000 ISBN 1 872 870 26 0 £10

Drug Trafficking and Criminal Policy Penny Green
See the Waterside **Criminal Policy Series** in the catalogue or at our web-site
1998 ISBN 1 872 870 33 3. £18

Women, Drugs and Custody Margaret Malloch
Looks at the interaction of the three strands of the title and their often competing agendas to show how all drugs present complex problems in a closed environment.
2001 ISBN 1 872 870 91 0 1 £16

The Longest Injustice Alex Alexandrowicz and David Wilson
Alex Alexandrowicz entered a Kafkaesque nightmare in which protestations of innocence only deepened his predicament. He served 22 years without adequate explanation. His own 'Prison Chronicles' are put into perspective by former governor and BBC *Crime Squad* co-presenter David Wilson.
1998 ISBN 1 872 870 45 7 £16

Introduction to Prisons and Imprisonment Nick Flynn
NOW REPRINTED. See **Beginners Guides** 1998, Reprinted 2002 ISBN 1 872 870 37 6 £15

Criminal Classes: Offenders at School Angela Devlin
Angela Devlin's highly acclaimed first work - which identifies areas at the schooling stage which influence and predict future offending behaviour. 'If you are in any doubt about the links between poor education, crime and recidivism, read it': Marcel Berlins *The Guardian*.
1996 Reprinted 1997, 2000. ISBN 1 872 870 30 9 £16.

Prison on Trial Thomas Mathiesen
Mathiesen's classic account in a SECOND ENGLISH EDITION.
See **Criminal Policy Series** 2000 ISBN 1 872 870 86 6 £19.50

All the World's a Cage Maggie Marshall (Novel) *See endpage*
2000 ISBN 1 872 870 83 X £10

The Prison Officer Alison Liebling and David Price
In association with *Prison Service Journal:* 'The most important book for HM Prison Service of the past 30 years': Phil Wheatley, Deputy Director, HM Prison Service. 'This outstanding book will be a major source of reference': Martin Narey, Director General. ISBN 0 952 8413 2 0 £10

Grendon Tales Stories from a Therapeutic Community
Ursula Smartt – With aForeword Lord Avebury ISBN 1 872 870 96 1 £18

As featured on BBC Radio 4
'A breathless personal slide through her year talking to some of Britain's most dangerous prisoners': *Community Care*
'A work of intimacy and frankness ... Concrete evidence that therapy does help expose the failures of the past whilst offering hope for the future': *Prison Service News*
'As readable as a novel . . . I could not put it down until finished': *The Magistrate*
'The tales are recounted in a style which allows the reader to read in colour . . . A tale well told and worth reading': *RPGA Newsletter*
'Indispensable reading . . . for practitioners and policy-makers alike': *Scolag Legal Journal*
'Several books have already been published about [HM Prison Grendon] but none with the depth of understanding that this author brings to Grendon Tales . . . Uplifting . . . A book that deserves a wide readership': *New Law Journal*

208 *Extracts from the Waterside Press Catalogue*

Prison Writing
Edited by Julian Broadhead and Laura Kerr

As featured in **The Guardian** *Prison Writing* is published annually in book form to promote creative writing among prisoners in the UK and beyond. The contents are of a high standard and cover a range of topics, prison-related and otherwise. **Many prisoners first saw their work in print** in *Prison Writing*. Some went on to be published in national newspapers and magazines and to attract the interest of book publishers. **Interviews** are a feature of Prison Writing, and interviewees have included **Eddie Bunker** ('*Prison Writing is doing a real good job. Keep up the good work!*'), **Martin Amis** ('*Writing depends on the only thing these guys have plenty of: solitude*'), **Howard Marks**, **Hugh Collins** and **Razor Smith**. A full list of the contents of each Waterside edition appears at www.watersidepress.co.uk
2001 Edition Number 15 2000 ISBN 1 872 870 87 2 £12 **2002 Edition** Number 16 2002 ISBN 1 872 870 40 6 £12 (Spring 2002) **Special two book offer:** Both the 2001 and 2002 editions for £25 inclusive of delivery (to be despatched together on publication of the latter).Prison Writing . . . We value your support

ANOTHER HIGHLY INNOVATIVE PUBLICATION . . .

the Geese Theatre Handbook Drama with Offenders and People at Risk
Edited by **Clark Baim, Sally Brookes** and **Alun Mountford**

The *Geese Theatre Handbook* explains the thinking behind the company's approach to applied drama with offenders and people at risk of offending, including young people. It also contains over 100 exercises with explanations, instructions and suggestions to help practitioners develop their own style and approach. The materials can be readily adapted to other settings including conflict resolution, restorative justice and interpersonal skills training.

With easy to follow directions and **with over 100 practical exercises and instructions**

ISBN 1 872 870 67 8 Price £19.50.

Inside Art Creativity and Crime Mary Brown

Now rescheduled for 2002. The significance and importance of art for people seeking to come to terms with their offending behaviour and rebuild their lives – with the connection between the creative impulse and criminal offending explored. Further details to be announced. ISBN 1 872 870 89 9. £16

WATERSIDE PRESS • DOMUM ROAD • WINCHESTER • SO23 9NN
☎ **Tel/Fax 01962 855567**

Direct mail prices quoted Please add £2.50 per book p&p (UK). Cheques '**Waterside Press**'
Firms, organizations and public utilities can be invoiced for orders of over £25 in value.

VISA • MASTERCARD • SWITCH Etc

Orders can be placed by E-mail: **watersidepress@cs.com** Online bookstore **www.watersidepress.co.uk**

Please give a day-time telephone number – and/or e-mail address
Attention is drawn to the Consumer Protection (Distance Selling) Regulations 2000 (SI 2334) for customers' rights.